FRANCE AND BOTANY BAY
The Lure of a Penal Colony

Colin Forster

MELBOURNE UNIVERSITY PRESS
1996

Melbourne University Press
PO Box 278, Carlton South, Victoria 3053, Australia

First published 1996

Text © Colin Forster 1996
Design and typography © Melbourne University Press 1996

This book is copyright. Apart from any use permitted under the *Copyright Act 1968* and subsequent amendments, no part may be reproduced, stored in a retrieval system or transmitted by any means or process whatsoever without the prior written permission of the publisher.

Typeset in 10/13 pt Sabon
Printed in Malaysia by SRM Production Services Sdn. Bhd.

National Library of Australia Cataloguing-in-Publication entry

Forster, Colin, 1926– .
France and Botany Bay: the lure of a penal colony.
Bibliography.
Includes index.
ISBN 0 522 84715 3.
1. Penal colonies—New South Wales—History.
2. Deportation—France—History. 3. New South Wales—History—1788–1851. I. Title.
994.402

FRANCE AND BOTANY BAY

Contents

Acknowledgements		ix
Note on Terms		x
Introduction		1

I Learning about Botany Bay, 1788–1831

1	Support for a Penal Colony	7
2	Emerging Opposition in the 1820s	42
3	The Great Parliamentary Debate, 1831	55

II Stalemate, 1831–1848

4	The First History of Australia	72
5	Tocqueville and Australia	92
6	*Histoire de Botany Bay*	118
7	Penal Colonies and Parliament	128
8	The Role of the Navy	143

III The Triumph of Transportation, 1848–1854

9	Napoleon III and French Guiana	155
10	The Navy and New Caledonia	166
	Epilogue	170
Abbreviations		176
Notes		177
Select Bibliography		186
Index		195

Illustrations

Plates

Plan of Port Jackson, 1802, by C.-A. Lesueur Muséum d'Histoire naturelle du Havre	*facing* 22
View of the *Uranie* from the observatory, Port Jackson, 1819, by Alphonse Pellion Bibliothèque nationale, Paris	23
Panorama of Port Jackson showing the French camp, 1802, by C.-A. Lesueur Muséum d'Histoire naturelle du Havre	38
Port Jackson in August 1825, from a drawing by Edmond de la Touanne National Library of Australia, Canberra	38
The town of Sydney and the entrance to Port Jackson, 1802, from a drawing by C.-A. Lesueur National Library of Australia, Canberra	39
Cox's River, west of the Blue Mountains, 1819, from a drawing by Alphonse Pellion Bibliothèque nationale, Paris	39
Title page of the first history of Australia, by Ernest de Blosseville, 1831	86
Title page of the book in which Beaumont and Tocqueville first assessed transportation to Australia, 1833 Bibliothèque nationale, Paris	87

viii   Illustrations

Title page of Jules de la Pilorgerie's 1836 reply to Blosseville's 1831 history Bibliothèque nationale, Paris	102
Plan of the convict barracks, Sydney, 1819, from a sketch by Louis de Freycinet Bibliothèque nationale, Paris	103
Fort Macquarie in 1825, with *L'Espérance* at anchor, from a drawing by Edmond de la Touanne National Library of Australia, Canberra	134
Government gardens in Sydney, 1825, from a drawing by Edmond de la Touanne National Library of Australia, Canberra	134
Macquarie Lighthouse in Sydney, 1826, from a painting by Louis de Sainson Bibliothèque nationale, Paris	135
The entrance to Sydney Cove in 1826, from a painting by Louis de Sainson Bibliothèque nationale, Paris	135
'Vooloo-Moloo', Port Jackson, in 1831, from a drawing by Barthélemy Lauvergne National Library of Australia, Canberra	150
Sydney in 1831, showing the Rocks area and Fort Macquarie, from a drawing by Barthélemy Lauvergne National Library of Australia, Canberra	150
The penitentiary at Port Arthur, Van Diemen's Land, in 1839, by F.-E. Pâris Musée de la Marine, Paris	151

Text illustration

'Rhum' and drunkenness in the early years of penal settlement Bibliothèque nationale, Paris	*page* 68

Acknowledgements

For professional assistance in all aspects of this book I am deeply indebted to Honore Forster.

The generosity of the French Embassy in Canberra made possible the provision of illustrations and, in particular, I should like to thank the Cultural Attaché, Laurent de Gaulle, for his enthusiasm and support for the project. To obtain the illustrations the co-operation was required of the Bibliothèque nationale and the Musée de la Marine in Paris, the Muséum d'Histoire naturelle du Havre and the National Library of Australia; the contribution of Angus Mackenzie of the Australian Embassy in Paris and Beryl Knight of the National Library was appreciated.

Kris Alilunas-Rodgers and Barry Howarth gave valuable advice on translation, but the style and errors are my own.

The writing was completed as a Visiting Fellow in the Economic History Program, Research School of Social Sciences, Australian National University. Members of the Program, headed by Professor Graeme Snooks, provided the physical and intellectual support. I thank them warmly.

Note on Terms

Botany Bay, so named by Captain Cook, was the site originally chosen by the British government for its penal establishment in New South Wales. In France, as elsewhere, the name was commonly used over a long period as a descriptive term for the British penal colonies in eastern Australia. In this book, the context indicates the appropriate meaning.

Only limited use is made of French terms and, when their meaning is not clear, they are explained in the text. Nevertheless, the translation of several terms is worth stating briefly at the outset.

anglais; Angleterre: English; England. In French usage the terms often meant 'British' and 'Great Britain'.

bagne: penal institution in which inmates worked in the naval dockyards.

forçat: prisoner inmate of the *bagne*.

rapporteur: reporter for a parliamentary committee. Translated as 'spokesman' for the committee in his appearance in parliament.

réclusionnaire: prisoner sentenced to longish term of imprisonment with work in a prison called a *maison centrale*.

Introduction

In 1852 the British government ended the transportation of convicts to the eastern colonies of Australia. In the same year French transportation began: the first common criminals left their prisons for camps in French Guiana. One year later the French flag was raised in New Caledonia, and this act was officially justified solely by the desire to establish a penal settlement. In 1868 what was probably the greatest penal experiment of all time was formally brought to a close with the ending of transportation to Western Australia. Only one year earlier, France had announced that henceforth New Caledonia would be the only destination for hard-labour convicts from continental France and that their work would lead to a thriving colony. As the British system of expulsion of criminals, combined with colonial development, crumbled and vanished under the weight of criticism, so the French system was established.

What accounts for such an ambitious penal venture so late in the day? Some other European governments dabbled with overseas penal establishments, but the scale and nature of the French effort were exceptional. It cannot avoid having an anachronistic air. Clearly there were immediate reasons, immediate pressures on the French government, but more importantly transportation was the outcome of a current of French thinking that had a long history. It was a history intimately associated with Australia, and a symbolic date and event for the basis of this thought could well be 1788 and the arrival of the first convict fleet in Botany Bay.

The British settlement of Australia was begun by convicts. Fifty years after the first landing they still made up about two-fifths of the population. In all some 160 000 convicts were transported. Such a novel and vast undertaking has been intensively analysed. Australian historians have had a natural interest in the social behavior and the economic development within this part-convict society. Contemporary British administrators attempted to assess carefully the effects of transportation on convict reform, on the resulting society and on crime in Britain. The study of the effects of transportation has concentrated inevitably on the two countries most affected—Australia and Britain. However, what has not been sufficiently noticed is that the interest in and the influence of the system of transportation were felt much more widely. Never again have European eyes examined Australia so closely. And this was particularly the case with France.

The extent and depth of European interest reflected in part a fascination with the new world so recently opened up in the South Seas. But just as important was the penal aspect. The transportation of convicts to Australia commenced as the modern penal debate was developing. Late in the eighteenth century a number of countries began to replace corporal chastisement with restraints on liberty as the penalty for crime. The form that such restraint should take became one of the great social issues of the Western world. How to combine the often competing claims of deterrence, punishment and reform with the maintenance of costs within acceptable limits? The British were never sure that they had got it right in Australia, and frequently changed the conditions under which the sentence of transportation was served. There was, however, much in the Australian example to attract other countries. Not only did it seem that important penal objectives were obtained by ejecting criminals, but at the same time these very criminals could be used to create a flourishing colony. Nowhere were these sentiments felt more keenly than in France— the greatest power in Europe, a country with a strong maritime tradition and one that had lost one empire and was seeking after 1814 to create another.

The first years of the settlement of Australia coincided with the French Revolution. The accompanying revolution in social thought in France saw the immediate beginning of imprisonment as the normal punishment for criminals. But a quarter century of social upheaval and war meant that it was not until 1814, with peace and the Bourbon restoration, that France could realistically consider the option of a penal colony. The example of Australia prompted considerable support for transportation, but after some delay influential champions of a revamped prison system emerged. The decision whether to persist with prisons or to transport criminals became a major one for successive French governments. This was an issue which could not be settled by theory alone, and both sides felt their case turned critically on the results obtained by Britain through transportation to Botany Bay.

Did the history of Botany Bay demonstrate that a penal colony could be a more effective response to crime, viewed both penally and economically, than a prison at home? Did it also demonstrate that convicts could be the foundation for the development of a free and prosperous community that could be a centre for French trade, migration and influence? Even if the answer to both questions was yes, could the conditions at Botany Bay be replicated in a later era? These questions were at the heart of the French penal debate, and the answers required comprehensive information about Botany Bay, which itself was continually changing. It was also accepted that even a very favourable view on the desirability of a French Botany Bay had to be considered within the context of such factors as the extent of French power, naval ambitions and the availability of a satisfactory site.

This study centres on the influence of Botany Bay on the development of French penal policy in the nineteenth century. It demonstrates the great interest shown by the French in acquiring knowledge concerning the effectiveness of transportation, knowledge which was obtained from sources as diverse as French visitors, Australian newspapers and British parliamentary papers. In turn, this information was the basis for an outpouring of publications in France putting the case for and against penal colonies. The Chamber of Deputies focused attention on it in two great debates in 1831 and 1844. The navy roamed the world searching for a comparable site. While Australian historians have not adequately appreciated the wider impact of Botany Bay throughout Europe, equally French historians have not recognised its pivotal role in the establishment of their own penal system.

It was primarily the penal interest that directed French attention to Australia. However, any assessment of the penal success of transportation necessarily involved an assessment of the social and economic success of Australian society as a whole. So that while French observations on Australia were in the main stimulated by penal concerns, they had in fact a much wider focus. In particular, three outcomes of the French response to Botany Bay are of far greater significance than their immediate influence on penal policy. The first was the production of the first scholarly history of Australia. Written by Ernest de Blosseville and published in 1831, the *Histoire des colonies pénales* . . . was both a response to an intense desire for information and an attempt to influence policy. Its status has never been recognised. It brought a reply in the form of another major history in 1836, Jules de la Pilorgerie's *Histoire de Botany Bay* . . . The third outcome was the involvement of Alexis de Tocqueville in the debate. His observations on American democracy are, of course, famous. Almost unknown is the fact that in 1833 and 1836 he wrote extensively and critically on the transportation system and the resulting Australian society. The works of these three authors are sufficiently important to be considered as historical studies in their own right, rather than solely in terms of their contribution to the penal debate in France.

I
Learning about Botany Bay, 1788–1831

1
Support for a Penal Colony

In the middle of the eighteenth century the Pacific remained an area largely unknown to Europeans. France, as a great power with maritime as well as continental interests, in the forefront of intellectual enquiry, could be expected to play a major role in the opening up of this area over the next half century or so. In fact, war, fiscal problems and internal instability severely limited French participation during this crucial period.

Between the end of the Seven Years War in 1763 and the beginning of the American War of Independence in 1775, several French exploratory voyages were made. None could be called an unqualified success. The most influential was that of Louis-Antoine de Bougainville, who published an account of his circumnavigation in 1771. A second edition followed a year later. Although Bougainville did not make any important discoveries, his voyage was hailed in France as an outstanding achievement. He was honoured at court and sought after by scholars. The crossing of the South Pacific, the sojourn in Tahiti and his return with a Tahitian stimulated widespread interest in the entire region.[1]

The results of the French exploration were quite overshadowed by the success of Cook's three famous voyages, accounts of which were quickly produced in French. The first appeared in 1772, the second in 1778 and the third in 1782. All promoted further interest, along with further feelings of rivalry, and the French government took up the challenge. Very careful planning, adequate resources and high hopes were behind a new expedition to the Pacific. Led by Jean-François de Galaup de Lapérouse, it was primarily one of geographic discovery and scientific research, but commerce and geo-politics were also important considerations.[2] Lapérouse's two ships sailed in 1785 but, having accomplished many of the purposes of the voyage, were last seen by Europeans when they left Botany Bay in February 1788. Such was the mystery and the concern over Lapérouse's disappearance that even the turmoil of the early years of the Revolution did not prevent the dispatch of a fresh expedition to try to discover his fate. This mission, which set out in 1791, under d'Entrecasteaux, was unsuccessful in its main aims and fell apart as the ship's company reacted to the revolutionary impulse emanating from France. In 1791 the decision was made to publish Lapérouse's journals, dispatched before he left Botany Bay, and this was accomplished in three volumes by 1797. His disappearance in the South Seas remained a challenge to French exploration.

The extraordinary venture of the transportation of British criminals across the world to establish a settlement in New South Wales in 1788 excited particular French interest. English works on the initial voyage and the early days of the colony appeared quickly in French. Beginning in 1789, Watkin Tench's *Voyage à la Baie Botanique* ... ran to a number of editions. Stockdale's *Voyage du Gouverneur Phillip à Botany Bay* ... appeared in 1791 and John White's *Voyage à la Nouvelle Galles du Sud* ... in 1795. The translator of White's book, Charles Pougens, thought the settlement would ruin England financially; and in a comment presaging the coming penal debate, and possibly influenced by recent French history, wrote: 'the only real advantage ... is to have contributed to the introduction of a less barbarous jurisprudence and to have suggested to the government the salutary idea of commuting the death penalty to a simple deportation'. And he went on to implore his country, and some leaders by name, to do away with the death penalty: 'let us kill the crimes, but not the culprits'.[3] Apart from these translations,* English newspapers

---

*The last translation to appear in the 1790s was the very popular adventures of George Barrington, *Voyage à Botany-Bay* ... (Paris, 1798). Barrington, a convict, was something of a folk hero in England. He became a chief constable in New South Wales. The accounts of his life are fraudulent. (*Australian Dictionary of Biography*, vol. 1, pp. 62–3)

and journals provided another source of information for widespread French comment and speculation. A very early example occurred in a 1789 prize-winning eulogy of Captain Cook by a parliamentarian, Pierre-Edouard Lémontey:

> Travelling prisons conceal in their bowels a criminal population and vomit this frightful mixture of tainted and depraved men on to the coasts of New Holland. Oh sensitive philosopher, avert not your gaze: work and necessity on a desert shore will purify these dregs of the great cities. Perhaps a strong and hard-working nation will emerge from a vile rabble of convicts, as in other times a swarm of ruffians founded the empire of the Caesars. Life everywhere is born of corruption. It is to fetid dung that we owe both the golden harvests and the dazzling vine.[4] *

In spite of the French interest in the Pacific and in Australia, it is remarkable that in this period of almost continuous revolution and war even one expedition of exploration and scientific research was mounted. This was Nicolas Baudin's voyage of 1800–1804, for which the instructions related particularly to uncharted portions of the Australian coastline. War with Britain required a passport endorsing the enterprise. In the event, the expedition spent five months at Port Jackson, from June to November 1802, and this provided the opportunity for a first-hand account of the settlement by its naturalist, François Péron. He obtained a considerable fame in France and, since his remained the only important observations by a Frenchman until the 1820s, they were of particular importance in influencing early French opinion.[†]

---

*Lémontey had another vision of Australia's future: 'The position of New Holland will make it one day the meeting place of the world. An English colony will soon attract others to its fertile shores; China will perhaps place there its superfluous population; the reclusive Japanese will come there to mingle with the great human family; the European and the Malay, the American and the Asiatic will meet there without astonishment.' (P.-E. Lémontey, *Éloge de Jacques Cook*, pp. 53–4)

†A different view, reported in *Moniteur* of 3 January 1803, was given in an address by Citizen Toulongeon on the foundation of colonies: 'The settlement that the English government has formed at Botany-Bay invites the attention of the observer, of the philosopher; it is the first time anyone has dared to fashion a society from all that is wicked in another; success, and even success proven by long experience,

The report on the voyage appeared in a number of volumes. The first, by Péron, entitled *Voyage de découvertes aux terres australes* . . . , was published in 1807. While in Sydney the naturalist had travelled extensively and established close relations with prominent residents. His description of the settlement opened in glowing terms: 'how astonished we were at the flourishing state of this singular and distant colony'.* His portrait of the settlement emphasised the physical accomplishments and the advanced state of development that it had reached. He hardly mentioned the penal aspect and the role of the convicts, except to dwell on the change in the convicts' morals that transportation had brought about:

> The colony's population was for us a new subject of astonishment and reflection. Never perhaps has a more worthy object of study been presented to a statesman or philosopher. Never perhaps has the happy influence of social institutions been proven in a more striking and creditable manner than on the distant shores of which we are speaking. There, brought together, are those terrible ruffians who were for so long the terror of the government of their country: thrust from the bosom of European society, consigned to the extremities of the globe, placed from the first moment of their exile between the certainty of punishment and the hope of a more happy fate, encompassed by constant surveillance, inflexible and assiduous, they have been forced to lay aside their anti-social behaviour. The majority, having atoned for their crimes by a hard bondage, have rejoined the ranks of the citizens. Obliged to concern themselves

---

would scarcely justify such an undertaking'. (p. 414) And Toulongeon thought the society carried the seeds of its own dissolution. Anyone who did well would try to leave and then would conceal his origins. Moreover, the government divided the colonists into two classes, deported and free, and these two groups would never unite.

*Other members of the expedition were also impressed, and Baudin himself in a dispatch to the Minister of the Navy in 1803 wrote: 'I should warn you that the colony of Port Jackson well merits the attention of the Government . . . People in France and elsewhere are far from being able to imagine how large and prosperous the English have been able to make this colony in the space of fourteen years—a colony whose size and prosperity can only increase further each year through the efforts of the Government'. (F. Horner, *The French Reconnaissance*, p. 273)

with the maintenance of law and order to safeguard the property they have acquired, having become nearly at the same time husbands and fathers, they are bound to their present state by the most powerful and beloved ties.

The same revolution, brought about by the same means, has taken place in the women; and miserable prostitutes, gradually restored to more proper principles of conduct, are today bright and hard-working mothers of families.[5]

This historical volume took the expedition as far as Port Jackson, but the remainder was not published until 1816. Péron died in December 1810 with most of the narrative written, and its completion had to wait on the availability of his fellow traveller, Louis Freycinet, who was writing another volume on navigation and geography. It was in thirty-five pages of this 1816 historical volume that Péron's developed and expanded views on the colony were recorded.[6] He began by discussing the conditions associated with free settlement, but then turned to the position of the convicts where the laws had 'the same spirit of wisdom and justice'. The convicts were contained and improved by fear and hope: fear of very severe punishment and hope of remission of sentence and eventual prosperity. When freed, the ex-convict had all the rights of a free man, and they 'appear almost always honest and circumspect'. The habit of hard work obtained during their bondage made them in this aspect superior to free migrants. They were successful as farmers and in arts and commerce, and Péron predicted that in less than thirty years many would make fortunes. The transformation of the women showed 'the triumph of the legislation and the ultimate in social improvement'. Most men were single, but the marriage of convict couples improved their behaviour, was generally happy and produced an outstanding new generation. Because of the viciousness of some of the criminals and their harsh treatment, the words 'Botany Bay' still might provoke horror, but this would surely change and all would 'better understand the wisdom of the directions which regulate and guarantee the brilliant future to which it is called'. Péron's description of the colony concluded with sections in which he praised the expansion of trade and the financial system.*

France entered the period of peace with only one account of the Australian penal settlement by a Frenchman. It acclaimed the economic development of the colony, but it also gave a wholehearted endorsement of the British transportation system and of the beneficial effects on the transportees. For a considerable period and for many Frenchmen it remained the only assessment of the penal settlement. It was a point of departure for the emerging transportation debate and was one which opponents of transportation felt they had to counter.

FRANCE IN 1814: THE LAW, PRISONS AND PRISONERS

The government of the Restoration inherited a penal philosophy and system which had changed decisively in the period of Revolution and Empire. The weight of sentences had shifted from corporal punishment to imprisonment, and an emphasis on vengeance and deterrence was broadened to include reform. Before the Revolution, the 'modern' prison in which those sentenced could spend long periods did not exist. Prisons were places where people were detained by court procedures before their real punishment. This could be death, physical chastisements like branding, whipping or placing in stocks, banishment (local or national), and occasionally fines or short periods of detention.[7] The punishment closest to imprisonment was to be oarsmen in the Mediterranean galleys; given the conditions on the galleys, whatever the period of the sentence, it was often for life. By the middle of the eighteenth century the galleys had been decommissioned, and this type of prisoner was then sent to work in *bagnes*—institutions in which inmates worked in the naval dockyards. The four best-known and longest-run of the *bagnes* were Toulon (1748–1873), Brest (1749–1858), Rochefort (1767–1852) and Lorient (1794–1830).[8] The population of the *bagnes* was about 5400 in 1789.[9]

---

*In footnotes, Freycinet updates some of Péron's material. His principal source is John Turnbull, *Voyage fait autour du monde en 1800, 1801, 1802, 1803 et 1804*...

1 Support for a Penal Colony

In keeping with the spirit of the Declaration of the Rights of Man, legal procedures were dramatically changed in 1791, and a scale of offences was drawn up and related to prison sentences of different lengths. Types of prisons also indicated the nature of the crime and the sentence. The death sentence remained, and *bagnes* were retained in what was intended as a temporary expedient for those sentenced to hard labour. A new development was the introduction of deportation for life, but it was restricted to second offenders and then only after they had served their second sentence in France. In introducing this half-hearted measure, the spokesman for the committee on legislation explained that, although some well-informed people favoured deportation, it failed to meet the important test for punishment: 'distant from the place of the crime, [it] failed . . . to render the example present and lasting'. It was also, he felt, insufficiently repressive for most criminals. The actual legislation was intended to meet both these objections as well as expelling the incorrigible from France.* After discussion with the navy minister the committee favoured a penal settlement not in an existing colony but 'on the divers lands of the African coast'.[10] In fact this legislation was never drawn on to deport common criminals, although over the next twenty years several hundred political deportees were shipped off to various parts of the French empire, none of which was found to be altogether suitable for this purpose.

The penal code was rewritten and made more repressive under Napoleon in 1810, but a hierarchy of prisons remained the basis of the system. Earlier, in 1801, Napoleon had declared himself in favour of the transportation of common criminals:

> This measure is urgent. It is in accord with public opinion, and is prescribed by humane considerations. The need for it is so obvious that we should provide for it at once in the Civil Code. We have now in our prisons 6,000 persons who are doing nothing, who

---

*In 1791 the French were strongly influenced by English legal institutions, and in this instance it has been claimed that they had the example of Botany Bay in mind. See F. de Barbé-Marbois, *Observations sur les votes*, p. 11. They were also aware of English criticisms concerning the penal effectiveness of Botany Bay.

cost a great deal of money, and who are always escaping ... Transportation is imprisonment certainly, but in a cell more than thirty square feet.[11]

Notwithstanding his view, the code of 1810 retained deportation only for political offences.*

Throughout the period the *bagnes* continued to receive prisoners, so that they held an estimated 16 000 near the end of Napoleon's rule.[12] These institutions and their inmates, the *forçats*, posed a special challenge to those who wished to change the penal system. The regime there was one of hard labour, and the *forçats* were paired together in chains, which could range from light to very heavy. Twice a year, those sentenced to *bagnes* were assembled in Paris and in a humiliating fashion were marched across France to their respective ports.[13] They were 'legendary figures, objects of fascinated horror among the general population'.[14] Of special concern were the *forçats libérés*—those freed at the end of their term. Whatever their original offence, it was generally agreed that they emerged from the *bagnes* as hardened criminals and that they were the main source of serious crime.

More generally, France entered the Restoration with a newly established penal system centred on the prison. In theory, individual prisons were designated according to type of prisoner, length of sentence and expected behaviour. However, there was little agreement on the philosophy behind the prison system, the bureaucracy was inefficient, the buildings were inadequate and unsuited for their purpose, and conditions in the prisons were often appalling. In short, the system was in a mess and decisions were needed about its future course of development.[15] One strand of thought saw an important role for penal colonies.

In February 1819 the French government established a committee to consider the question of sending prisoners overseas to a penal

---

*Legally, deportation (*déportation*) after 1810 applied to political offences only and meant exclusion from France for life under some constraints in a French colony. In the ensuing penal debate it was very often (and confusingly) also given the meaning of 'transportation' of common criminals as used in British law.

1 Support for a Penal Colony

colony. In part its action stemmed from the increase in the numbers sentenced to deportation for political reasons after the Restoration. It was claimed that between 1815 and 1817 the Minister of the Navy had been unsuccessful in a search for a satisfactory penal site,[16] so that political offenders were perforce imprisoned in France. But pressure built up quickly for a penal colony as a solution not only to problems for the navy in administering the growing number of *forçats* in the *bagnes*, but also to more general problems associated with prisons in France. Indicative of this growing sentiment is a fifty-page memoir by M. Forestier, dated 14 October 1816. Forestier was an important bureaucrat, a Councillor of State of the Committee of the Navy and Colonies and later an influential member of the 1819 Committee.* In his memoir he raised most of the issues around which debate would focus for decades.[17]

Forestier began by drawing on Blackstone, 'the most learned jurist in England', to the effect that modern criminal laws should have as their aim 'to reform the offender, to remove his means of relapsing into crime and by his example to keep in check his fellows'. In these developments he considered that England had gone far: 'Nearly all the crimes which involve the death penalty, are punished by deportation. A new continent offers the convicts a new homeland, a new life, hopes of fortune and prospects of pardon'. At the same time the colony would grow and prosper. Contrast this with France where the prisons and *bagnes* were costly, produced little work and were schools of crime from which prisoners emerged more dangerous than when they entered. It was therefore necessary, Forestier concluded, 'to follow England's example and found a colony for deportation. Justice, morality and good policy demand this establishment, and when so many interests tend towards the same goal they should be speedily satisfied'. Such a colony should also be open to free migration, and the more it was examined the more necessary it was to 'render homage to the excellence of the English system of colonisation'.

---

*The Council of State was a very important advisory council to the government. At the time it divided into five committees of which one was Navy and Colonies.

For the administration of such a colony, Forestier fell back on the model provided in Péron's observations of Port Jackson in 1802, where he felt work and wise and severe laws had transformed criminals into useful farmers; and 'what is still more astonishing, women formerly lost to debauchery, have forgotten their previous degradation and have become hard-working mothers of families'. The French government, therefore, should 'follow the system of colonisation of our predecessors', as set out in Péron's account.

In these matters Forestier was able to make confident recommendations. It was a different matter when it came to naming a satisfactory location for a settlement. From one of the 'numerous' memoirs that he said had been submitted to the government, he drew some general requirements: the place should be 'circumscribed, isolated, distant' with 'a healthy climate and a fertile soil'. Nowhere open to the French—French Guiana, Senegal or Madagascar—quite satisfied him. Possible areas appeared to be occupied by the colonial powers—Britain, Spain, Holland and Portugal. And in the end he was forced back to the lame recommendation of negotiating the occupancy of Crete, then part of the Turkish empire. What is clear from Forestier's memoir is his unbounded enthusiasm for a penal colony, the supporting evidence for which he found mainly in Péron's account of Sydney in 1802.

In January 1819 there were two important submissions to the Minister of the Navy and Colonies, Baron Portal, concerning *bagnes*. One, from Baron Degérando, a Councillor of State, was a plan for improvement in the regime in the *bagnes*. The other, written by Admiral Willaumez, argued for the establishment of a penal colony of *forçats* in Guiana.* Both writers were later appointed to the 1819 Committee.[18] Their plans, 'joined with many others which, for a long time, had been presented for the same object, were sent to a committee'.[19] One other influence should be mentioned. Interior Minister Lainé, in a report to the

---

*C. Schéfer claims that Portal, as Director of the Colonies (1816–19) had from 1816 already thought of *forçats* as a source for a colonial workforce, and that Willaumez's plan was the direct cause of him setting up the committee. (*La France moderne et le problème colonial*, p. 192)

1 Support for a Penal Colony

King in November 1818 on begging, prisons and *bagnes*, recognised both the case for deportation of *forçats* and the problems associated with it. He called for more research and public discussion to assist the government in making a decision.[20] In fact, information was already being sought from England: in June 1817 the French Ambassador had been asked 'to procure for the department of the navy, documents on the laws and regulations in use at Botany Bay'.[21]

The high-level committee of ten, chaired by Count Siméon, deliberated for only four meetings. The principal question put to it was: 'Is it fitting to substitute . . . the punishment of deportation for that of hard labour [*travaux forcés*]?'[22] The committee appears to have had little difficulty in rejecting the existing system of *bagnes* and deciding on some level of deportation.[23] Forestier was able to draw on his 1816 memoir, and he argued that gaols only made people worse: 'I found that in establishing the colony of "Sydney-Cove" the English had solved this problem; and that the same means would lead us to the same results'.[24] It was the second question—'What place should be chosen for the stay of the convicts?'[25]—that caused real difficulties. Nowhere in the French empire was acceptable, and Forestier appears to have won the committee over with an argument for south-west Australia.[26] However, Lainé attended the last session and, although he endorsed the Australian site for which he thought France had a legal title based on prior exploration, he raised serious concerns about possible British reactions.[27] In the event the committee was indecisive: there was no report and nothing was officially communicated to the ministry.* Possibly there was an understanding that the navy should seek out a possible site for a penal colony. Certainly, Portal almost immediately approached the *Commandant et Administrateur* of Guiana with a view to establishing a colony of *forçats* there. He was rebuffed; opposition was 'violent and unanimous', mainly because of its expected effects on white status in a country where there was a black slave

---

*A draft of the minutes indicates that the committee concluded in favour of 'a point on the western coast of New Holland, or one of the islands of the Pacific'. (Hyde de Neuville, 'Rapport au Roi', p. 692)

population.[28] In 1821, in a memorandum to the minister, Forestier regretted the lack of any action. He thought that 'interests still more weighty, if that is possible, and the protracted work of the Chambers have absorbed all the thoughts of the Government'. Suggesting that the times were now more favourable, he again recommended south-west Australia or Crete.[29]

BARBÉ-MARBOIS AND THE CHAMBER OF PEERS

Soon after the meetings of the 1819 Committee, Comte François de Barbé-Marbois, who became the most knowledgeable, outspoken and influential of the opponents of deportation, drew on its discussions in a debate in the Chamber of Peers, the upper house of the French parliament. He himself had been deported without trial to Guiana for political reasons in 1797, and he liked to refer to himself as a *déporté non-jugé*.[30] On 30 March 1819 he submitted a proposal to the Chamber of Peers for a law to substitute some other appropriate punishment for deportation, 'the execution of which is recognised as impossible'.* Supporting his proposal Barbé-Marbois put forward three main arguments. First, the knowledge of the impossibility of deportation had upset the sentencing policies of the courts, and very few had been so sentenced; it was also unjust that 50 to 55 men sentenced to deportation should be held at the prison of Mont Saint-Michel until a site for their deportation could be found. Second, to establish and maintain a penal settlement France would need a sustained period of peace or at least freedom to use the seas for peaceful purposes. Third, it was most unlikely that France would find a suitable site for a penal colony, but even if it did, consider the problems as exemplified by the English experience in Australia:

> New Holland, as vast as Europe, will perhaps sustain in future centuries 60 million inhabitants. Now a few savage tribes are scattered there. The English, with most humane intentions and in

---

*He appears to have been prompted by the attempt in the Chamber several weeks earlier to revoke some emergency legislation dating from 1815. This legislation, designed to deal with the situation following Bonaparte's final departure, placed emphasis on deportation for serious political offences. (*AP*, 6 Mar. 1819, pp. 180–4)

1 Support for a Penal Colony

order to restore vicious men to virtue through their interest in their own welfare, have founded there, at enormous expense, the greatest establishment for deportation that has ever existed. Today this nation, after thirty years of efforts, seems to recognise that this is not how a regular and happy society is attained. Economy and morality are the basic requirements for it.

Although, Barbé-Marbois continued, the English had sent out free farmers who have prospered, they were unhappy in a society where a mixture of the free and the condemned had led to general corruption and undisciplined convicts. Moreover and most importantly, he argued, the costs to England were so great that it would have abandoned deportation to Port Jackson were it not so committed. The cost to France of a similar undertaking would be equally large.[31]

The response in the Chamber of Peers was to establish a committee of five, including Barbé-Marbois, to consider his proposal. It reported its rejection—four to one—to the Chamber on 22 April. Its main reason for rejection was that since 1810 the French penal code specified deportation for a group of narrowly defined, basically political, offences. In addition, some temporary legislation had recently let to an increase in the number sentenced to deportation, but it still totalled only 111. This, it was pointed out, was in total contrast with numbers transported from England, so that much of Barbé-Marbois' argument was irrelevant. No great expense would be involved in deportation since France would not need a colony like that at Botany Bay. Was there any chance that deportation could become a more general punishment? Not at all. This might happen where there were 'arbitrary governments, especially in weak hands',[32] but such a description could not be applied to France, with its precise penal code. If Barbé-Marbois wanted alternative penalties to deportation, the only candidates under the existing system were hard labour for a term in the *bagnes* or, less severely, a significant term in prison with work (*réclusion*); and these, it was suggested, would be less acceptable to political prisoners, not least because of the humiliation associated with them:

Those condemned to either of these two punishments must be fastened *in the iron collar of a pillory in a public place with a sign, exposed to the gaze of the people.* (Art. 22.)

Those condemned to deportation do not suffer this disgrace, which would be for them worse than death, even one accompanied by the songs and dances of savages.[33]

The single aspect of his case on which the committee agreed with Barbé-Marbois was that the sentence of deportation was not being executed, and that it was unsatisfactory to hold these prisoners in Mont Saint-Michel until a place was determined. From the situation, however, it drew a conclusion, the opposite of that of Barbé-Marbois: deportation should be enforced, not abolished. Accordingly it proposed this amendment: 'The King will be beseeched to have presented to the Chambers a law which organises the mode and assures the execution of the punishment of deportation'.[34]

In his reply in the Chamber to the committee, Barbé-Marbois attempted to argue that under the existing penal code large numbers had in fact been sentenced to deportation, and that in any case the future might provide such numbers. He then shifted his ground: 'Another circumstance will perhaps yet arise to increase the number of deportees by several thousand'. In explanation, he said that information provided by 'the ministry' had stated that discussions had recently taken place between the representatives of several departments concerning the employment of *forçats* overseas. He therefore felt that he could legitimately raise important questions about the success of large-scale deportation, and these inevitably led him to a discussion of the Australian experience. He argued that this type of deportation failed the two most important tests of the usefulness of punishment—deterrence and reformation. For the first of these, the sentence was not observable and might even be attractive:

The offender, the *forçat*, deported an immense distance, will be withdrawn from the gaze of those who could be turned from crime by the sight of his punishment. His fault is known; his punishment is not, or if other offenders know what deportation entails, there is nothing in the nature of this punishment to alarm criminals; perhaps they are even sufficiently depraved to desire it. Deportation has existed for thirty years in England, and for thirty years the number of crimes has grown at a frightening rate. Let us fear a similar result and profit from this sad experience.[35]

Deportation had also failed, Barbé-Marbois claimed, as a means of reforming criminals, and here he found the Australian experience even more damning: 'Not only is it not obtained by deportation, but the official reports received from New South Wales have shown that all kinds of disturbances have made disastrous progress'. He admitted the prosperity of the colony, but in colourful language proceeded to attack its morality:

> The efforts of wisdom and humanity are foiled by the affluence of the deportees, of whom a great number is of the type of convict who fills our *bagnes*. These corrupt men are no longer in a state of captivity there; they communicate and trade inevitably and freely together; they tell each other the discoveries that they have made in criminal skills, they boast about them, they admire each other. They are not seen, as elsewhere, shamed and friendless. They form secret societies; they impose secret rules the better to assure their impunity; they distribute ranks among themselves according to their respective competency, and the more daring, the more wicked, are the chiefs of these detestable societies. The savages who approach them often receive dreadful lessons from them, and, at the beginning of the settlement, these savage tribes had thought that the vices of these outcasts from society were the ordinary products of civilisation. Drunkenness, the passion for strong drink, an unrestrained debauchery, an idleness against which punishment does not succeed, the theft of livestock and sheaves on the plantations, murder and violence of every kind, such are the practices which, among the convicts, replace the openness and moderation necessary for the relations between men in society. They burn down a church in order to dispense with being present at religious services. They burn the very crops, and they revenge themselves on a public officer or on a magistrate by setting fire to the stores which contain their own provisions and clothing which would be distributed to them.

It is observed that the women, who elsewhere are certainly not inferior to the men in virtue, surpass them in depravity in the state of deportation. Thus this punishment has served only to make mankind more vicious and sinful.[36]

Indeed, Barbé-Marbois observed, all these effects were exactly as predicted by Jeremy Bentham twenty-five years before.* But it was not only that deportation to New South Wales failed as a punishment; many convicts escaped and some had the audacity to return to their former homeland. And, of course, there were the costs of the settlement: 'They are so big that this nation [England], the richest in the world, finds them disproportionate to their benefit'.[37]

The committee had rejected Barbé-Marbois' claim that deportation was 'impossible' in the sense that there was no satisfactory site available. He now returned to the subject, pointing out that he could obtain some support from the fact that no deportation had occurred in the last twenty-seven years. But he placed much more emphasis on information about the 1819 Committee that the government had 'readily' provided, and from which he quoted:

> Among the *forçats* who are in the *bagnes*, there are some who, in execution of their sentence, should be deported at the completion of their punishment in chains.
>
> Several persons were charged by different ministers to examine the means of deporting overseas. No plan was decided on. The torrid climate, the safety of the inhabitants, absolutely rule out French colonies as a destination. One appreciates the numerous difficulties which could impede the establishment of a penal colony in New-Holland, and at the same time it was considered that, except for a particular consideration,† this would be the only place suitable to receive these deportees.[38]

---

*Jeremy Bentham, philosopher and reformer, was the most important of the early English critics of transportation to Australia. He argued for the use of a circular prison, a panopticon, at home. For a brief account of Bentham's views on this issue, see J. B. Hirst, *Convict Society and its Enemies*, pp. 10–15.

†The 'particular consideration' to which the government referred was, of course, possible British reaction.

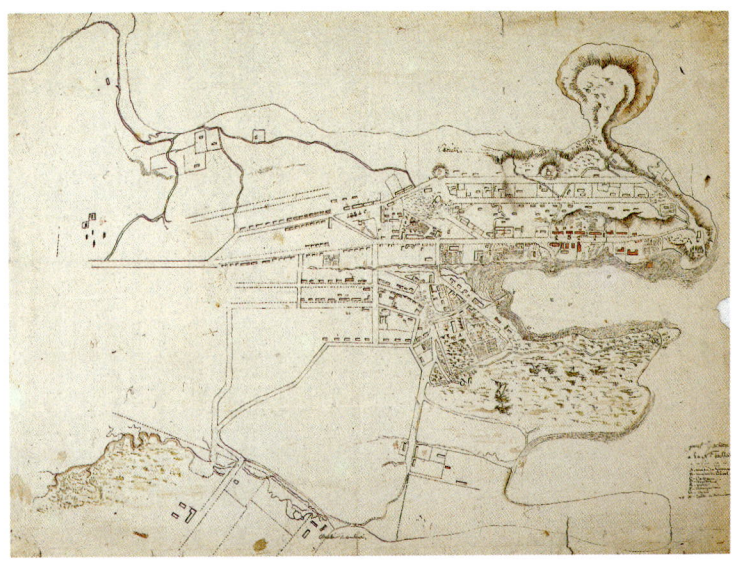

The Baudin expedition in Sydney, 1802: C.-A. Lesueur's plan of Port Jackson [Collection Lesueur du Havre 16074-1, Muséum d'Histoire naturelle du Havre]

Port Jackson: a view of the *Uranie* from the observatory painted in 1819 by Alphonse Pellion, a member of the Freycinet expedition of 1817–20 [Rose de Saulces de Freycinet, *Campagne de l'Uranie. Journal de Madame Rose de Saulces de Freycinet. D'après le manuscrit original . . .*, Paris, 1927, Plate 25]

With this authority to hand, Barbé-Marbois claimed that, if he could show Australia was not a suitable location for deportees, then he would have shown that deportation in general was impossible. What he drew on in explanation was obviously the experience of extreme deprivation at Port Jackson for the first years. Imagine, he said, that in spite of all the difficulties a French colony had been successfully established for several years in Australia, there would still remain an insurmountable drawback:

> But New Holland is 6,000 leagues away. We have on the route neither port of call, nor settlement nor commercial stations scattered on the Ocean which, a short distance apart, form for another people a chain joining the mother country to its most distant settlements.[39]

These considerations meant journeys of seven or eight months at sea, and any delay in the flow of supplies, any natural disaster affecting food supplies in the colony, would lead to famine and the colony's destruction. It was up to the committee, Barbé-Marbois concluded, if it persisted with its amendment, to show that deportation to New Holland could be effectively organised.

In the event the Chamber took no positive action and simply adjourned Barbé-Marbois' motion. In the debate it was generally accepted that under existing law only political offenders could be sentenced to deportation and that currently the numbers were small. Barbé-Marbois' criticism of the large penal settlement in Australia was therefore considered inapplicable to the French situation. As one member put it:

> If different ministers are occupied with the possibility of deporting the *forçats* who fill our *bagnes*, if the government, recognising this possibility, presents to the Chambers a draft bill to authorise this transport, then we shall hear the noble author of the motion . . . reproduce his researches and reflections whose opportuneness will no longer be contested.

In a concluding comment, the Minister of the Interior said that some deportees had been pardoned and that the immediate problem was what to do about sixty-nine deportees held at Mont Saint-Michel. Personally, he thought Senegal was a possibility.[40]

In a broader context, the significance of Barbé-Marbois' argument in support of his attack on deportation was that he brought together two themes which were to be central to the emerging penal debate. One was deportation on a large scale, especially of *forçats*, which many would see as a solution for a number of problems associated with punishment. The other was the extent to which the demonstration of the possible success of such a policy would hinge on an assessment of the results obtained by Britain in Australia. Barbé-Marbois was, of course, a passionate opponent of deportation, and he acknowledged a debt to H. G. Bennet whose work attacking transportation had just been published in England.[41] He had access then to the very recent criticisms being raised in England concerning the effectiveness and cost of the Australian penal settlements. Nothing in the debate suggests other speakers were as well informed. Although defeated, Barbé-Marbois could have drawn satisfaction that his opponents had been forced to emphasise that the law limited deportation to some specified political offences only.

PERCEPTIONS OF TRANSPORTATION 1820–1828

During the 1820s a climate of opinion developed in France in favour of transportation. It was spurred by what was perceived as a high and rising rate of crime, which was associated particularly with recidivism. And the problem of recidivism, in France itself, would of course be solved by transportation for life. Looking back on the decade from 1831, a historian of the period, Ernest de Blosseville, wrote:

> ... numerous voices demanded for France an establishment like England's penal colony. Properly alarmed by an increase in the number of those convicted ... seeing moreover in our *bagnes* and in our prisons only schools where all the secrets of immorality are taught, all of France seemed to rise to ask, not for new punishments against the crimes which afflicted it, but for effective measures to prevent crime. Publicists could not remain apart from this great movement of public opinion. Various writings, most notable for the wisdom of their principles and the absence of declamation,

soon threw fresh light on a question of such general interest, and most papers kept readers informed.[42]

An editorial comment in 1828 in the semi-official journal of the naval department thought the argument for transportation won:

> One could say that the question appeared morally resolved; and if it was a subject raised several times in the *Annales maritimes et coloniales*, it was less to discuss it than to hasten its accomplishment and to advise on means of soon putting into execution a project that so many people still consider infinitely salutary for the country.[43]

Both the above sources could be regarded as favouring the establishment of penal colonies, and therefore perhaps interested in exaggerating the extent of public support. But a similar assessment was made by those opposed to this view. Barbé-Marbois in 1828 noted that numerous departmental governments favoured deportation, 'and undoubtedly they expressed the sentiments of the population'; and he added that it was 'an opinion which seems to be shared by so many good minds'.[44] Similarly, Maurice Alhoy in 1830 referred to the 'general infatuation' in France for a penal colony. He noted:

> ... the great fame of the English settlement in New Holland; everywhere it is only a question of Botany Bay, of this miraculous land, so that it would be said that it is enough to arrive in order to become good and virtuous again. In France, Botany Bay is the unanswered argument of the partisans of reform ...[45]

During the 1820s the departmental governments mentioned by Barbé-Marbois increasingly felt that public order was threatened by crime committed by *forçats* who had served their time. During these years they passed motions expressing support for deportation as a means of keeping such men out of the country. Some specifically stated that they favoured a penal colony like the one at Botany Bay. By 1827 the number of departmental governments which had formally endorsed deportation was at least 41 out of a total of 86.[46] Their votes obtained considerable publicity, and were often used to illustrate the widespread nature of support for penal colonies. This popular demand for penal colonies and their association with Botany Bay had been stimulated by Péron's 1816 account, which had been republished in 1824. His views received strong support from another French observer, Jacques Arago who, while draughtsman on the expedition captained by Freycinet, spent a little over a month in Sydney in 1819. Presented to the general reader in the form of letters to a friend, Arago's lively story of his visit, *Promenade autour du monde* . . . , was published in 1822. And what general reader could not but be impressed by his description of the operation of the transportation system and the resulting settlement?

> Thieves were devastating England. Prostitutes were ruining families; a corner of the earth, almost at the antipodes of London, offered a safe refuge from storms; some whale fishermen, and an experienced captain, gave a glowing description of this country; a philosopher conceived a noble and philanthropic plan. Ships employed by the state are loaded with those whom the metropolis disavows as its children; they arrive in New Holland . . . The thief forgets his crimes in an active and hard-working life; the prostitute becomes a wife and mother, and only recalls her aberrant behaviour in order to detest it; her children receive lessons in probity and honour from her; land is shared out by a wise, impartial and strict Governor, who gives with discernment and refuses with firmness; it is brought into cultivation by strong arms which demand riches from it of which they will no longer have to be ashamed. Those mighty trees which had been raised with so much difficulty over the centuries fall and roll on the earth which had nourished them. Spacious buildings replace smoke-filled huts; a lively and radiant population is restless, eager for pleasures in those very places where savages gave themselves up to murderous combat but a short time ago. Obscure paths become broad and level roads; a city rises, a colony is formed, Sidney [sic] becomes a flourishing town.*

---

*Possibly to avoid any misunderstanding by the reader of his praise of the settlement, Arago declared: 'For my part, I avow that the word *English* never resounds painfully to my ear, whereas *english Nation* distresses it'. (J. Arago, *Promenade autour du monde*, vol. 2, p. 269)

1 Support for a Penal Colony

And what of the town itself?

> I do not want to give you a description of the town which I've just passed through; I'm under a spell, and prefer to let my imagination have a rest. Magnificent townhouses, majestic mansions, homes of taste and extraordinary elegance, fountains decorated by sculptures worthy of the chisels of our best artists, spacious and well ventilated apartments, sumptuous furniture, horses, carriages and gigs of the most exquisite elegance, vast storehouses: would one believe that all this can be found four thousand leagues from Europe. I assure you my friend, I thought myself transported into one of our most beautiful cities.

When Arago turned to the moral transformation wrought in the convicts at 'Sidney Cow', he was equally rhapsodic:

> And these culprits that England has spewed out, are they not formidable enemies of the citizens' peace of mind, there where their flight is easier, there where live independent people disposed to welcome them? Again you are mistaken, dear sir: there the forger is employed in useful work, which at first gives him land, then esteem, and finally honours. There the thief, abjuring his blameworthy habits, often attains the magistracy, and even becomes here the scourge of thieves. I have seen a swindler, now honoured with the just confidence of the Government, bestowing upon the children of Sidney as much by his example as by his teaching, principles of the strictest virtue and the greatest honour. One would say that the air of this country, though savages breathe it, purifies the mind and makes every noble sentiment grow within it.[47]

Arago wrote for the public. Other writers attempted to influence penal policy as much by directing their arguments to the Department of the Navy and Colonies. In 1828, the minister commented:

> Since the year 1819 up to today, several works have been published, as much on the question of colonisation of *forçats* as on improvements to introduce in the regime of the *bagnes*; others, in greater numbers, have remained unpublished: most contain useful views that the administration is eager to turn to account.[48]

To suggest the type of argument advanced in favour of transportation in these works, a brief outline will be given of two of the better-known pamphlets. The first, published in 1826 by J.-F.-T. Ginouvier, was a thirty-two page memoir addressed to Count Chabrol de Crouzol, Minister of the Navy and Colonies. In the strongest language, Ginouvier claimed that France was being swamped with crime; in the *bagnes* criminals became more corrupt; when released they created havoc in society and the system of surveillance was useless: 'Repentance is only a word for he who has the vocation of robbery and murder'. Now, society 'clamours for deportation . . . in a distant land, where they may be able to regenerate themselves and live out their lives without making criminal attacks on others'. He argued strongly for French Guiana which 'will be for France what New South Wales is for England. Our colony will be like Sydney: free colonists will derive great advantages from legal slaves'.[49] In general, the new colony would be modelled along the lines of Botany Bay: freed convicts would prosper and would not want to return to a life of shame in France. Guiana would prosper and France would benefit.

The second pamphlet, *De la colonisation des condamnés . . .*, was sixty-seven pages in length and was published in 1827. It was written by Benoiston de Chateauneuf and drew some material from Ginouvier.* Benoiston de Chateauneuf noted that deportation had been the subject of a good deal of writing: 'I come to join my ideas to those of others'. Again, he identified the growth of crime as the problem. Some saw a solution in religion but he disagreed: deportation was the answer. A particular problem was the growth in numbers of ex-convicts resulting, as he saw it, from the healthy life in the *bagnes* which permitted convicts to live a long time. When freed, convicts led a miserable existence because they were rejected by the community, and they often returned to

---

*Benoiston de Chateauneuf was a distinguished statistician and demographer, and a prolific writer. In his entry in Quérard, *La littérature française contemporaine* (vol. 1, 1842, p. 276), the following comment is made on his penal pamphlet: 'M. Ad. Gondinet, who, in the 'Revue Encyclopédique' (vol. 33, p. 556), has reviewed this work, ends by saying "that it recommends itself by a host of interesting observations, presented in an elegant form." It contains also some very intriguing statistical facts'.

crime. England solved the problem by sending convicts to America, and on its loss they settled 'Sydney-Cow'.[50] He then outlined in very favourable terms the treatment of the convicts and the economic growth that had taken place. For statistics of growth he drew on Wentworth's 1824 account, which had been used in an article in the *Quarterly Review*, which in turn was republished in French in the *Revue britannique*.[51] Is this picture, he asked, exaggerated? He was aware, he said, of the abuses and disorders of the early years—there had been the account of Collins, for example, and 'for a long time Jeremy Bentham has been critical of them', but such a state of affairs was inevitable when the population was wholly criminal and the administration was inadequate. But what Benoiston de Chateauneuf wanted to emphasise was the moral improvement that took place in the convicts and the quality of the succeeding generation: 'Behold human perfectibility'. A good example, he said, could be found in Barrington's description of his life. The relative costs of penal colonies and prisons, he continued, could not be decided, but prisons, including Bentham's circular prison, did not reform criminals. What finally justified penal colonies was 'the creation of a new people and of new markets for commerce'.[52] On all sides, he said, there was support for deportation, and he strongly urged the government to act.

On the final page of his work, Benoiston de Chateauneuf drew attention to an essay competition which related to the establishment of a penal colony. In 1827 the Mâcon Society of Agriculture, Science and Literature set competitors the subject of devising both an alternative punishment to hard labour and the means of protecting society from freed *forçats*. The winner was M. Quentin, and his entry was published in 1828.* Both the

---

*The full question was: 'Outline, for the replacement of hard labour, a punishment which, without ceasing to satisfy the needs of justice, leaves less degradation in the soul of the condemned; propose measures to take in the meantime so that freed *forçats* are no longer driven to misery by a public opinion which rejects them, and so that their presence no longer threatens the society which receives them'. (Quentin, *Mémoire*, p. 2) Quentin does not appear to have any other connection with the penal question. On the title page of his work, *Mémoire sur les forçats*, he is described as a retired lieutenant-colonel of the cavalry, a member of the Legion of Honour and a *Chevalier de Saint-Louis*.

competition and the published result brought widespread interest and discussion, and indeed the government commended Quentin's work and acted on some of his recommendations when, in 1828, it began to separate *forçats*, according to the seriousness of their crime, by sending them to particular *bagnes*.[53]

Quentin favoured the introduction of a limited form of deportation, part compulsory, part voluntary, which would be applied to non-political prisoners. He felt unable to recommend the deportation of all *forçats*, not because of the English experience at Botany Bay, but because of differences between the French and English societies. He argued that a penal colony depended heavily on convicts deported for life, and that the greater severity of English law produced a better type of life-deportee. And if deportees for a term were considered, again the severe English law provided less-criminal types. French term-deportees, moreover, were more likely than the English to return home because 'they prefer their native soil to all other, and . . . are not as fitted for colonising as the English or Germans'. The outflow of these freed deportees would be disruptive for the colony, and would mean no solution to the problem of crime currently being committed by freed *forçats* in France. That French deportees would be of lower quality than English deportees was bad enough, Quentin argued, but for two reasons a successful French penal colony would need convicts of superior quality. In the first place, as established by the English government 'and published in its journals', it was much more costly to keep convicts in England than to transport them, whereas the reverse was probably true for France. There were two reasons for this difference. Through work, French *forçats* pretty nearly met their maintenance costs, provisions being less expensive than in England, and 'the Frenchman consuming less than the Englishman'. In the second place, the foundation costs of a penal colony would be high for France because French entrepreneurial drive was not as strong:

> We do not have in France these daring capitalists who voluntarily leave their homeland to go across the seas to increase their wealth by settling there. English deportees find in New Holland planters who employ them, and for whom they take the place of negroes

1 Support for a Penal Colony

and servants; but it will not be the same in a French colony. Our capitalists will not risk their funds there, at least in the early years: that is why our deportees themselves will have to be settlers and planters ... Thus the government will have to make ... outlays which in the English colony are made in part by private investors.[54]

Quentin mentioned slavery as an alternative to the *bagnes* but, as he said, 'who would dare propose the establishment of slavery in a country which is the centre of civilisation of the entire world?'

This influential document did not extend transportation as a general punishment as far as most of its supporters would have wished. Quentin did, however, accept the argument that penal colonies on the Australian model were a success for the English. Moreover, he did recommend the taking of the crucial step of establishing a penal colony outside France for some common criminals.

Throughout the decade, the Chamber of Deputies appears to have favoured deportation and the founding of a penal colony for *forçats*. There was no debate specifically on this issue, but the opportunity for discussion arose on the presentation of the budget for the Ministry of the Navy and Colonies, especially that part which dealt with expenditure on the *bagnes*. At the beginning of the decade, in May 1821, the spokesman for the budget committee said that getting rid of the *bagnes* was a 'generally desired improvement'. They were costly and the prisoners in them plotted revenge on society. The government was trying to get them out of France: 'The intention and will are very positive, the difficulty is in the execution'. There was no wish to throw the convicts on to totally inhospitable shores, and the committee could only 'hope that the efforts and reflections of the government will lead to a prompt and satisfying solution'.* Only one speaker, Laisné de

---

*In April the Minister for Justice had admitted that the government was 'very embarrassed' at not having a place for the deportation of political prisoners. He went on to say that the government 'has had frequent communications with the Minister of the Navy, who has arranged several operations, as a result of which the very great difficulty encountered in the attempts to set up a place of deportation has become apparent. It is a colony of quite a different type from others which it might be necessary to establish'. (*AP*, 16 Apr. 1821, p. 23)

Villevesque, took up this issue in the general debate. He attacked *bagnes* for being costly and for breeding crime. On the other hand, agricultural work in a penal colony leading to land ownership would morally transform convicts: 'it is thus . . . that New South Wales has risen swiftly to high prosperity and already numbers 30,000 inhabitants'. He went on, somewhat prophetically:

> . . . can we see without blushing from shame, without feeling an intense desire to copy, England, and in former times Spain, covering the world with its colonies? One day 200 million people will speak Spanish and English.

And he summed up: 'national interest, the glory and honour of France, plain economy, thus commend this colonisation to the attention of the government'.[55]

In 1825 the budget committee applauded changes taking place in work practice in the *bagnes*, and in a few words seemed to give up hope on deportation: 'information shows that it is impossible to create settlements for deportation, like those of New-Holland; wherever there are settlers, they would want to leave'.[56] One year later, and the budget committee had reversed this view and returned to its position of 1821. The spokesman said that the committee had discussed the conditions in the *bagnes* and the dangers that freed *forçats* posed for society, and had concluded that deportation was essential:

> The most cogent grounds of morality and public safety, even the interests of these unfortunate men whom society has cast from its midst, and who are condemned to die of misery, or to resort to new crimes after their liberation to obtain subsistence, demand that the government take a measure similar to the one which England has so happily tested in its settlement at *Botany-Bay* . . .[57]

Unlike 1821, this time the committee claimed that it 'has good reason to believe, from information supplied, that the government is seeking the means to realise it'.[58] In the debate there were two relevant and important contributions. One was from du Hamel, whose views could probably be taken as representing the naval establishment.[59] The other speaker was the minister, who could more formally speak on behalf of the government.

Du Hamel, who at one time had been the administrator of a *bagne*, emphasised that it was not the administration of the *bagnes* but the very institution that he wanted to attack: 'The correspondence of the prefects and of the attorneys general, the votes of the departmental governments, personal, administrative experience all call for a great change'. On the average, he said, there were about 10 000 *forçats* who were costly to maintain, and annually about 2000 were released on society worse than when they were imprisoned. What France must do was follow the example of its neighbour:

> Instead of being a permanent cause of fear, anguish and expense for their country, English deportees go, colonising distant lands, to find there new morals, a new existence; what prodigious developments these convict settlements have experienced in the 38 years from the first deportation! ... to 1815, 17,066 persons have been conveyed to Austrasie [sic] or New Holland and to New South Wales. Numerous hard-working families cover the fertile soil, formerly uncultivated and uninhabited; several towns have been founded: Port Jackson, Botany Bay, Sydney. This latter town is populated by more than 7,000 inhabitants; it possesses several newspapers, some scientific establishments. Few freed convicts have wanted to leave so prosperous a situation; honoured in their new homeland, in the old one they would find again the everlasting impression of their past crimes.[60]

Using British figures to 1821 du Hamel argued that transportation to New Holland had been cheaper than imprisonment at home; thus 'calculations of economy again come to justify these measures of high humanity'. The lesson for France:

> We are therefore able to hope for the same success, by taking the same trouble, the same care. These offspring, justly banished by the motherland, will offer it useful colonies in the future and in their purified posterity, and will make it forget the mistakes of their founders.[61]

By easy extension, naval thinking went from penal colonies to colonies in general. Penal colonies were obviously part of an expanded empire and required an expanded navy. Du Hamel drew attention to 'a painful contrast. What a colossal extension has taken place in the colonial system of our neighbours!' Now, 'this insatiable people' covered the world, and their expanding empire went hand in hand with expanding trade. France needed such trade and this called for 'naval and merchant shipping, and these two fleets cannot exist without numerous and vast colonies'.[62] *

When the Minister of the Navy spoke he pointed out that to substitute deportation for hard labour in the *bagnes* required a change in the penal code, which was not in the hands of his department. Moreover, a change in the law affected the future, and it could not be used to change sentences already imposed. However, he agreed that it was desirable that measures be taken to stop habitual criminals being freed into society; and, bearing out the comment of the budget committee, he continued:

> Instructions have been given to seek out in various parts of the globe places where a system of deportation could be established according to circumstances which would have been foreseen by the law. Our neighbours have this advantage on us; they have purchased it through enormous outlays from which today they gather the fruit. This important matter will not be lost from sight.[63]

Certainly an encouraging but non-committal comment. What had the Department of the Navy and Colonies been doing?

DEPARTMENT OF THE NAVY AND COLONIES 1820–1830

It has been shown how, following the Restoration, thinking within the department had turned to the deportation of *forçats* and to the establishment of a penal colony. The department was at least partly responsible for setting up the 1819 Committee whose conclusions broadly endorsed the naval view. This view could be seen, somewhat narrowly, as stemming from problems for the navy in its responsibility for the operation of the *bagnes*. More generally, and following its crushing defeat in the war, the navy would be seeking the rebuilding of French naval power, commensurate with

---

*Du Hamel would make the same general points in the budget debate in 1827, and then continue: 'I know that the king's ships explore the seas to try to discover a new *Botany-Bay*'. (*AP*, 8 May 1827, p. 678)

France's position in the world. Such a navy would require at the very least provisioning points throughout the world, but more broadly a navy required colonies and colonies required a navy. A penal colony, especially one in a new land in the still partly explored southern ocean, would be a most desirable step within this policy. The ability of the navy to accomplish such a significant measure depended, of course, on available resources and its place in the context of the government's foreign and domestic policies. Within this framework a number of questions are thus suggested. Did the department remain an important influence in pushing for a penal colony? Did it actually seek out and promote specific sites? Was it inspired by the example of British actions in Australia?

The 1819 Committee, influenced by the example of Botany Bay, favoured the establishment of a penal colony in south-west Australia. Leslie Marchant, historian of French naval activity around Australia, argues that the navy followed up the committee's findings with firm action but, because it was let down by the captains of the two ships it dispatched to assess the potentialities south-west Australia, France lost its opportunity to establish a colony there.* It is true that neither commander carried out that particular assignment, but doubt must be cast on the resolve of both the navy and the government.

The first expedition was commanded by Louis-Isidore Duperrey. He submitted a plan of circumnavigation for scientific research to the department in October 1821. It was approved, and in early 1822 there was included in his itinerary the instruction to examine the suitability of south-west Australia, especially the Swan River area, as a possible site for a French settlement.† No significant change was required in his scientific plans, nor any reduction in the duration of his voyage. In fact he did not leave France until

---

*'... both men failed their country and their superiors in a time of need.' (L. R. Marchant, *France Australe*, p. 234.)

†"For a number of years, searches have been carried out in the most distant and inaccessible countries, in order to find there a place with anchorage and a port, which, because of its fertility and mildness of climate, might be able to take a settlement formed solely by Europeans. The point on which eyes are generally fixed, is situated on the western shores of *new holland* along the banks of the *Swan* river'. (AM, BB4, 1000, plaquette no. 2, 'Mémoire pour M. Duperrey')

August 1822, three and a half years after the 1819 Committee met, and did not return until March 1825. The second expedition took place several years later. Hyacinthe de Bougainville set out in March 1824, returning in June 1826. Marchant appears to be arguing that favourable reports from the captains would have spurred the navy to make a settlement, and 'the mid 1820s was the opportune time to do this'.[64] Given the dates of return of the two navigators, this would have required a very prompt response, but nothing in the French actions suggests urgency. On the other hand, the British, in response to concerns about trade and control of the continent, acted with vigour—Melville Island was occupied in 1824 and King George Sound in December 1826.* The commander at King George Sound was instructed to make it plain to any Frenchman he might meet that all of New Holland was British.[65]

Duperrey's expedition yielded a report to the department by two of its officers, R. P. Lesson and Dumont d'Urville, in favour of penal colonies for King George Sound and New Zealand. It does not appear to have been considered significant, and Lesson commented that it was 'no doubt thrown away'.[66]† Much more influential was a work by another officer on the expedition, Jules de Blosseville, who was approached by the Minister of the Interior to present a plan for the colonisation of south-west Australia.‡ Blosseville put it this way:

---

*There are other problems in Marchant's account. No reason is offered for the change in early 1826 in 'official opinion . . . away from establishing a French colony in "Leeuwin Land"', except to suggest that New Zealand would be more salubrious. There is also the conflicting claim that 'the time for Britain to have felt real concern was years before, from 1819 to just after the Spanish intervention in 1823 when real French proposals existed and when real moves were made by the French in regard to "Leeuwin Land" [a name for south-west Australia]'. (L. R. Marchant, *France Australe*, p. 246)

†Lesson did reply to a letter in the *Annales maritimes et coloniales* which argued that the Falklands could be 'our Botany-bay'. He rejected that site and he also emphasised that establishing a colony was not a simple matter. The English had been casual in their approach to Botany Bay, but 'today success unexpected and singularly lucky has crowned the work of inexperience and chance'. (2, 1825, p. 540)

‡E. de Blosseville suggests that the original approach came from Franchet d'Esperey, the Director of Police. (*Jules de Blosseville*, p. 54)

1 Support for a Penal Colony

> Deeply impressed by the fascinating spectacle of the English colonies in Australia, I wished that this example should not be lost on France, but my position and age made my wishes vain. I did not think that my views were of any consequence, when in 1825 the minister of the interior asked me for a report on the establishment of a penal colony. I delivered it and my ideas appeared to meet with approval.[67]

Blosseville had been a keen observer of the Australian colony when Duperrey's ship had spent two months at Port Jackson in early 1824. He mixed freely among the people and sought out information. He met 'missionary Nicholson . . . who, at the same time, in a long letter related to him the progress of the penal colony, the discoveries of lands in the interior, the industries, the settlements and the plans of our antipodes'.[68] Blosseville acknowledged his use also of Wentworth, 'historian and panegyrist of the English settlement'.[69]

In his report, dated January 1826, Blosseville examined the experiences of countries which had attempted to establish penal colonies, and concluded that only England had succeeded with 'wisdom and forethought', using two systems: forced exile and voluntary migration. In New Holland the English government acted on what it had learnt from problems with transportation to America: it transported the convicts and kept authority over them; good conduct meant liberty; and great distance made return difficult so that convicts tended to adopt a new homeland. There were, he continued, many costly mistakes in the early years and the colony languished until free, hard-working men arrived, became owners of land and got convict services; 'Then one saw the works of a small number of farmers outdo in an instant all those that the government undertook itself'. Since then, prosperity has grown 'despite the mistakes, often repeated, of the administration'. There follows a hyperbolic description of the colony where 'sixty thousand inhabitants find abundance'.[70]

So much for the benefits for Australia, but England too had gained substantially:

> While thus deporting the scum of the population into healthy and temperate countries, England has attained internal peace, improved

the behaviour of the people, reduced the number of executions, made economies on its costs of police and transformed criminals, vagrants and wretches into hard-working and peaceful citizens.[71]

England had also given birth to a people who added to its power, had created a haven for excess population, extended the civilised world and increased trade.

What, Blosseville asked, could France learn from this venture? It was a 'gratifying hope' to think to equal the English success. Nevertheless, France could learn from English mistakes; it could go more directly towards its goal and obtain 'results still more astonishing'. So was there a suitable site anywhere on the globe? Finding real problems with French Guiana, Madagascar and the Falklands, Blosseville went on to recommend strongly south-west Australia and he submitted his plan for an exploratory voyage.[72]

Notwithstanding Blosseville's eloquent plea for south-west Australia, the attention of the navy had turned away firmly from this area by the beginning of 1826. It would seem that caution concerning Britain prevailed. After his return with Duperrey in March 1825, Dumont d'Urville had almost immediately proposed a new scientific expedition. The proposal was accepted, but the additional naval instructions made no mention of south-west Australia.[73] Instead, although they firmly dwelt on the continued interest in establishing a penal colony for *forçats*, on the English model, now emphasis was placed on a possible site in New Zealand:

> Independently of the interest which would be attached to similar particulars under the military and naval reports, there would be very great interest as well in the discovery there of a place which was suitable for the formation of a colony to which the criminals that our present laws condemn to chains would be deported. For a very long time we have been taken up with schemes to copy what the English have done in this manner on the eastern coast of new holland; but we have always been stopped by the difficulty in finding a place which was appropriate for a similar settlement. It is necessary that the latitude be such as to permit Europeans to work there without succumbing to excess heat and fatigue, and that it does

The Baudin expedition in Sydney, 1802: C.-A. Lesueur's panorama of Port Jackson with the French camp in the foreground [Collection Lesueur du Havre 16063-1, Muséum d'Histoire naturelle du Havre]

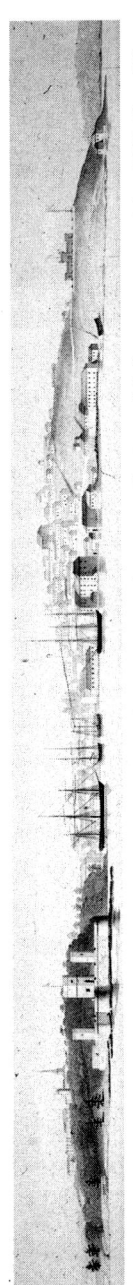

Sydney, Port Jackson, in August 1825, from a drawing by Edmond de la Touanne [H. de Bougainville, *Journal de la navigation . . . Atlas*, 1837, Plate 54]

The Baudin expedition in Sydney, 1802: view of part of the town of Sydney and of the entrance to Port Jackson, from a drawing by C.-A. Lesueur [F. Péron and L. de Freycinet, *Voyage de découvertes aux terres australes* . . . Atlas (by C.-A. Lesueur and N.-M. Petit), Paris, 1807, Plate 37]

View of Cox's River, west of the Blue Mountains, New South Wales, in 1819, from a drawing by Alphonse Pellion [L. Freycinet, *Voyage autour du monde* . . . *Atlas historique*, 1825, Plate 98]

not become a place of those sicknesses . . . which are the scourge of a great part of america.

The instructions then stated very specifically that Dumont d'Urville was to report on aspects of the territory in New Zealand being offered by Baron Thierry:*

> . . . and principally on the possibility of forming there, under his auspices, a colony of the type of that at Botany Bay; it is to this identification that you will have to apply yourself during the time that you are exploring the coast . . . of New Zealand.[74]

Again there is the expression of interest and the taking of preliminary steps concerning the location of a penal colony, but again there is the absence of any note of urgency. Dumont d'Urville was away for almost three years, not returning to France until February 1829, and he returned to a France in which a marked change was taking place in the penal debate and more generally in the whole political environment.

Concern over the possible English response to a French settlement in Australia was still being discussed in 1827. The occasion was the return of some papers by the Director of Police to the Minister of the Navy and Colonies on 8 May.[75] The papers related to 'the project conceived and discussed in his ministry for the deportation and colonisation of *forçats*'. For his part, the Director thought freed *forçats* and *réclusionnaires* posed the greatest threat to society, and that deportation without return, 'rather like the emancipated convicts of New South Wales', was the answer. Apparently unaware of the British action or the orders to Dumont d'Urville, he agreed with the naval papers that the south-west of New Holland, especially King George Sound, was the best place. In his view it was available to the first occupier, but it was up to the minister to clarify this promptly. If this were so, action should be speeded up, 'and above all to secure for the Government of the King, by taking possession of the position indicated, the capacity to found there a settlement as soon as he

---

*Charles, baron de Thierry, was a French adventurer who claimed that he had purchased land from the Maoris.

judges it expedient'. But what would England do? Almost certainly, he thought, it would occupy King George Sound if it got wind of French intentions.

Along with the return of the naval papers, the director sent to the minister a report prepared in his own department on crime and punishment. It was in three parts. The first dealt with the numbers of imprisoned *forçats* and *réclusionnaires*, the second with the dangers to society posed by them when freed—the director believed that they committed 90 per cent of serious crime. The third section covered remedies, of which deportation was in his view the best, and here 'the example of England comes to the support of this assertion'. Accordingly he then outlined the history of English transportation and on this basis surveyed possible sites for a French penal colony, again favouring King George Sound. He continued:

> As for the regimen that it would be appropriate to establish in this colony of deportation, the only model that exists currently, I find in New South Wales. It can be referred to with so much more advantage as the English administration at first made some big mistakes that it has successively corrected and, so instructed by its experience, it has brought this colony to a point of prosperity that it would not have been easy to foresee at the start.[76]

In his description of the colony the director drew heavily on the Bigge Report of 1822* and he also noted Blosseville's memoir. He also attempted to estimate the costs of deportation for France, using the British figures to 1821.

To sum up: during the 1820s the Department of the Navy and Colonies remained firm in its view that a penal colony modeled on the Australian experience was needed. It sent expeditions to the South Seas to discover a satisfactory site. In particular, attention centred on south-west Australia, about which there had been

---

*Appointed as commissioner of inquiry into the colony of New South Wales, J. T. Bigge arrived in Sydney in September 1819. His three reports were printed by the House of Commons, one in 1822 and two in 1823.

encouraging reports. But the approach adopted by the department to this area, following the meeting of the 1819 committee, was tentative and lacked determination. By 1826 the focus had shifted to New Zealand, but the approach remained leisurely. Concern over the British response was obvious in French discussions. French power was limited. As recently as 1818 there had been an army of occupation in France; at the beginning of the decade the navy was pitifully weak. Although recovery was rapid, British naval hegemony remained and French foreign policy and action centred on Europe and the Mediterranean.* Jules de Blosseville was at least partly right when he complained in his 'Projet . . . Suite' of 1829 of the failure to establish a penal colony: 'Let us not always blame England; let us blame ourselves, it deserves its success through its activity'.†

---

*The minister responsible for the re-creation of the navy under the Restoration was Baron Portal. Comparing French naval power in 1825 with the period before the Revolution, he wrote: 'At that time, the combined forces of France and Spain were equal to the forces of England; then a great naval victory would have been able to make us masters of the sea. Things are greatly changed; England has acquired such a great superiority, that we can no longer contend hand to hand . . . it is necessary to seek to do the harm to its trade that we can no longer do to its navy. (*Mémoires de Baron Portal*, pp. 273–4)

†A similar point was made in the same year by the editor of the *Revue britannique*. In a long footnote to an article on the plan for a British settlement at Swan River, he wrote: 'Perhaps this new attempt at colonisation will at last bring us out of our inertia. Thanks to this inertia, the English race tends to prevail everywhere to our exclusion'. (24, 1829, p. 99)

2
Emerging Opposition in the 1820s

THE PRISON REFORM MOVEMENT

Dissatisfaction with the results obtained by the prison system within France was one of the principal impulses behind the deportation movement. The ramshackle system inherited from the Napoleonic period did not accord with the framework specified by law. To a significant degree improvement was a matter of economics, especially the provision of resources to provide more satisfactory buildings and to permit the separation of different types of prisoners. Improvement of the system also meant, for many, the moral rehabilitation of the prisoners. This aim had its origins in terms of the development of penal philosophy within France, but it was strongly influenced by the ideas and penal practice of other countries, especially Britain and the United States.

'In 1819', wrote Catherine Duprat, 'the dawn of reform saw the age of the *philanthropes*'. Their activities centred on the Société royale pour l'amélioration des prisons, an institution created by Interior Minister Decazes, with the patronage of the King and the presidency of his nephew. Its 321 founding members came from a wide spectrum in terms of politics and occupations, and Duprat claimed: 'No other association was more brilliant in its time, none was able to boast such a collection of notables'. The society worked for the physical and moral improvement of prisoners but, notwithstanding its prestigious associations, its activities were checked by the growth of political reaction early in the 1820s; it had a brief resurgence from 1828.[1] A somewhat similar group of reformists founded the Société de la morale chrétienne in 1821; committees were formed to specialise in various social problems,

2 Emerging Opposition in the 1820s 43

one of which was that of crime and punishment. And it was through this society that Charles Lucas, probably the most famous of French prison reformers, first obtained wide public recognition. Lucas, then aged twenty-three, won the society's essay prize in 1826 for his attack on capital punishment, *Du système pénal et du système répressif en général, de la peine de mort en particulier.** Included in this work were critical assessments of transportation as a method of punishment and of Botany Bay as a penal colony. This appears to be the first published attack on the penal success of Botany Bay, which at the same time puts the case for the alternative of penitentiaries.

In his introduction Lucas gave half a dozen pages to a discussion of penal colonies (pp. lvii–lxiii). He noted that all were agreed on the necessity to get rid of *bagnes*, but not on what should replace them. In his view there were two systems available: one was the system of deportation used by England, which he considered was then discredited in that country and likely to be abandoned; the other was along the lines of the American penitentiary system with 'its marvellous successes'. What principally concerned Lucas in this introduction was the misrepresentation of Botany Bay 'which has popularised in France the idea of deportation'. And, it was not just France that had been misled, but Europe. Indeed, 'criminals in England do not hesitate to steal to get themselves deported. It is the first time perhaps that one has seen the punishment decreed against the crime become an inducement to commit it'. Then again, the claim had recently been made that 'this *marvellous* transformation ... the complete *regeneration* of the guilty, was the goal of the settlement founded by the English at Botany-Bay, and this goal has been attained'. The source given for this observation was Freycinet. Yet, continued Lucas, he had conversed with Freycinet on this matter and he had agreed with him 'that the only advantage of Botany-Bay was to deliver England of a population of criminals', and that it was little concerned with moral

---

*It was a double triumph for Lucas, as his work also won a competition initiated by Comte de Sellon at Geneva (see J. Pinatel, 'La vie et l'oeuvre de Charles Lucas', p. 123). Lucas devoted a long life (1803–89) to the cause of prison reform.

regeneration. For Lucas, it remained astounding that in France there was so much important support for deportation:

> ... such has been the intellectual shock given by all these marvellous stories of Botany-Bay, that for a moment the government itself, while listening to the whole nation repeat in chorus the verse of the poet of *la Pitié*,* almost yielded to these harmonies as did Euridice to those of Orpheus.

The weakness of the government to which Lucas referred was the establishment of the 1819 committee. But he believed that the situation had changed:

> Today the government, although it renews with each naval expedition the recommendation to search for a suitable place for deportation, has quite got over, I believe, the notion of colonising with criminals.
>
> Well, may it turn its gaze, which it is finally averting from the system of colonisation, back towards the penitentiary system.

Lucas gave more extensive treatment to deportation in the twenty-one pages (pp. 329–49) of part three, chapter V, entitled 'Of Deportation—Of the System of Colonisation at Botany-Bay'. As in the introduction, he began by noting the unanimity of opinion concerning the abolition of the *bagne*; 'and what is very remarkable is that everywhere the remedy of the same evil is recommended with the same unanimity'. It could not be claimed that this 'general infatuation' with colonising was based on any past French success.

> But all the suspicions have vanished before the great fame, on the continent, of the English colonial settlement in New Holland, this immense land as vast as Europe and destined to nurture in future centuries sixty million inhabitants. Everywhere it is only a question

---

*In a footnote Lucas quotes from Delille's famous poem, *La Pitié*. L'abbé Jacques Delille (1738–1813) was one of the most celebrated French poets. He wrote this poem in 1803:

> Eh! qui ne connaît pas le consolant spectacle
> Qu'étale de bandits ce vaste réceptacle,
> Cette Botany-Bay, sentine d'Albion; etc.?

2 Emerging Opposition in the 1820s

of Botany-Bay, of this miraculous land, so that it would be said that it is enough to arrive to become good and virtuous again. In France, Botany-Bay is the unanswered argument of the partisans of reform.

But Lucas believed that he had an answer for these partisans:

> I am not unaware that I am going to bring about disenchantment among them by re-establishing the truth in all its light from irresistible documentation. This work is necessary, because I have to prove the superiority of the penitentiary system over the system of colonisation and justify the preference that I have granted it.

In a footnote Lucas referred to the sources on which he was going to draw: the Bigge report (Bigge is referred to throughout as Biddge); the unpublished journal of Lesson who, on Duperrey's expedition, had spent two months in Sydney in 1824; conversations with Duperrey himself and several of his officers; and conversations with officers from Freycinet's expedition, particularly Gaudichaud and Guémard, 'whose names are known in the world of learning'. Completing his claims to authority, Lucas wrote: 'I shall take care to cite other sources where I have drawn on them'.

In assessing Botany Bay, Lucas thought it ought to be examined from two points of view: as a 'colonial settlement', and as a 'settlement of reform and punishment'. Various authors including Wentworth had shown how, after the early difficulties, the colony began to prosper after the crossing of the Blue Mountains. As a result, 'considered on the colonial aspect, the success of the settlements in New Holland is therefore certain and even prodigious'. But what of the penal side? Lucas was impressed by Bigge's criticisms, especially 'where he says that of a *hundred* convicts, *eight* or *nine* are of irreproachable morals and have a respectable character, although *as yet the obviousness of it has not been very clearly demonstrated*'. Lesson's journal described the bushrangers, the pickpockets and villainous convicts, and he had received letters from Sydney which said that it was 'full of thieves, and that all the gallows are in action'. This description of an immoral society was, Lucas asserted, confirmed by Mellish's account which had been translated and published in the *Revue britannique*.[2] What if transportationists claimed that a better system would bring better results? For instance, should convicts be sent to inhabited colonies where public morality had already been established? But, asked Lucas, what French colony would be suitable or would accept convicts? The example of the United States did not suggest a favourable response. There, Benjamin Franklin had challenged Britain: 'Would you be very comfortable if your country were sent rattlesnakes?' Yet the problem at Botany Bay was that there were not enough honest people; the population consisted of officials, convicts, free migrants, emancipists, children etc., and 'among them there is no fusion possible'. Lucas' conclusion therefore was that Botany Bay was a penal failure, and that deportation would work only as a part of a repressive system. In such a system it should be confined to a very limited number of offences, such as recidivism with murder or political conspiracy against the state.

Lucas was the most notable of a number of prison reformers who, towards the end of the decade, began to write systematically on the nature of the prison system and on the line of development it should take. In this type of work the analysis was confined to the penitentiary system, and transportation was mentioned only incidentally. Lucas himself published a two-volume work in 1828–30 on the penitentiary system in Europe and the United States.* He felt he could be dismissive of transportation:

> We do not have to expand here on this method of punishment, in order to expose all its ineffectiveness, the flaws, the dangers even generally felt and acknowledged in England where the government, ruled by the force of circumstances and enchained by the enormous expenses of the first settlement, is no longer free to repudiate this system. All its efforts to combat the bad effects are reduced to curtailing the number of transportees by retaining the condemned in the hulks.[3]

---

*He was awarded the Montyon prize in 1830 by the Académie française for his book's contribution to mores. In the introduction to the first volume (p. xxix), he finds support for his opposition to transportation in a speech by James Mackintosh to the House of Commons.

2 Emerging Opposition in the 1820s

When he came to look back on this period, Lucas saw his opposition to penal colonies in a more dramatic light:

> There was such a craze for the Botany Bay system . . . Well, without other support than that of conviction, we dared, alone against all, to oppose this thoughtless infatuation of the country with discussion of principles and verification of facts. Soon to our voice was joined another more important, that of the venerable Barbé de Marbois.[4]

While Barbé-Marbois, as early as 1819, had reminded the Chambre des Pairs that the improvement of prisons was an alternative to deportation,[5] explicit rivalry between the two systems and their penal philosophies appears to have emerged only towards the end of the 1820s. Then, those supporting prison reform within France appeared to seize the intellectual high ground. They were assisted by the re-appearance of Barbé-Marbois in the debate.

BARBÉ-MARBOIS' ATTACK ON DEPORTATION, 1828

In 1828 Barbé-Marbois published a powerful and influential attack on deportation, *Observations sur les votes* . . . It was prompted by expressions of support for the deportation of freed *forçats*, which were made during 1826–27 by 41 of the 86 departmental governments.* His work was addressed to the Dauphin as president of the Société royale pour l'amélioration des prisons. Barbé-Marbois was a founding member of this society, and on the opening page of his text he reminded the Dauphin that the adoption of deportation would be a set-back to prison reform within France, 'fruits of nine years of efforts and perseverance'. Very briefly, Barbé-Marbois suggested that the two-and-a-half years that he had spent as a deportee gave him authority but would not destroy his impartiality. Unusually for an opponent of deportation he, again briefly, argued that the crime problem posed by freed *forçats* was overstated, and that the petitions of the departmental governments showed an 'imitative concern'. But the

---

*The French term *conseils-généraux de départements* has been translated throughout as 'departmental governments'. This may give an exaggerated impression of their power. They were councils responsible for the administration of the departments.

central theme of his sixty-four pages of text was a sustained and critical analysis of the Australian penal settlement, and it appears to be based almost entirely on English sources.*

Barbé-Marbois argued that ideally a penal colony should be in an area that was isolated, distant, unsettled and with a good climate, and that nowhere in the world seemed to meet these requirements anywhere near as satisfactorily as '*les Terres australes*'—Australia and New Zealand:

> It was therefore natural that the supporters of deportation judged them suitable for such a settlement. It is their project that I propose to examine, and the observations which can be made about it are applicable to all other projects of this nature.

Central to French projects for deportation, Barbé-Marbois continued, was the example of England, and it was the English experience with its penal colony that he accepted as his challenge:

> In order to succeed in knowing if we are able, in the same way as the English, to apply deportation to the condemned, in order to understand the effects it has had in England, I have had to refer only to the history of Botany Bay; I have to relate only the principal circumstances surrounding it, and that is what I am going to do. I won't make the bad worse, I won't suppress the good.[6]

The following fourteen pages concentrated on the difficulties, disappointments and failures associated with the initial settlement and the experiences of the colony over the first ten years or so. As

---

*In E. de Blosseville's view, 'the illustrious deportee had recourse to the greater part of the English works of which knowledge was lacking with his supporters and even with a large number of his opponents'. (*Histoire des colonies pénales*, p. 40) In the text, Barbé-Marbois mentions as sources Collins, Bigge, Barrington and governors' reports. In 1827 Barbé-Marbois asked the English Ambassador if he could obtain for him the reports of any recent committees examining the Australian settlements. The ambassador passed the request on to the Colonial Office, mis-describing Barbé-Marbois as a 'member of a commission appointed to enquire into the expediency of establishing a '*Botany Bay*' for the reception of convicts'. The Colonial Office commented: 'There is no official report excepting Mr Bigge's, which could be of use. Collins's New South Wales and some later publications may be of service in showing the progress of our settlements at Botany Bay and the other settlements'. (CO, 201/188, pp. 240–1)

2 Emerging Opposition in the 1820s 49

for the effects on the convicts, with very few exceptions, 'deportation did not reduce at all their extreme depravity, and these men kept in the colonies all the vices they had in Europe'. The convicts' vices were extensive but they also hated work. Some escaped. Of those whose term had expired, some returned unreformed to Europe, others remained and were a blight on the community: 'insolent and arrogant, they torment the honest and peaceful inhabitants'.[7]

To be fair, Barbé-Marbois wrote, he had to report that in the same period 'notable improvements' had taken place, though he did not believe this would weaken his case against French deportation. Famine was overcome. Punishment and discipline finally made convicts less ungovernable, and those who became land owners had an incentive to improve morally. From then on a genuine colony began to emerge based on free migration, and great progress was made in agriculture and trade and in public and private construction. As a result, 'the establishment of transportation which originally was the principal purpose of the foundation of these colonies, will soon be no more than an adjunct to it'. It is basic to Barbé-Marbois's theory of penal colonisation that the changes which had now created prosperity had resulted from free migration: 'the important improvements have taken place only over the last eight years, and disorders lasted thirty'.[8]

From this overview of the colony, including Van Diemen's Land, Barbé-Marbois turned to a more intensive discussion of the treatment and behaviour of the prisoners and the operation of the penal aspects of the colony. Drawing heavily on Bigge, he discussed critically over fourteen pages such subjects as work and work practices, women prisoners, sexual imbalance, types of convicts, emancipists, robber bands, alcoholic spirits and the costs of the penal establishment. On the basis of this analysis of this 'first and great test' of deportation, Barbé-Marbois felt that he was able to draw some conclusions which bore on the French proposals. First, those who proposed deportation believed it necessary to combine a free and penal colony. Barbé-Marbois believed this was impossible. He argued that the precedent which was often cited of the deportation of British convicts to North America was irrelevant, because there the colonies were founded and dominated by free men who set a moral example for the small minority of deportees. By contrast, New South Wales was founded by scoundrels, and 'undoubtedly, it is to be feared that many years must pass before New Wales and Van Diemen are delivered of these bad seeds'. Second, deportation was not simply a method of getting rid of criminals: it was also a punishment and, for it to be effective, escape had to be impossible. But even the English, with their command of the seas, could not prevent escapes. Third, deportation had been a penal failure for England: it was not a deterrent and indeed this punishment had encouraged crime; deportees who returned were worse than ever; in an about-face the English authorities now sometimes substituted imprisonment in the hulks for deportation. For Barbé-Marbois, 'these great tests appear decisive'. But, he continued, suppose that 'after thirty-three years of useless search',[9] the French government identified a site for a penal colony and went ahead with a settlement. It would, he argued, be a grave mistake, and the settlement would fail within a few years. The reasons, which he developed at length, were those he had already advanced in 1819: the great cost, maritime difficulties without ports of call and exposure in times of war.*

In conclusion, Barbé-Marbois drew on the authority of Jeremy Bentham to support the view that in general deportation did not answer the purpose of penal laws.† What the alternative should be he felt ought to be the subject of a separate study; but as 'an infallible means to reduce the number of crimes in France', he recommended the provision of education for children, appropriate to their station in life:

> The expense will not be great; if it were, it is at this cost that we shall obtain internal peace for the realm and that we will correct

---

*Barbé-Marbois drew attention here to the government's current interest in finding a penal site and, in an apparent reference to Dumont d'Urville's expedition, he stated that New Zealand was being explored, 'perhaps with this hope in mind'. (*Observations sur les votes*, p. 53)

†He mentions a number of Bentham's criticisms: deportation was a sentence for crimes of differing severity; being out of sight of the community, its effectiveness as a deterrent was reduced; it did not improve the morality of the criminal.

2 Emerging Opposition in the 1820s

behaviour depraved by ignorance and idleness. Each must contribute to the cost, competency along with wealth; and if there were to be some difference, the richer should be the more eager to contribute for they are the most exposed. They are also the best educated and they should appreciate more the value of knowledge. Thus for them it is proper to procure work for the poor; and this method of providing charity benefits more than others those who give it and those who receive it.

Any penal colonies, he wrote, should be established on uncultivated land in France, not overseas: 'They will not cost the hundredth part of what it would be necessary to spend to establish a place of deportation in New Zealand'.[10]

The case made by Barbé-Marbois could have been put more coherently, but his status and his own penal experience, along with the apparent knowledge he brought to bear on the subjects of deportation and Botany Bay, appear to have combined to make this an effective document. It was cited extensively in contemporary references.* His biographer, E. Wilson Lyon, claims that Barbé-Marbois had been asked to respond to the departmental governments by publishing the journal of his own deportation, but that he thought a more telling reply would be an analysis of Botany Bay; the resulting distribution of this work 'in the departments ... aided materially in silencing the demand for the effective applications of deportation'.† This assessment is supported in a paper in the colonial records which summarises the development of the deportation case: 'M^r De Barbé-Marbois checks the movement by two considerations, chiefly by the expenditure'. The *Annales maritimes et coloniales* almost immediately published an

---

*Most notable was the almost immediate reference (Aug. 1828) to Barbé-Marbois's argument in the report on *bagnes* made to the King by the Minister of the Navy, Hyde de Neuville. ('Rapport au Roi', p. 694)

†(*The Man Who Sold Louisiana*, p. 175) These were also the opinions of Barbé-Marbois (*Journal d'un déporté non-jugé*, p. ii) E. de Blosseville was not convinced: 'M. de Marbois, a not over-naive man, believed however with an impeturbable naivety, that he had reduced to silence forty-one departmental governments; and he expressed it without too much modesty'. (*Histoire de la colonisation pénale*, p. xxx)

extensive extract from the work; it introduced it by noting the widespread support in its own pages for deportation, and then continued:

> But a weighty voice, and one which deserves being heard because it is that of virtue, of experience and of devotion to the public good, has been raised to tear us away from these illusions: we therefore invoke the complete attention of our readers to the observations of the Marquis de Marbois.[11]

In the next two years two memoirs by supporters of deportation attest to the influence of Barbé-Marbois' criticisms. Their replies took different routes: one accepted his criticisms of Botany Bay, the other rejected them. The first was not published until 1840 but it had been presented to the Minister of the Navy and Colonies in 1828; its author, a ship's lieutenant, did not identify himself but appears to be Mortemart de Boisse.[12] While the purpose of his sixty-one page memoir was to advocate the establishment of a penal colony in the Falklands (Malouines), he recognised that the cause of deportation had suffered a setback:

> A man universally respected, famous for more than one reason, and whose name alone gives authority, M. de Barbé-Marbois, has pointed out some faults of the English system of deportation, and scarcely has he spoken, than discouragement has seized us.

Why, he asked, are the numerous partisans of deportation so cast down? 'I can see nothing other than the prestige produced by a great name'. The problem with these supporters, he argued, was that they did not have new ideas, that they accepted the English experience too slavishly; 'being only imitators, it has needed only some quotations to overturn their plans'. The answer to Barbé-Marbois was to accept the criticisms, 'to combat victoriously the defects he recounts, to remedy the evil, that is the way to respond'. Thus France had to abandon the route taken by England in Australia, and supporters of deportation had to demonstrate that:

> the disastrous results of its method of deportation are the consequence of a defective system, and not that of an impracticable project; let us show that it has been turned from the principal goal

by mercenary views, to which it has sacrificed the colonisation by the convicts; and by following step by step in the work of M. de Marbois, where all its faults are outlined, let us try to discover the origin, neutralize the effect and apply the remedy to the evil.[13]

And for some thirty pages that is what Mortemart de Boisse does. He argues, for instance, that New Holland was not a good place for a penal settlement, and that a settlement in the Falklands would not face the same problems. More generally, he refuses to accept the Botany Bay experience as a crucial test for the success of a French penal colony, and he concludes that France was now in a position to achieve its penal aims through deportation.

The second memoir, dated January 1830, was not published. It was written by B. de Basterot, who said he was inspired by Hyde de Neuville's 1828 report on the *bagnes* which had called for a fresh examination of the problems there. Basterot saw his work as a counter to Barbé-Marbois, and it too was presented to the Dauphin in his capacity of president of the Société royale pour l'amélioration des prisons. It was fifty-one pages long and included a map of Australia.[14] In it, Basterot argued that there were two ways to deal with convicts: the American, the penitentiary system, and the English, deportation. These would not be discussed theoretically or in the abstract, he wrote, because it was possible to examine 'the two systems in operation and the various results that they have produced'. Basterot assessed the writings of a number of supporters of penitentiaries, and found them all unconvincing. He then turned to examine the case of New Holland. Certainly, there had been great difficulties there early on, but the statistics for 1821 showed 'brilliant results'. And he was able to quote sections from Barbé-Marbois which credited convicts with an important contributory role in this success. Those opposed to deportation, he believed, were searching for objections. They claimed it did not reform convicts, but Peter Cunningham's recent work was full of praise for the qualities of the emancipists.* An

---

*Basterot drew on a review article of P. Cunningham's *Two Years in New South Wales* for this assertion. The article, first published in the *Quarterly Review*, was translated and republished in R*evue britannique*. The translator appended an interesting note: 'We have already directed the attention of our readers to New

admitted problem was whether deportation was a sufficient deterrent, but in Basterot's opinion it was if it were genuinely for life. As always the problem for France was to find a suitable site. After surveying various possibilities, Basterot returned to New Holland where 'the genius and enterprising spirit of England already yield so many fine and marvellous results'. It was no use, he wrote, having vain regrets about a lost opportunity at the Swan River which France could have occupied a few years before, and he recommended an area on the north-west coast described by Baudin, Freycinet and King. Would this project be too costly? No. On the basis of the English transportation costs to 1821, and benefits such as trade, it would be much cheaper than either *bagnes* or penitentiaries.

In conclusion, Basterot surveyed the widespread support for deportation, 'which naturally results from the obviousness of the success of England in this measure'. Against it there was a 'lone powerful voice', that of Barbé-Marbois, but his attitude was to be expected given his own unhappy experiences. Basterot therefore recommended an immediate expedition to the partly unknown coast of *la terre de Witt* where, if the assessment was favourable, a penal colony should be quickly established.

South Wales, and the other parts of Australia . . . But nature, like society, shows itself in this new world with aspects so varied and so bizarre that the subject is very far from being exhausted. Moreover, civilisation advances so quickly there, that one would have soon lost track of it, if one did not ceaselessly keep in touch with its progress'. (*Revue britannique*, vol. 16, 1828, p. 70)

3
The Great Parliamentary Debate, 1831

It is clear that in the last years of the 1820s influential arguments were being put forward against the transportation of common criminals. The government's indecision was shown in the 'Rapport au Roi' by the Minister of the Navy and Colonies, Hyde de Neuville, in August 1828. In this document he set out the common view on *forçats* and recidivism and then discussed the popular solution of transportation. He thought that there were two important questions concerning a penal colony that needed to be answered before any thought could be given to changing the existing legislation. One was the location of the colony, and the other was whether it should be 'in imitation of the establishments created by the English in New South Wales'. After surveying the literature on these subjects, noting especially what emerged from the 1819 Committee, and the publications of Quentin and Barbé-Marbois, he simply drew attention to the disagreements and moved on, along the lines of Quentin's advice, to recommend a reform of the *bagnes* whereby *forçats* would be separated according to the length of their sentences.[1]

The last positive act by the government in relation to transportation had been in 1826 when Dumont d'Urville was requested to report on the suitability of New Zealand for a penal colony. He did not return until 1829 and by then the government was not in a position to consider ambitious penal ventures. Increasing dissatisfaction with the government of Charles X led to the revolution of 1830 and the crowning of Louis-Philippe as King of the French. The new government was reformist in nature, and one of its early tasks was to begin a review of the legal system. In

September 1831 the Chamber of Deputies set up a committee to examine draft legislation, and in November it reported back to the Chamber.[2]

Referring to punishment, the spokesman for the committee, Dumon, began by declaring that although the existing prison system was a great advance on past practice, he thought that the future lay with a form of penitentiary system based on work and isolation. Such a change, he believed, would take several years to bring about, and meanwhile some immediate reforms should be made. One related to the government's proposal to deal with the anomaly of political prisoners sentenced to deportation being kept indefinitely at a 'special place' in France. The proposed solution was simply to remove the sentence of deportation and substitute for it what was actually occurring. Dumon stated that the committee endorsed this course of action, but he admitted that the proposal had brought some 'rather lively protests'. Several royal courts had expressed their regret at the renunciation of a punishment for which 'the settlement, known under the name of *Botany-Bay*, had proven the good effects: they have renewed the wish for the foundation of a penal colony, a wish which has already found voice in the departmental governments of 41 departments and in the budget committees'. The committee therefore felt that it should spend a little time on this matter. Dumon pointed out that the sentence of deportation in France was confined to political offences, and therefore its abolition did not involve the question of the English-style deportation of criminals that some wished to introduce. No one had actually been deported since the Restoration; and 'from that time to the present (as the archives of the navy ministry attest) there have been continual efforts to found a penal colony ... [but] not even the probable site of the future colony has been decided'. In these circumstances the government was asking the Chamber to abolish deportation, and indeed the committee saw dangers in its retention. What English 'transportation' did was to rid the country of recidivism: 'the penal colony of Botany-Bay is a kind of liquidation of crime to the profit of the motherland. That is its principal and most incontestable advantage'. But with only a small number of political offenders

3 The Great Parliamentary Debate, 1831

who could be deported, such a gain was not open to France. Moreover, how would French political deportees be treated in a penal colony? If they were free there, would the punishment be too light? Would they escape? On the other hand, if they were imprisoned there, perhaps the penalty would be excessive. But the committee thought the main danger of deportation lay in the possibility of the exercise of arbitrary authority for political vengeance in a distant colony.

The committee would probably have been wise to have left the matter there. However, giving as its reasons the great interest in deportation and the fact that penal reform was now under discussion, it thought it should present its more general conclusions. Essentially these related to the establishment of a penal colony for *forçats* and *réclusionnaires*, whom it regarded as the French equivalent of the transported English criminals. It thought that the question of a penal colony could be viewed under three heads, the first relating to problems of establishment. What was required was a healthy country, temperate, with fertile soil. Otherwise penal colonisation 'disguises a condemnation to death under a condemnation to deportation'. These considerations, along with the attitude of free settlers and the effects on black slaves of seeing degraded white convicts, ruled out existing French colonies and suggested some uninhabited location. The committee, nevertheless, felt it 'probable' that France would 'easily' secure for itself a satisfactory possession, and that diplomatic arrangements could be made to cover any difficulties in the event of a war. As to other problems in establishing the colony:

> ... the risks of famine and contagious diseases, the dangers of floods or the raids of savages, the necessity for very powerful means of repression. The example of England proves that these difficulties can be overcome by suitable sacrifices.

Having disposed of the physical problems in the establishment of a penal colony, Dumon turned to the second question, that of costs. The evidence showed that up to 1821 English costs for New South Wales, 'better known under the inexact name of Botanay-Bay [sic]', were appreciably lower per convict than for that country's hulks or penitentiaries. In France, however, the position was different. Costs in prisons and *bagnes* were lower than in England, but probably the costs of transporting the prisoners and supplying the colony would be higher. Thus the committee felt itself unable to resolve whether considerations of cost favoured a penal colony or penitentiaries.

There remained the final point at issue—the success of deportation as a penal system. Did it serve as a sufficient deterrent to crime? Clearly the committee thought it almost certainly did not:

> England well understands this, since it continually restricts, either legislatively or in fact, the employment of deportation. Do not these restrictions give substance to what is told about wretches who commit a crime to obtain their transportation, and who see in this punishment only the novelty and risks of a great voyage? What exact intimidatory effect can be produced by a punishment which is worsened or mitigated by a thousand fortuitous happenings, as unknown to the judge who pronounces it as to the guilty person who faces it, and which, earned in one world and applied in another, has nowhere the authority of a lesson nor the efficacy of an example.

What of deportation as a method of obtaining the moral reformation of criminals? Again, Dumon's report revealed that the committee had grave doubts:

> On all sides the example of Botany-Bay is cited: on this question again assertions clash, evidence is contradictory; and while on one side is celebrated the prosperity of the colony and the marvels of repentance produced there, on the other is drawn a hideous picture of this society of crime where unbridled corruption wears out ruthless repression.

As authority for this disagreement, Dumon cited the works of two supporters of the results obtained at Botany Bay, Péron and E. de Blosseville, and of one opponent, Barbé-Marbois. He then turned to the opinions of Dumont d'Urville, based on short visits to Sydney (1826) and to Hobart (1827), who had expressed a strong desire to enlighten the committee. Dumont d'Urville had emphasised the growth and prosperity of the colony ('which already even disquiets England'), but its moral state was another matter. In his view the three groups, consisting of convicts, emancipists and free settlers, behaved like artificial castes separated by jealousy, intolerance and hatred. Emancipists were prosperous, 'but few fortunes seem respectable'; in the main they were excluded from public office, and they were significantly involved in crime and disorders. As for the convicts, 'the most severe discipline barely controls them; the rod governs them'. Their moral improvement was 'very rare'—scarcely one in five were so reformed—and obstacles placed by England to their return nearly always converted temporary transportation to a permanent one.

The committee's formal conclusion was that it was unable to decide whether this unhappy state of affairs was peculiar to New South Wales or the inevitable consequence of a penal colony, and it therefore called for the government to order 'a thorough examination of the possibility and benefits of deportation'. Meanwhile it regarded the substitution of the sentence of detention for life in place of the sentence of deportation for political offences as indispensable.

Almost two weeks later, on 23 November, the draft Bill was presented for debate in the Chamber. Before discussion took place on individual clauses of the Bill, there were some general preliminary observations by members. One of them, Gaëtan de La Rochefoucauld (son of the famous prison reformer La Rochefoucauld-Liancourt), took up the question of deportation. His views suggested that the government and the committee might have misjudged the reception that the attempt to abolish deportation would receive in the debate. He saw advantages in deportation for political offences, and indeed he considered that, through providing an alternative to execution, its existence as a punishment had possibly saved the lives of a number of people in the 1790s. But La Rochefoucauld quickly moved on to argue in favour of deportation for *forçats*: the *bagnes* corrupted and made criminals worse, and gave no benefits to society. On the other hand:

> The following has long been said: Give a thief, a murderer even, a legacy, an inheritance, any wealth, he immediately becomes the most honest man in the world. That is the real benefit of

deportation. It provides land, work and comfort. One can be virtuous and happy; it is therefore probable that one becomes honest and lives well.

But what had motivated such very widespread support for deportation?

> Much less the liberty of the condemned than their removal; much less their benefit than our safety. Our committee and the ministry itself, while acknowledging the huge number of second offences in France, agree that Botany-Bay preserves England from them, and when this happy effect of deportation is recognised, it isn't quickly established! More than that, it is refused, it is abolished . . . !

Why was it, La Rochefoucauld continued, that after fifteen years a suitable colony has not been found for convicts? After all, the French colonies were home to French citizens and soldiers, so they could not be too unhealthy. He closed on an enigmatic note. Perhaps he was referring to an official interest in New Zealand following the reports of Dumont d'Urville:

> Indeed you have found at this moment a favourable opportunity that you should not let escape.
>
> I won't expatiate on this subject. Diplomacy imposes silence upon me; but it is for the government to take advantage of our foresight and to realise our hopes.[3]

As soon as the clause in the Bill which abolished deportation was presented to the Chamber, an amendment to remove it was moved by the first speaker, Delpon.[4] During the debate the amendment was modified by Odilon Barrot, its final form being:

> So long as the government has not established a place of deportation determined by the law, the punishment of deportation will be replaced by imprisonment.

The sentence of deportation would thus be retained, but the punishment would be imprisonment only until a site for deportation was declared and the real intention of the sentence could be carried out. In his address, Delpon drew on the authority of

3 The Great Parliamentary Debate, 1831

La Rochefoucauld-Liancourt to argue in favour of deportation. He considered deportation to be both a humane and effective punishment, and without it Barbé-Marbois and others would have lost their heads in the 1790s. On the question of the desirability of deportation for common criminals, and bearing in mind the absence of a penitentiary system, the actual state of French prisons and the increasing recidivism, it was not good enough merely to be told that France did not have a penal colony. But this did not mean that he would support the establishment of such a colony 'on the murderous shores of Senegal or in the pestilential swamps of Cayenne'. Why not Patagonia, which had been recommended by one of France's most illustrious sailors? It offered immense advantages over the countries occupied by the English colonies of deportation. 'It is there, gentlemen, that it would be fitting to form our Botany-Bay, our Sydney'. This opening address set the tone for the succeeding debate, in which, as will be shown, the main speakers—for and against the committee's proposal—canvassed the penal issues which had been raised in the previous decade.

But de Podenas, the following speaker, after restating the difference between French and English deportation said he was more influenced by the fact that, in the French scale of punishments, deportation would be more severe than the imprisonment envisaged in the legislation. Thus the committee's proposal to abolish deportation would be an amelioration in keeping with the current spirit of reform, and it did not compromise public order. The next three speakers quite ignored the France–England distinction, and spoke only of the deportation of common criminals. The first, Chalret-Durieu, affirmed that a satisfactory site for deportation could be found in America, New Holland or Africa. Moreover, deportation was preferable to imprisonment because it offered the chance of reform and a normal life: 'What I say is supported by the example of English deportees at Botany-Bay, where convicted persons have become honourable citizens'. Developing his Australian theme, Chalret-Durieu continued: 'Don't we have the possibility of sending deportees to the still uninhabited shores of New Holland? Are we not able to found settlements there, to do at last what the English have done?' English evidence suggested that its colony was relatively cheap to run, and there were gains in having a colony. Moreover, deportation would reduce the need for the application of the death penalty, as it had in England.

The next speaker, de Tracy, said that even if France had a place for a penal colony he would oppose deportation. If the colony were unhealthy the deportees would die. On the other hand, if it had strong positive qualities the deportees could be better off than honest citizens at home. There was, indeed, factual support for this last point:

> In England people get themselves convicted precisely for what they call the expense of the voyage. Why is that? It is because in New Holland one isn't badly off at all; living, once one has arrived there, is more agreeable than at certain social levels in England. And it should not be that a punishment, while mocking morality, becomes advantageous.

But for de Tracy, 'the purpose of punishment is reformation', and this would not be obtained in a penal colony. In New Holland, for example, free settlers established no relationship with deportees, and any possible improvement in the latters' morals was destroyed by new consignments of criminals. Moral improvement could be obtained only in penitentiaries, and he strongly recommended their early introduction into France.

In his speech Odilon Barrot strongly criticised the way in which the prison system, especially the *bagnes*, grouped all types of prisoners together: 'This regime is bad. There is universal opposition to it and its reform is sought'. He went on to discuss the two proposed courses of reform—penitentiaries and deportation. It had been claimed for deportation that the possibility of a new life might reform convicts, and this argument could not be dismissed. It had not been proven incorrect for the United States nor for 'those populations of New Holland which have become the elements of a very prosperous commerce and industry'. In these circumstances, he suggested, it would be a mistake to abolish deportation in an 'absolute, irrevocable manner', and he urged

3 The Great Parliamentary Debate, 1831

the government to establish a penal colony to which it could 'transport the condemned'.

When the committee's spokesman, Dumon, joined the debate, he again attempted to separate the Botany Bay experience from political deportation. He claimed first that as the law stood, the sentence of deportation was illegal because in the circumstances it actually meant imprisonment. Next, he argued that deportation was a bad sentence for political crimes, and questioned the sending of political deportees to such a place as Botany Bay. The general evidence about it might be contradictory, but 'more than half [the convicts] are in prisons; for them it is scarcely more than a *bagne* at the end of the world'; most of the others worked for settlers in harsh conditions and under continual surveillance, and this type of regime was quite unsuitable for political deportees. Dumon was moved once again to make some more general points about Botany Bay. In particular he dwelt on the subject of the convicts' moral improvement: there had been strong condemnation in England of the lack of such improvement, and 'just as the romance of Botany Bay was being exploited in France in a most infatuated fashion, the state of that colony was truly deplorable'. It offered the 'most disgusting spectacle'. Subsequent moral and economic advance was brought about by free settlers. And, as before, Dumon drew support from the testimony of Dumont d'Urville. These assertions about Botany Bay brought Delpon, the initial mover of the amendment, back into the debate, and he contrasted the 'hideous picture' painted by Dumon with what was revealed in the work of Cunningham, *Two Years in New South Wales*, who reported that of the two populations, emancipist and free, it was the emancipists who were the more virtuous.

As the president of the Chamber named the next speaker, Mauguin, the impatience of members began to show and cries of 'to the vote!' thereafter commonly greeted successive speakers. Mauguin went over familiar ground when he said that he was prepared to believe that deportation could bring moral reform, but for him the most important argument was that France had no suitable site and was unlikely to find one in the near future: 'Don't let us say that there is a possibility of carrying out this punishment;

for this would be to ask for the arraignment of all the successive ministers over forty years. (A voice:Yes!—laughter)'. In any case it would be too costly: 'I ask you, can we afford the expenditure as England has done to set up Botany-Bay?' In Mauguin's view, more consideration should be given to penitentiaries. This latter point was taken up by Odilon Barrot, who intervened to argue that even if the penitentiary system lived up to the hopes of its supporters, there was no reason why it could not co-exist with deportation.

A significant split took place in the ranks of the supporters of the government when a member of the committee, Mérilhou, said that he thought that it was the amendment and not the draft legislation which best caught the intention of the committee. Turning the debate back to Botany Bay he stated that he wanted to disagree with Mauguin on the subject of costs. English parliamentary papers contained proof that it was very much cheaper to send convicts to Botany Bay than to prison, and he believed France could make similar savings. But in searching for a place to send deportees he thought the ministry had been dilatory: 'Let us not therefore take a course which proscribes a practice to which England owes the foundation of a colony which, in a few years, will rival the finest possessions of Great Britain'. Moreover, after speaking with Dumont d'Urville and reading the account and the documents provided by him, he said he had reached a very different conclusion about the social state of the colony from that of the committee's spokesman:

> Look at what the documents from Australia show. It has been said again that there are two societies existing together; this is a mistake by the spokesman, and I am going to specify it. I have no intention of calling in doubt the facts that he avouched; but I think that he has considered these facts from a different point of view than my own.
>
> We two members of the committee have been able to consider the same facts each according to our personal judgement, and it is my personal judgement that I have the honour to develop from this tribune.

3 The Great Parliamentary Debate, 1831

> What do we see at Botany-Bay according to the documents that we have both consulted? We see there a vast territory occupied by an ever-increasing population which builds towns, which digs waterways, which lays out roads, which continually clears the land so as to present the most impressive sight that human reason can imagine in a country which but lately, 40 years ago, was covered with forests.
>
> There are convicts, there are descendants of convicts; there are families who descend from people who voluntarily transported their homes and destinies to this new world.
>
> Does this mean that there are two different societies? No, Gentlemen, there is one single society whose members are able to occupy various positions, but who all make up one and the same society . . .

Mérilhou then proceeded to argue that assigned convicts were transformed by work and discipline, were able to be paid and could sometimes amass a small fortune. Sometimes pardoned before their sentence was complete, they could become part of the one society which, as papers from the colony showed, was 'neither more nor less, and perhaps less rather than more depraved than that of the homeland'.

Another member of the committee, de Rémusat, at once felt he had to disagree. There was no doubt that Botany Bay was an economic success, but penally it was a failure. Order was maintained only by 'terrible repression'; and society was divided into two, as distinct and 'more insuperable perhaps than that which is raised in the Antilles between whites and blacks'. More generally, de Rémusat focused on what he took to be the basic issue. He accused opponents of speaking only of English transportation and Botany Bay, when the real subject matter was French deportation. By doing so, by moving the amendment to keep deportation possible, they were attempting to push the government towards transportation: 'it imposes on it a sort of moral obligation to work at it'.

In a short response Odilon Barrot attempted to accomodate de Rémusat's point: 'We have been involved in speaking of our deportation, because English deportation is only a more extended application of the principle of French deportation'.* For his part he hoped to see deportation extended to cover civil crimes. But the final speaker for the amendment, Salverte, went much further. Deportation somewhere, he pointed out, had always been possible, but what was needed, and what was not now available, was a settlement which would take *forçats*:

> The aim of this amendment is therefore to force the government to found such a settlement as soon as possible, because, by the admission of all the speakers, and by the admission even of those who have criticised Botany Bay fairly harshly, the good results of such an establishment have been recognised.

This view having been firmly stated, the amendment was put to the Chamber and carried by 'a large majority'. The Chamber of Peers agreed and accepted the amendment in March 1832.

This lively and extended parliamentary debate took place in the context of a climate of opinion which felt strongly that the response to crime in France required some fundamental change in the French prison system. The new French government was reformist in many ways, and its attitude towards the prison question was perhaps symbolised by its appointment in 1830 of Charles Lucas, a man dedicated to the introduction of a penitentiary system, as inspector-general of prisons. The government gave no indication of any interest in the establishment of a penal colony, and indeed a regime preoccupied with survival during its early years was unlikely to engage in a bold colonial adventure. However, when it attempted to remove the sentence of deportation for political offenders, it encountered popular opposition. Opponents in parliament had a different agenda: they wanted to keep the option of transportation of common criminals within the framework of prison reform. Accordingly they took over the debate on political deportation, and succeeded in pressing their case for a

---

*At this point the Minister for Justice, Barthe, intervened briefly. Again the distinction was made between English and French deportation, and it was suggested that the deportation of French criminals was of sufficient importance to warrant discussion at some other time in its own right. He did admit that both the committee's proposal and the amendment solved the current legal problem of the government associated with its inability to carry out the sentence of deportation.

3 The Great Parliamentary Debate, 1831

penal colony. Government supporters tried to meet them on their own ground, and argued that the future lay with a penitentiary system. But the debate did not centre on the penal effectiveness of penitentiaries, about which indeed there was not a lot of information; instead it concentrated on the role of penal colonies as exemplified by Botany Bay. Not surprisingly, the two sides drew opposite conclusions from its penal history, but the emphasis on one particular aspect was unusual. Some attention was paid by speakers to the transportation of criminals as a punishment and as a deterrent to crime. Some discussion took place on costs. But the main issue in making a judgement on Botany Bay, the core of the disagreement, appears to have been the extent to which transportation had led to reform in the behaviour of the convicts, and had ultimately permitted them to lead useful and crime-free lives.

No doubt a variety of reasons contributed to the 'large majority' eventually obtained by the transportationists. It would have been obvious to members who broadly supported the government that this was not an issue of great importance to it. The negating of its proposal was not a major rebuff and no change was required in its deportation policy. Moreover, recent elections had brought into parliament a high proportion of new deputies; party structure was loose and discipline slight. To a significant degree members would have felt free to vote on this issue according to their individual views.[5] They would have been aware of the broad popular support for a penal colony and the navy's endorsement of it. At the same time, support for transportation could accomodate within it very different emphases on the roles in a penal structure of punishment, deterrence and reform. In the event, a motion was carried which implicitly endorsed the Botany Bay experience and which urged the government to establish a French equivalent. It was to be another twenty years before anything like this goal was achieved.*

---

*In his seminal work on the development of the French prison system, *Surveillir et punir: naissance de la prison*, Michel Foucault hardly mentions deportation. Writing of this period he states that deportation was 'essentially to ease the financial burden required by the whole apparatus of detention'. (p. 284) This view is not supported by the evidence above. He also says that 'England abandoned [deportation] from the beginning of the 19th century'. (p. 278)

'Rhum' and drunkenness beside the prison in the early years of penal settlement: a fanciful sketch of a Sydney scene by an unnamed artist [M Alhoy, *Les bagnes*, 1845, p. 419]

II
Stalemate, 1831–1848

The year 1831 had closed with the Chamber of Deputies putting strong pressure on the government to establish a penal colony—along the lines of Botany Bay—for common criminals. But it was not until 1848 that the conditions began to be established which finally led to the introduction of transportation. In the intervening years, between 1831 and 1848, transportationists were active: pressure was applied in parliament; publications setting out the virtues of Botany Bay continued to appear; the navy actively searched for an overseas penal site. There was an attempt—which ended in failure—to establish a colony in New Zealand; a settlement in the Marquesas was partially successful. But success in putting their policy into action was denied the transportationists, partly because of the strength of their opponents, who favoured the establishment of penitentiaries in France.

Before discussing these developments, three remarkable studies of the Australian penal colonies by Frenchmen will be examined. In 1831 Ernest de Blosseville published his history—the first history—of Australia; in 1836 Jules de la Pilorgerie published his history in reply; between these two events, in 1831 and 1836, Gustave de Beaumont and Alexis de Tocqueville produced their own assessments of transportation to Australia and the lessons which they believed France could draw from them. None of these studies has ever received the recognition that its importance warrants. They will therefore be examined not only for their contribution to the French penal debate, but also as historical documents of wider significance.

4
The First History of Australia

The first history of European settlement in Australia was published in Paris in 1831 under the title: *Histoire des colonies pénales de l'Angleterre dans l'Australie*. Its author, Ernest de Blosseville, was a young Frenchman of thirty-two years. Then of no established reputation, he nevertheless moved in intellectual circles and had Chateaubriand as a patron and Tocqueville, his contemporary, as a friend. His book stemmed in part from a family connection with Australia, but more generally it was a response to the keen French interest in Australia and the effectiveness of the English transportation system. His view that Australian history demonstrated the success of transportation, as a means of dealing with crime and as a method of colonial development, provoked a critical reply in a second French study of the history of Australia, Jules de la Pilorgerie's work, *Histoire de Botany-Bay* . . . Blosseville returned to his subject matter in 1859 when he published a new edition of his work entitled *Histoire de la colonisation pénale* . . . In this edition the terminating date of the history was extended from the original of 1830 to 1857. Blosseville's 1831 history is a substantial volume. There is a preface of 9 pages, an introduction of 59 pages and text of 447 pages. As authority for the text an annotated bibliography of 68 pages is provided. It is extraordinary that this history appears to have been unappreciated, indeed largely unknown, in Australia. No doubt language has been a barrier.

It is a bold and always disputable claim that a particular history is a country's first. In fact there has been only a limited amount of analysis of early Australian historiography, but the most recent and the most valuable study is that by Stuart Macintyre.[1] He distinguishes between three types of historical writing in the period before 1900. The first consists of the work of writers who were participants in the events of the foundation years—Phillip, Collins, Hunter, Tench and White—or who were travellers and explorers. They published accounts largely based on their own experiences and, as such, they are records rather than histories. The second type of writing is identified as beginning with William Wentworth in 1819 and ending with John West in 1852.[2] These writers, Macintyre considers, are historians in as much as they reveal an 'ordering principle', an interpretation. Each was concerned with the application of political authority and its effects on society. Each argued for different policies, a different society. They were involved men of affairs and, 'lacking a substantial body of documentation ... drew heavily on testimony or first-hand experience'.[3] Their histories were presented as chronological narratives. A third group of writers, Macintyre argues, emerged after self-government was obtained in the 1850s. Rather than attempt to influence the policies of the British government, they found a new theme in the progress of the colonies. 'They were concerned with recording what Macaulay had described as "the history of physical, of moral and of intellectual improvement" which in this case was measured in flocks and crops, bricks and mortar, and then in the civilisation these made possible'.[4] Dealing with the early period, their narratives still tended to be organised around the administrative decisions of governors.

In this framework Blosseville's history overlaps the second and third types of writing. He wrote in part to influence government policy—in his case, the French government—and he also emphasised the physical development of the colonies, the moral improvement in the ex-convicts and the establishment of civilisation. If David Collins, the most important and comprehensive of the early writers, cannot be judged a 'true' historian, then in terms of precedence only Wentworth's name can be raised. But Blosseville's work is of a different genre altogether. Wentworth produced a strange mishmash of information: the first (1819) edition of his work does have a long historical section, 'Operation of the existing System of Government in the Colony for the last fifteen Years'.

But much of this section is discursive and/or contemporary comment, and although it is retained in the second (1820) edition it is dropped entirely from the third (1824) edition. In the preface to the 1819 edition Wentworth referred to this work as a 'hasty production' for which he relied 'in a great measure' on his memory.*

Blosseville's history offers the immediate contrast of the scholarly use of wide-ranging sources. His formal bibliography of 'principal works' contains forty-one entries, and his thoughtful approach to their use is indicated by his annotations.† Consider, for example, his assessments of the two important authors already mentioned, Collins and Wentworth. He begins his comment on Collins' work by describing it as 'the most authentic and detailed account that exists of the first years of the English settlement in New South Wales'. He regards it as the work that still may be 'consulted most fruitfully'. His one criticism of Collins is what he sees as a common fault of English travellers, an 'over-supply of details'. On the other hand, there is, he says, the English criticism of 'the alleged aridity of the better French accounts'. Blosseville notes that much of the minutiae has been pruned from Collins' second edition, but most importantly he wishes to acknowledge his debt: 'We must not conceal how useful he has been for us'.[5]

Blosseville offers a much more qualified view of William Wentworth's usefulness:

> This history of a nation 31 years old, written by one of its sons, is of great interest. But the reader should be on guard against an exaggerated feeling of nationalism. More order in the composition, better balance between the different parts, could be wished for.

---

*Mark Hutchinson argues that Wentworth was not writing history: 'historiographers may see [in him] a fore-runner, or pre-cursor, to an historical view of the Australian experience . . . he does not represent the thing itself'. See his 'W. C. Wentworth and the sources of Australian historiography', p. 78.

†In his study of Australia, Hyacinthe de Bougainville commented that Blosseville 'presents a complete bibliography of Australia, accompanied by reviews which put the reader, curious to go back to the sources, in a position to choose among these works the one which he is most interested in consulting'. See his *Journal de la navigation autour du globe*, p. 469.

4 The First History of Australia

Too often, Wentworth forgets his role as a historian in order to argue, like a true lawyer, against his opposing party, Commissioner Bigge. The English Reviews have criticised, not without reason, the dictatorial tone, and the *foolish language* [italicised in English in the original] of Wentworth.

In spite of these critical remarks, the first historical work by an Australian is to be commended for its new insights and accounts of facts not reported by any traveller. With proper caution, there is much to be learnt in this interesting book.[6]

In two places Blosseville draws attention to other source material he has drawn on. In the preface he notes his indebtedness to *La Revue britannique*, the *Edinburgh* and *Quarterly Reviews*, the *Asiatic Journal*, the *Nouvelles annales des voyages* and notes made by three members of a French ship which visited Sydney in 1824. Again, at the conclusion of his formal bibliography, he especially mentions the *Revue des deux mondes*, the *London and Paris Observer*, the Reports of the Australian Agricultural Company and 'official documents printed by order of the House of Commons'.

Undoubtedly Ernest de Blosseville's interest in Australia was stimulated by the activities of his younger and more famous brother, Jules. A naval officer, Jules had accompanied Duperrey on his voyage to the South Seas and had spent two months in Sydney in 1824. On his return he submitted reports to the French government in 1826 full of praise for the penal and economic success of the English colonies, and recommended that France follow this example. There is evidence of Ernest's interest as early as 1827 when he published in an edition of one hundred copies his *Revue de divers écrits concernant les forçats et la déportation*.[7] An explanation of the immediate circumstances surrounding Ernest's commitment to his own book is offered by his biographer, Louis Passy: Jules had engaged to write a journal article on the penal colonies in Australia but, on being called away for the French Algerian expedition of 1830, he bequeathed to his brother some notes which became the beginnings of Ernest's book. Ernest later wrote that he was inspired by his brother and two of his shipmates (Lesson and Gabert); he began a 'simple article' which grew to a pamphlet, and 'one day it turned out that the slim pamphlet had become a book'.[8]

In his 1831 preface Blosseville makes no direct reference to any influence from his brother. Essentially he sets out material relating to what he considers to be a great social problem—crime and its punishment. He points to the unanimity of opinion in France concerning the dangers to society posed by freed *forçats*. Prisons make criminals worse: recidivism is a major source of serious crime. However, he continues, there is no similar unanimity on what society's response should be; most people favour the establishment of penal colonies, although they have only limited knowledge of the great test of the effectiveness of penal colonies carried out in Australia with 'such prodigious success'.[9] It is this lack of information resulting from the limited quantity and quality of French language publications on Australia that his book is to remedy.

The long introduction to his history ranges widely and develops a number of themes: the attempts by various countries including France to dispose of convicts overseas; the growth of support in France for penal colonies; the opposition to penal colonies especially from supporters of penitentiaries; a sustained attempt to rebut the penitentiary argument and defend transportation. Finally, there is a brief discussion of sites previously proposed for a French penal colony. As in the preface, the great success of the Australian penal colonies is asserted, but Blosseville argues that France could do better:

> without making all the mistakes which have so sadly characterised the first attempts of Great Britain. Time has revealed the flaws of an administration without a coherent plan; the lesson will not be wasted.[10]

THE CONTENTS

The epigraph to Blosseville's preface, attributed to Beaumont and Tocqueville, indicates an important aspect of his intentions: 'Books of theory abound: practical works are not to be found'.[11] His 'sole aim', he writes, was 'to bring together in the form of an historical summing up the various documents' that were available.

4 The First History of Australia

This would enable him to present the 'facts' relating to Botany Bay to inform an ignorant public, to counter the opponents of penal colonies and thus to influence policy:*

> An historical account will report facts whose consequences and application will come naturally to mind. The good sense of the public can be trusted to distinguish in these annals of a few days, what should be copied, what should be avoided.[12]

Blosseville felt that writing Australian history posed a special challenge, and that this should be formally brought to the readers' attention. Something quite novel was required:

> The history of the English settlements in the southern lands presents no resemblance to subjects previously dealt with by historians. This has resulted in continual difficulties for the author. He is allowed none of the familiar features of historical writing: none of those dazzling exploits which holds one's attention; no deliberative oratory, no heroes, no wars, scarcely a few light skirmishes. Certain to be judged according to the rules imposed on historians, most often forced to resort, in spite of the subject's importance, to the more familiar forms of statistics and of voyages, he is resigned to recognising that, in an account which hardly ranges outside mundane matters, the surrender of all conceit by the author was absolutely necessary. Perhaps this confession will give him some claims to the indulgence of his readers.†

This 'nature of the subject' was also Blosseville's explanation of the greater space in his history which he gave to the early years of settlement. To present all the facts:

---

*When, in his introduction, Blosseville surveys arguments concerning transportation and penitentiaries, he confesses that in this instance he has not simply supplied the 'facts': 'This intention of being impartial has not been rigorously carried out. It is difficult to let pass the opportunity to defend the system which appears best to satisfy at once justice and humanity, the interests of both society and the guilty, by joining punishment and reform'. (*Histoire des colonies pénales*, p. 59)

†Reference is made to 'forms of statistics and of voyages'. This is a literal translation. In the early nineteenth century, the meaning of 'statistics' was the collection of facts relating to a country's extent, population, resources, etc. 'Voyage' could mean the account of a voyage.

... he has had at first to stress minute events the repetition of which would have entailed too much boredom. In proportion as the nation grows, the account returns to more narrow confines. Finally, a general picture of the current state of a civilisation so suddenly improvised concludes a work which could be considered fanciful were it not for the proximity of the events.[13]

The conventional historical section of Blosseville's work ends at about 1822, after which, as will be shown, a slightly different approach is adopted. The history is presented in chronological form: after four chapters on the historical background to transportation and two on the voyage to Sydney, chapter 7 begins: 'The 26th of January should be inscribed with honour in the annals of civilisation'.[14] From that point the account is related by chapters to the administrative periods of particular governors, although individual governors might be given more than one chapter. As Blosseville mentioned, the earlier period is given more space: Arthur Phillip's five years are allotted 129 pages; Lachlan Macquarie's eleven years take 50 pages. Avoidance of repetition may be relevant, but perhaps a more straightforward explanation is the greater human interest in the initial settlement—the shock of the new, the drama, the near-catastrophe. Possibly not irrelevant also is the number of detailed accounts in English of those first years on which Blosseville could draw.

Overall, the history tells the story of a penal settlement founded in desperate circumstances at the end of the world, of the difficulties faced and overcome, and of eventual success by the 1820s when it had developed into a thriving colony—part-penal, part-free. But of course there is more to it than that. For instance, no history of the period can avoid judging the settlement in penal terms, and debate in England, France and Australia on transportation and penal colonies was usually passionate. Supporters and opponents put their case most positively. What is interesting in Blosseville's work in this regard is both the mildness and realism of his support, and the limited amount of direct attention that he gives to this topic.

Consider Blosseville's views on the convicts themselves. There is no sympathy for them as such, although he is careful to distinguish political from common prisoners. Looking at 1788 he

4 The First History of Australia

emphasised their poor pioneering qualities both in skills and motivation. He noted the turbulence, the disorders and the punishments imposed—and replied to critics:

> Opponents of penal colonies have often wished to turn to account so disproportionate a number of sentences in so short a space of time and with so small a population. They should have given more attention to the petty nature of the offences and the need to make examples.[15]

Similarly, he noted how beneficial it would have been if convicts who had proven their trustworthiness could have been put to guard the supplies. As it was, Phillip had to choose custodians:

> ... before having been able to know with sufficient certainty the reform of these men whom he was going to present as models to their fellow convicts. The result of these flawed arrangements was easy to predict. The operations of the domestic economy became disordered, and supervisors, much less known by their superiors than by their subordinates, too often failed to have a desirable influence.[16]

When, in 1789, convicts of good conduct were selected for the night watch in Sydney, Blosseville acclaimed the outcome:

> The good results of this institution could not be in doubt; they soon surpassed the hopes of the governor. More than one district of London was less safe, during the night, than the streets of Sydney.[17]

After almost four years of settlement Blosseville considered the early disorderly period to be over; crime had diminished, and indeed early thefts had been in part prompted by need. He thought that the policy of pardons and assistance for ex-convict settlers were most important in this improvement. Thereafter Blosseville gave little attention to the convicts as such. Usually they were discussed only incidentally in reviewing society as a whole. Thus, in summing-up at the time of Governor Hunter's departure:

> Undoubtedly the behaviour of the new settlers was not beyond reproach; a few state buildings burnt down; provocations against the indigenous people, frequent excess of debauchery, brawls, escapes, attempted piracy on seized ships' boats, too often reminded

the governor of the origins of the society entrusted to his care. He was obliged to struggle against idleness and bad faith, against the dangers of exaggerated moderation and excessive rigour; but firmness joined with justice was sufficient to maintain order, and by clemency without weakness, Hunter managed to make his administration cherished and respected.[18]

Changes in the penal system in the 1820s brought Blosseville's approval: transportees were required to have a minimum sentence of seven years; the care and conduct of the convicts on the transports were more closely supervised. He believed that moral reform was becoming increasingly common along with better understanding between masters and servants. However, a danger accompanied any softening of the system: 'the feeling of terror which was imparted in the first years of the system of deportation has already lost some of its force in England'. But although courtroom wits spoke frivolously of 'the sentimental excursion to Botany-Bay', and although there were instances of crimes committed with transportation in mind, Blosseville thought the problem not sufficiently important to condemn the system; in any case, 'the reputation for severity of the last governor, Sir Ralph Darling, has almost completely put this abuse to rights'.[19]

Yet in judging the penal success of the Australian colonies, Blosseville was not primarily interested in transportation as a punishment and as a deterrent to crime in Britain. His main concern was the extent of reform in the character of the convicts as shown by their behaviour when freed. And in fact he believed that it was this behaviour which had led to so much of Australia's economic and cultural development. In his history he cited the careers of Ruse and Barrington, but emancipists as a group (as with convicts) were dealt with in passing, until he reached an assessment of Macquarie's regime. This takes the form of a consideration of the circumstances surrounding the Bigge inquiry. Blosseville began by discussing the long-standing criticisms of New South Wales in England which had gathered strength during Macquarie's governorship. More specifically, Macquarie was accused of permitting breaches of trade regulations and, more importantly, of excess expenditure. But Blosseville felt that the underlying motive for the attacks on Macquarie stemmed from his social behaviour, exemplified by his custom

> of receiving the families of emancipists and of emigrants with completely equal respect and courtesy; as if the very institution of the colony had not made this conduct a pressing duty for him. He had, it is true, pushed the application of a principle, just in itself, a little far. To close his home to whomsoever would not follow his example was an act of impolitic intolerance in a system of complete tolerance; it was to provide a pretext for cries of oppression and proscription.[20]

In the attack on Macquarie in the British parliament Blosseville singled out the criticisms of Bennet and Brougham; he also noted Brougham's letter to Lord Sidmouth. The government's response in setting up the Bigge inquiry was, Blosseville concluded, partly for its own political reasons. What did the inquiry discover?

> Here it is necessary to point out another striking example of historical uncertainty. Scarcely ten years have passed since the inquiry. We have all the documents of the legal process before us; we have been able to consult disinterested witnesses, and yet such a spirit of vexation has presided over the attacks and replies, that a large number of facts remains in doubt .

Nevertheless, Blosseville had no doubt as to Bigge's partiality and attacked him and his report. He observed that Bigge was a relative of Bennet; and, chosen 'to bring together evidence in support of an accusation, he has surpassed the hopes of his principals'. Blosseville strongly criticised particular aspects of the inquiry and concluded: 'His inquiry became a veritable defamatory lampoon: consequently his conduct, contrary to the spirit and even the letter of his instructions, was severely criticised by Mr Forbes in the House of Commons'.[21]

The social setback to the emancipists' cause was acknowledged by Blosseville but, in his view, it was unimportant in the more general context: freed convicts had been successful in the new colonial society; at the end of the 1820s he saw them as 'the richest class of the colony and the most active part of the population'.

He reported that in Sydney commerce, emancipists were regarded as more trustworthy than emigrants, and by the same logic the worse their former reputation the more reliable they were. Why? Because they had to be so very careful and act to avoid the least suspicion. 'This is not perhaps the triumph of morality, it is one of self-interest; but the result for society is the same'.[22]

Blosseville believed, as we have seen, that the history of Australia was most unusual and posed special problems for historians. But he saw the nature of that history changing in about 1822. It was still an unusual history and still required special treatment, but the period 1822–30 related to a society now more familiar to European eyes. This change required him to move from the 'forms of history to those of statistics'. In the introductory chapter to this section he observes that the country's infancy is over, and he presents his picture of the 1820s:

> Now having reached man's age, in everyday contact with European civilisation, these colonies have barely retained a singular appearance. The period of eight years that we have yet to cover shows astonishing progress, but without obstacles overcome, without remarkable events. Periods of good fortune are barren for history; these eight years, which ensure the existence of Hobart Town and Sydney for a boundless future, will occupy little space in their annals. They have brought about valuable improvements, consolidated inexhaustible resources, but naturally, through force of circumstances. So many new nations nowadays rise on distant shores; the struggle of civilisation against barbarism is so continually presented to our eyes in so many different climates, and this struggle brings in its wake as much disaster and strife to the land which once was Greece as to newly-born Colombia, that peaceful conquests cannot catch general attention. Risen from nothing in a world without match, while other peoples build on ruins, the young society whose history we trace has already effaced, in the speed of its progress, the singularity of its origin. More fortunate, more civilised, possessing more assurances of security than its American sisters, it no longer has to claim the tokens of interest that weakness attracts; but it is able to dazzle by unforeseen riches. It is left to us to trace its picture again.[23]

Following this introductory chapter the chronological approach is abandoned and the next five chapters deal with various aspects of the period 1822–31. While they certainly have more of an air of providing information, of giving a description, they nevertheless retain an historical character. Certainly this was Blosseville's opinion when he produced his new edition in 1859. He removed his reference to a change in his method of approach, and with a minimum of rewriting the five chapters—all relating to 1822–31—were classified thus: social conditions, administration, commerce, agricultural progress, nascent colonies. The headings of these chapters also give some indication of the broad scope of what Blosseville considered to be the subject matter of his history before 1822. As has already been suggested, there is no concentration on the penal aspects of the colony. The title of Blosseville's book is a correct description of the contents: he has written a general history.

RECEPTION AND INFLUENCE

There was an immediate, personal triumph for Blosseville following the publication of his book. In 1832 the Académie française awarded him the Montyon prize, consisting of a gold medal and 3000 francs for the work 'most morally useful'.[24] This was a distinguished prize awarded annually. In the following year it was bestowed on Beaumont and Tocqueville for their report on American penitentiary systems, and several years earlier Charles Lucas had won it for his book on penitentiary systems in Europe and America. The subject matter of these prize-winners indicates the French preoccupation with the issue of crime and punishment. Blosseville must also have been pleased that his book appeared just in time to be used in the parliamentary debate of 1831, which climaxed the push for penal colonies during the 1820s.

How did critics greet Blossevilles's book? Looking back from 1859 he observed that:

> Several periodicals, especially some reviews, spoke of it in favourable terms; some extensive and justified judgements were made of it by writers such as M. de la Renaudière, M. de Montvéran, M. le comte de Salvandy; in Holland, by M. Van West; in America by M. James Mease.[25]

He did not mention the notice given the book by an American, D. B. Warden, a resident of Paris and an editor of *Bulletin de la Société de Géographie*, who wrote that the book deserved:

> ... the attention of all those who follow the progress of civilisation. It contains a multitude of very interesting particulars on the colonies of New South Wales, the difficulties that it had to overcome, its sufferings, its turmoil and its growth.[26]

It is surprising that the book was not reviewed in the *Annales maritimes et coloniales* until 1837. This journal, as a semi-official naval publication, naturally favoured the dissolution of the *bagnes* and the establishment of penal colonies. It is not, however, surprising that the anonymous reviewer was most enthusiastic and that he reviewed it more as an argument for transportation than as a history. He believed the book provided for parliamentary and government discussion 'all the evidence for the great contest between deportation and the penitentiary system, and we can reduce these disputes to more simple terms'. On Blosseville's role as historian, the reviewer thought that he had consulted 'all the original sources', and that he was astonishingly successful in involving the reader's sympathies in the fortunes of the early settlement. He summed up:

> ... a work which is destined to produce a pleasing revolution in our penal code; a conscientious work which was absolutely lacking in France, and which reveals at once a skilful historian and an enlightened friend of the public good. In it are to be found a profound judgement, a diverse and ever-growing interest; a proper style, free of those pretentious sentences, of those neologisms so common nowadays when Ronsard has again found admirers, and yet a style full of energy when the situation calls for it.[27]

Blosseville's book was not translated into English and it might have passed almost without notice in England had it not been picked up by the *Foreign Quarterly Review*, an important journal whose policy was to review books not available in English translation.[28] Henry Southern wrote a long review of sixteen pages, using it in large part as a vehicle to express his own views. As a

Benthamite, Southern thought colonies in general an economic liability, and the Australian penal colony a social disaster; he strongly supported penitentiaries at home. Southern considered that Blosseville's desire for a French penal colony was based less on penal reasons than on the French envy, widespread but groundless, of the wealth and glory of Britain's colonial empire. If Blosseville was really interested in a penal colony *per se*, why had he not given a close analysis of the costs and benefits of transportation? As it was, 'the subject of transportation is treated in no other way, than as a matter of narrative'. The book as a whole was, in Southern's eyes, a general, but nonetheless good history of the Australian colonies:

> We have, it must be said, an able abridgement of the materials which present themselves in abundance for the history of the gradual rise and progress of the settlement. In forty years, the rapid rise of the colony, the nature of its population and the circumstances of the country have furnished a great number of details for the pen of the historian, and M. de Blosseville has handled them with that precision and exactness, not unusual with his countrymen, but very rare in England, where the business of compilation seems disdained by all who pretend to literary fame. It is, however, no easy task, and deserves both greater honour from the public, and a higher reward from the employer than is usually awarded to it. The command of a clear but rapid style, the art of narrating various events on the same scale, which the French call the *co-ordonnation* of facts, require a cultivated writer and a master of his subject. It is, however, only the mere historical branch of the question that this compiler can be said to have studied: and he has incurred a fearful responsibility by lightly recommending to his countrymen a measure, which he ought to have learned, is fraught with frightful evils both at home and abroad . . .[29]

Blosseville was pleased with the favourable comments that his book received, but he thought its reception was muted and he was obviously disappointed with its overall impact. It was a mistake, he thought, not to have used 'Botany-Bay' in the title of his work, as Pilorgerie had done in his reply. Although geographically inaccurate as the location of the settlement, 'Botany-Bay' was 'accepted at all levels of intelligence, has the good fortune to personify a system: it will remain'. More importantly, he saw the circumstances of 1831, with the revolution and the establishment in power of Louis-Philippe, as unfavourable. Internationally France was weakened: 'It was a time to lose rather than found colonial settlements. For a long time we would no longer be able to speak out loudly and firmly to rival nations'. But Blosseville also identified a more general change in attitudes in the influential circles which accompanied the new government—a government of which he did not approve. Rather bitterly he wrote:

> Reforms and progress were spoken of a lot. Improvement of prisons was the agenda and seemed easy to attempt, if not to realise entirely. The penitentiary system was better suited than penal colonisation to the commonplace nature of the times. Experiments could take place everywhere, even in the simple gaol of an arrondissement; there was no need for England's permission. The penitentiary had to prevail: it did prevail.[30]

It was Blosseville's misfortune that his book appeared just as the tide of feeling in favour of penal colonies was about to recede. For almost two decades the penal debate tended to centre on the type of penitentiary system which should be established in France.

In addition to this change in sentiment, it seems that Blosseville's book did not attract more attention because it lacked rigour and bite as a tract on the advantages of transportation. There was great French interest in the Australian colonies, but it focused significantly on their penal aspect and thus on the relevance of their experience for penal change in France. On the positive aspects of transportation, all that Blosseville appeared to have shown was that few freed convicts returned to Britain, that many freed convicts became good citizens in Australia and that by the 1820s the colonies were an outstanding economic success. Although he mentioned them, he did not firmly address such important questions as: Was transportation a sufficient punishment? What were the effects on crime rates at home? Was transportation more

HISTOIRE

DES

COLONIES PÉNALES

DE L'ANGLETERRE

DANS L'AUSTRALIE;

PAR M. ERNEST DE BLOSSEVILLE,

CONSEILLER DE PRÉFECTURE DE SEINE ET OISE.

> Delightful land in wildness e'en benign,
> The glorious past in ours, the future thine.
> CAMPBELL : *Lines on the departure of emigrants for New South Wales.*

PARIS.

ADRIEN LE CLERE ET Cᵢᴇ, IMPRIMEURS-LIBRAIRES,
QUAI DES AUGUSTINS, N° 35;
DELAUNAY, LIBRAIRE, AU PALAIS-ROYAL;
DANDELY, LIBRAIRE, PASSAGE DES PANORAMAS.

—

1831.

The title page of the first history of Australia, by Ernest de Blosseville, published in Paris in 1831

DU SYSTÈME
PÉNITENTIAIRE

AUX ÉTATS-UNIS,

ET

DE SON APPLICATION EN FRANCE;

SUIVI D'UN APPENDICE

SUR LES COLONIES PÉNALES

ET DE NOTES STATISTIQUES.

Par MM. G. de BEAUMONT et A. de TOCQUEVILLE,

AVOCATS A LA COUR ROYALE DE PARIS,
MEMBRES DE LA SOCIÉTÉ HISTORIQUE DE PENNSYLVANIE.

PARIS,

H. FOURNIER JEUNE, LIBRAIRE,

RUE DE SEINE, N° 29.

1833.

It was in the appendix to their analysis of the American prison system (1833), of which this is the title page, that Gustave de Beaumont and Alexis de Tocqueville made their first assessment of transportation to Australia.

costly than prisons? What proportion of convicts was genuinely reformed? What were the moral circumstances of a convict-based society? Did economic success begin only with the increasing number of free migrants? It mattered little that these questions were in the main unanswerable.

It was also true that Blosseville admitted some virtue in the penitentiary case. Its main weakness, he thought, was that ex-prisoners, even if reformed by the penitentiary system, were not accepted back into civil society. In contrast, there were great opportunities for ex-prisoners in the new society of a penal colony. In his concluding chapter Blosseville argued for combining the two systems—a point of view later to be taken up vigorously in both Britain and France. He believed the weakness of the penitentiary system could be overcome by establishing it not in the home country but in the penal colony, and he had this advice for the British cabinet:

> It is up to it to establish the union of penal colonisation and the penitentiary system. How many capacious establishments (the ever-growing prosperity of its southern colonies enables it to erect them), how many capacious establishments, formed on the combined model of the prisons of Auburn and Geneva, of Lausanne and Richmond, may receive on their disembarkment young transportees from Great Britain; how many others, the immense size of the land permits it, how many others, under an ever-active surveillance, and under the command of the law of silence, may be employed at useful land-clearing, and there, freed from the indispensable necessity of the poor house, the penitentiary system will bear all its fruit.[31]

TOCQUEVILLE'S REACTION

In the final years of the 1820s, Blosseville, Beaumont and Tocqueville became associates in the French bureaucracy and friends. Blosseville's book had recently appeared when Beaumont and Tocqueville returned from their study of prison conditions in America. Indeed, it is possible that it was Blosseville's interest in prisons that inspired his two more famous colleagues.[32] Their views now put them in opposing camps: Blosseville argued for penal colonies; Beaumont's and Tocqueville's American experience had made them committed supporters of the creation of a penitentiary regime in France. Their book and their advocacy were perhaps the catalyst for putting penitentiaries at the centre of penal debate and policy. Tocqueville studied Blosseville's book carefully while helping Beaumont draft their own, and his private notes are revealing. In evaluating Tocqueville's comments, the observation should be borne in mind that his private notes have 'a liveliness of tone—a maliciousness also—that are not found in their printed version'.[33]

Tocqueville began: 'This book is written with that common and facile style which characterises middle mediocrity. It flows like clear water'. For Tocqueville, there was insufficient discussion of the case for and against penal colonies, but he admitted that the author 'confines himself almost strictly within his title which is *the history* of the English penal colonies'. Even regarded as a history, however, Tocqueville found two major faults in the work. The first was the amount of petty detail along with a lack of attention to important issues such as colonial and transportation costs and the discipline and surveillance imposed on the convicts. He looked in vain for an 'accurate and living picture of what exists in Australia; and I remain with the confused ideas I had already'. The second and 'biggest fault' of the history was Blosseville's bias; in spite of his claim to impartiality, to be a presenter of facts, Tocqueville thought that the author 'brings to the fore all the facts favourable to this system and keeps in the background those against it'. In what could be interpreted as a tribute to Blosseville, but not meant as such, Tocqueville lined him up with his own principal opponent within the penitentiary camp: 'M. de Blosseville is the Ch. Lucas of deportation'. His final assessment was that the book 'is useful to have. But it is not to my mind a good book'. Nevertheless, Tocqueville admitted that it was this book that brought home to him the need to consider the question of penal colonies for France; and he rather endearingly continued: 'I shall try to bring to it so much the more impartiality because I write here for myself alone'.[34] And, when Beaumont and Tocqueville came to

4 The First History of Australia

write on penal colonies, they paid this tribute to Blosseville's work:

> In all that follows, we have often had occasion to turn to the book of M. de Blosseville. This work, whose author appears moreover favourable to the system of deportation, abounds in interesting facts and intriguing research. It constitutes the most complete document which has been published in our language on the English settlements in Australia.[35] *

The rider could be added to the last sentence that it was also the most complete document on this subject in any language.

History as a scholarly discipline was just emerging in the first half of the nineteenth century. In terms of subject matter, writers in the eighteenth century would have tended to agree with Gibbon that the main concerns of history were wars and the administration of public affairs. In the nineteenth century, it has been argued that 'historians (in Western Europe and North America) dealt largely with governments and great men, and with the development of national consciousness and the growth of political liberalism'.[36] The broader study of society as the subject matter of history did have its advocates, and Voltaire had been influential in strongly recommending it in the middle of the eighteenth century. To a degree this theme was taken up by several reformist French historians in the 1820s: Augustin Thierry, in his history of the Norman conquest of England, and Jules Michelet with his introduction to world history. Both took large subjects and treated them in a romantic manner. In the same period and mainly under Ranke's influence, the practice of the systematic use of primary sources as the basis for historical writing was in its infancy.

In this context it is again worth reviewing how Blosseville considered his work different from the conventional histories of the period. He began the introduction to his work with this jaundiced view of current historical practice:

---

*In *Democracy in America* (p. 305, n. 18) Tocqueville refers to Blosseville's 'excellent book on the English penal colonies'.

> Critics have often reproached bygone historians for the almost total absence of details concerning the native *mores* and early customs of the greatest nations. Reduced on nearly all points to the indecision of conjectures, doubting even the existence of the chiefs we call our first kings, we seek out with avid curiosity the least occurrences from the ancient chronicles; we examine shattered remains, the obscure archives of past ages; we seek to unearth some monument under the ruins of centuries, and, so as not to lose the fruits of our investigations, we nearly always end up by adopting some agreed fictions, which no longer deceive anybody, and which we do not however have the courage to repudiate.

He then contrasted this position with the writing of the history of more recent events:

> Very different are the nations which, born before our eyes, receive civilisation at the high level of development to which we have brought it through so many trials. Nothing uncertain in their annals . . . No place for the fictions of a golden age . . .
>
> Here there is no erudition to display, no model to follow. The history of the English penal colony, which is far from numbering fifty years of existence, presents to the writer no points in common with the accounts of the Greek and Latin historians or the chroniclers of the middle ages.[37]

Exaggerated though Blosseville's argument may be, he raises important issues and shows his uneasiness with his own project. In fact he wrote a curiously modern history. Although a general history, he relied heavily on the primary sources of the observations of participants in the penal colony and of visitors. Again, although most of his narrative was written around the terms of office of the governors, Blosseville's account centred on the life and circumstances of the colony, not the great men; at the same time he showed sympathy and understanding for the people in the settlement. There is no attempt, as was common at the time, to use wide-ranging theories of historical change. He was also writing what amounted to contemporary history, rather than the history of great events in the distant past. It would be hard to find other histories of the time that met these conditions.

4 The First History of Australia

Blosseville's achievement in his historical writing may stem not from any conscious choice, but rather from the nature of his subject matter. There were almost no secondary sources: he had, perforce, to use primary material. With his focus ostensibly on the success of transportation as a method of dealing with crime, Blosseville actually wrote about the fortunes and eventual social and economic success of a penal-based society. And, notwithstanding his Montyon prize, it is this which may have led to some contemporary lack of recognition of his worth as a historian. What a petty subject for a history: the fate of a penal colony in which after forty years the population numbered scarcely more than 50 000! There was little scope here for romantic writing, for great men, for sweeping interpretations of history. Students of history could ignore it; penologists found a general history insufficiently informative.

Blosseville appears to be a child of Ranke in affirming that he could produce the 'facts' of history, that the facts would speak for themselves. Was he being naive, or was this simply an attempt to bolster his argument? It is easy to understand Tocqueville's irritation at Blosseville's claim to impartiality. He was a biased historian. He was too dismissive of the critics of Botany Bay. But it is easy to see how the positive aspect, the formation, physically from nothing and morally with improbable material, of the flourishing society of the 1820s must have struck him. The modern historian is familiar with a far wider range of sources than was available to Blosseville. It would be unrewarding to seek in his work new material, new interpretations, new insights. What remains is a most interesting creation: a scholarly and first history of European settlement in Australia. Written in response to contemporary French interest, it is in part a period piece, but also in part a modern history.

5
Tocqueville and Australia

Alexis de Tocqueville achieved enduring fame with his observations and reflections on American society. He was also a distinguished historian and penologist. Not well known is that, as a result of his professional commitment to French penal reform, he was an interested observer and analyst of the system of transportation to Australia. He wrote on the nature and application of this system, and judged it by its effects on the rate and type of crime, on the convicts themselves and on the society that it produced in Australia. It is the purpose of this chapter to examine these views of Tocqueville and place them in the context of the French penal debate and Tocqueville's own penal philosophy. It begins by suggesting some reasons why such important writing has been overlooked.

The first part of Tocqueville's great work, *De la démocratie en Amérique*, was published in 1835 and quickly made the author famous. Yet already he had established a reputation in Europe and America in another field. His book *Système pénitentiare aux États-Unis*, jointly written with Gustave de Beaumont and published in 1833, had been critically acclaimed and had won the authors the prestigious Montyon prize in France. Tocqueville's writings on the nature of crime and the treatment of criminals were an integral and consistent part of his philosophy, and his expertise in this area became a central feature of his parliamentary career. Yet the book itself has an odd publication history. In France a second edition was published in 1836 and a third in 1845; there was then no other French edition until 1984 when it appeared in *Tome* IV of Tocqueville's collected works. The editor's introduction to this *Tome* relating to his penal writing is headed

5 Tocqueville and Australia

'Tocqueville Méconnu'—unrecognised Tocqueville,[1] but it is a Tocqueville who was well known to his contemporaries. The only unabridged translation in English was made by Francis Lieber and was published in Philadelphia in 1833.[2] It was republished in Philadelphia in 1868, and just over one hundred years later, in 1970, Augustus M. Kelley published a reprint of the 1833 edition.

Since it is in *Système pénitentiaire* that Tocqueville's writings on Australia are to be found, access to them has been restricted by the limited availability of the work; moreover, because they appear in the appendix entitled 'On Penal Colonies', and as part of the introduction to the second (1836) edition, the Australian content is not flagged. The actual subject matter of the appendix has been further obscured for English readers by its omission, along with other sections, from a popular abridged edition published in America in 1964; as the foreword to that edition stated, '[they] were omitted because they are of questionable relevance today; however relevant they may have been in the past'. Knowledge of the writing on Australia in the introduction to the second (1836) edition is even more difficult for English readers to acquire: it is of course not included in the 1970 Kelley reprint of the first edition.

Système pénitentiaire had its origins in the general dissatisfaction with the functioning of the French penal system at the end of the 1820s. A decade of debate had brought no decision as to what line of development should be followed. But the revolution and the formation of a new government in 1830 increased the pressure for some positive action. For Tocqueville and his friend Beaumont the change in government created both a difficulty and an opportunity. As members of the French judiciary, and with mixed feelings about the new regime, both thought it politically wise to be out of France for a time. They had already interested themselves in the penal question with which they had family as well as professional connections. Both had a wider interest in studying the new form of society in America, a country which was also an innovator in penal reform. This combination of circumstances saw them apply for and obtain leave to visit the United States as an officially sponsored mission to report on its penal system.

When, in October 1830, they made their tour proposal to the Minister of the Interior, they gave reasons why the penal systems of a number of other countries were not as worthy of study. England was rejected, in part because of its use of transportation:

> No one in this country is now unaware that the colonisation of Botany-Bay is a disastrous undertaking; but this type of deportation has already cost the English nation such enormous sums, that, in order not to lose the benefit from it, they persist with a system whose flaws have been recognised.[3]

This dismissal of the use of penal colonies is supported in a footnote using the authority of Barbé-Marbois: 'To get an idea of the drawbacks of Botany-Bay and to be convinced of the impossibility of France establishing anything similar, it is sufficient to read the report of M. Barbé-Marbois to the Society of Prisons'. The perfunctory nature of the dismissal, the failure to provide a detailed case, may indicate a conviction that the new reformist government already believed that any remodelling of the French prison system should take place within France.*

After an absence of almost a year Beaumont and Tocqueville returned to France in March 1832, and had completed their report by September. In it they reported favourably on two American penitentiary systems which, although rivals, were both based on silence, solitude and work. Under the Philadelphia system the prisoner was at all times confined to his cell, while under the Auburn regime work during the day was communal. Although the report fairly represented the joint ideas of the authors, its text appears to have been written almost entirely by Beaumont. In the text there is no discussion at all of penal colonies; it was, after all, a report on penal developments in America. However, on their return the two travellers found that the case for penal colonies had gathered strength. Parliament had rebuffed the government

---

*In 1836 Beaumont and Tocqueville wrote: 'In 1831, the administration had appeared eager to escape from the old routine followed until then, and the mission which was given to us to travel through the United States, in order to carry out an inquiry there into the theoretical and practical principles of the penitentiary system, demonstrated that it had improvement in mind'. (*OC*, vol. 1, p. 112)

in its attempt to remove the sentence of deportation from the penal code, and had put pressure on it to find a suitable site for a penal colony. Moreover, Ernest de Blosseville, friend and former colleague of Beaumont and Tocqueville, had been awarded the Montyon prize in 1832 for his book which emphasised the penal and economic success of transportation to Australia.[4] After reading Blosseville's work in May 1832, Tocqueville wrote that 'the examination of this work leads me to the examination of the very question of penal colonies and its relevance for France'.[5] And it was Tocqueville who wrote the appendix to *Système pénitentiaire* on this subject.[6]

The very logic of the report meant that Beaumont and Tocqueville were opposed to transportation as a penal solution. But it would also have been clear to the two ambitious young men, concerned to establish their reputation, that the impact of their report would depend significantly on the acceptance of penitentiary development within France as being the course that penal reform should take. At this late stage the case for the alternative had to be rebutted, and the preface to their report signals their intention to do so. In it they pointed out that a number of writers believed that the reform of criminals was impossible, and therefore deportation was essential. They continue: 'The system of deportation towards which public opinion in France seems rather *generally* favourable, appears to us to be surrounded by dangers and difficulties'.[7] The reader is then referred to the appendix on *Penal Colonies*.*

This appendix is some ten thousand words in length, and consists of a preface and three chapters. In the short preface Tocqueville repeated the claim already made that majority opinion favours penal colonies; and it was because the authors were so convinced of the dangers of such an undertaking that they were now writing. At the basis of the case for deportation, Tocqueville

---

*Quotations from the appendix are based on the author's translation of Tocqueville. No use is made of Lieber's 1833 translation. In his preface (p. i) Lieber, as a German, refers to his problems with English which have led to a 'want of that accuracy and precision of language, without which, in the ordinary course, no work ought to appear before its reader'.

argued, is a simple truth: 'without being cruel', criminals are removed from society and the crucial problem of recidivism is solved. Naturally, he continued, this has popular appeal, but deeper reflection leads to the conclusion that there are great, often insurmountable, difficulties in carrying out the project.[8]

Three categories of problems are identified and each allotted a chapter. The first chapter consists of a brief discussion of difficulties 'encountered in the legislation itself'. Tocqueville posed the question: 'to which criminals is the punishment of deportation to be applied?' If return to the mother country was to be forbidden, then deportation was much too severe a punishment for short-term prisoners and still too light for life prisoners. Non-return was essential because of recidivism, and certainly penal colonies did not change deportees in any moral sense. What they did was turn their thoughts from crime to a new and different future there, and this would not have occurred if return were possible. The English solution was to permit return, 'but they do not provide them with the means'. But the Australian experience had shown that a 'large number' of criminals, and these the most dangerous and clever, did return to England, while those unsuccessful in accomplishing this remained embittered and a threat to the colony. Deportation thus posed problems for legal theory, but there were 'still more insurmountable' difficulties in actually applying this policy.[9] *

Tocqueville examined these matters in Chapter 2, which draws heavily on the Australian experience and fills more than two-thirds of the appendix. Any colony, he argued, is difficult and dangerous to found, but the problems were multiplied for a penal colony. The chosen place must have a healthy climate suitable for Europeans. This was especially required for the convicts because, 'already weakened by the flaws which eventually led them into

---

*The question posed by Tocqueville does not appear to have been raised in Britain. According to L. Radzinowicz and R. Hood, 'It seems strange that despite the incessant flow of ministerial exhortations, judicial pronouncements, Colonial and Home Office papers, parliamentary enquiries, books, tracts and articles, nobody thought seriously to question whether, irrespective of its mode of enforcement, the punishment of transportation was justified for the crimes for which it was imposed'. (*A History of English Criminal Law and its Administration from 1750*, p. 484)

crime', and by the 'privations and strains' of confinement, they lacked the 'moral energy' which sustained free settlers. Tocqueville claimed that there were many in France who would not care if convicts were sent to their deaths; he found this view quite unacceptable: he was not opposed to the death penalty, but this would be death by 'evasion and deceit'.

It was also necessary in his view that a penal colony be a great distance from the homeland so that the deportee felt cut off and sought to establish a new life. Even so:

> ... the deportee of Botany-Bay, separated from England by the whole diameter of the globe, still seeks to clear a way through insurmountable perils towards his country. In vain does his new homeland offer him tranquility and comfort in her bosom; he thinks only of re-immersing himself quickly in the woes of the old world.[10]

For a penal colony the soil should not be too fertile or the countryside too attractive. Otherwise, deportees would be encouraged to escape, and they would then become a danger to the settlement. Moreover, if the land was inhabited by 'semi-civilised tribes', the danger was even greater. Escaped convicts would form alliances with the natives and, because of the superiority of Europeans, would usually become their leaders.

> We do not reason here on the basis of a vague hypothesis: the danger that we are pointing out has already made itself felt forcefully in the island of Van Diemen. From the first days of the English settlement, a large number of convicts escaped into the woods; there they formed gangs of bushrangers; they allied themselves with the savages, married their daughters and adopted some of their ways. From this cross was borne a race of half-castes more barbarous than the Europeans, more civilised than the savages, whose hostility has always caused anxiety to the colony, and has sometimes put it in great danger.

Overall, Tocqueville concluded, there were major obstacles in the way of finding a satisfactory site for a penal colony; but they were not necessarily, as England had shown, insurmountable. Suppose an appropriate site was discovered—what then? The cost of the initial establishment of the colony would be 'immense'; unmotivated convicts could not be relied on to support themselves and 'great calamities' would follow.

> We need only read the history of the English settlements in Australia to be convinced of the truth of this observation. Three times the infant colony of Botany-Bay has almost been destroyed by famine and disease. And it is only by rationing its inhabitants, like shipwrecked sailors, that it managed to wait until help arrived from the homeland.

Perhaps the incompetence of the English government had contributed to this situation, but it would always be a difficult one to avoid. In addition, the early days of a penal settlement lent themselves to disorder and revolt: 'The historians of Australia tell indeed of plots endlessly recurring, always foiled by the wisdom and firmness of the first three governors of the colony, Philip [sic], Hunter and King'.[11]

Tocqueville then proceeded to the next logical step in his argument. If a penal colony could be established and the difficulties of foundation overcome, what would be the consequences? The first question to be posed was cost. Would it be economical? Tocqueville had his doubts: 'while admitting that the upkeep of a penal colony costs the state less than prisons', one would also have to take into account foundation costs, transportation costs and the fact that prisons still had to be maintained at home. Taking the particular case of Australia, Tocqueville examined various estimates of cost thrown up by English parliamentary inquiries and noted especially the economies obtained by the system of assignment, under which the criminal became 'really a hired servant'. Nevertheless, taking everything into consideration, 'the savings that it is reasonable to expect from the system of deportation is on the whole reduced to very little, if they exist at all'. But for Tocqueville the question of cost was of secondary importance: 'The main question is to know whether the system of deportation ultimately reduces the number of criminals'. Transportation, he claimed, increased the number of ordinary criminals who were first offenders more than any fall in recidivism, because 'the penalty of deportation intimidates no one, and it encourages more than one to take the path of crime'. For many in England, 'deportation is scarcely anything else than emigration to the southern lands at the expense of the state'. This favourable view of deportation had been produced by the treatment of the convicts in Australia: in order to economise, 'England . . . frees the great majority, as soon as they set foot in the penal colony'. Also, 'to give them a future and to ensure through moral and lasting ties that they never return, it does all in its power to assist the emigration of their families'. Finally, on their release it 'distributes land to them, so that out of idleness and vagrancy they are not led back into crime'.[12] It was no wonder, he concluded, that the amount of crime and the number sentenced to transportation had grown rapidly in England.*

In Tocqueville's opinion, the supporters of deportation were unable to deny the substance of these problems. Accordingly, they had shifted their ground and now maintained that at least the system led to rapid colonial development, which 'soon returns more in wealth and power to the motherland than it has cost her'. For a number of reasons Tocqueville rejected this defence of deportation. Rapid growth of the convict population in New South Wales had meant increased cost of surveillance, and the construction of prisons for the convicts was being recommended: 'it is the European system with its faults, transported 5,000 leagues from Europe'. Moreover, the dumping of convicts would cause bitterness and indignation in the colony; this had happened in America, and in Australia 'the same murmurs are already heard'. Once Australia was able to do so,

---

*His final conclusion concerning the growth of crime in England drew on a letter of Bathurst, the Secretary of State, and the wording is confusing. Translating Bathurst, Tocqueville wrote that, as the fear of transportation had gradually diminished, so 'crimes increase in the same proportion'. He then added in parenthesis and in italicised English: 'They have increased beyond all calculations'. Bathurst's actual words were: 'Many circumstances however have since concurred to render the Punishment [transportation] lighter in itself, to diminish the Apprehension entertained in this Country of its Severity, and to break down all proportion between the punishment and the Crimes for which it is now inflicted'. (Bathurst to Commissioner Bigge, 6 Jan. 1819, *HRA*, 1, 10, p. 5)

it would stop deportation, and 'the outlays on its penal colony will be lost for England'. For Tocqueville, the feelings in the colony towards the motherland resulting from deportation were one of its more unhappy results:

> Nothing is sweeter, in general, than the sentiment that links colonists to the land of their birth.
>
> Memories, habits, interests, prejudices, all still join them to the homeland, in spite of the Ocean that separates them. Several nations of Europe have found and still find a great source of strength and glory in these ties of a distant fellowship. One year before the American revolution, the settler, whose forebears had left the shores of Great Britain one and a half centuries ago, still said *home* when speaking of England.
>
> But the name of the motherland recalls to the deportee only the memory of sometimes undeserved miseries. It is there that he has been unhappy, persecuted, guilty, dishonoured. What ties join him to a country where he has most often left no one behind interested in his fate? Why would he wish to establish commercial connections or friendly relations in the mother country?
>
> Of all the places in the world, the one where he was born seems the most hateful. It is the only place where his history is known and where his shame has been made public.
>
> It can scarcely be doubted that these hostile sentiments of the settler are continued in his race; within the United States, this rival of England, the Irish are still recognised by the hatred that they harbour for their former masters.

As for the colonies themselves, the penal system meant a future full of 'tumult and wretchedness'. Taking the example of Australia, Tocqueville pointed out that there society was divided into four distinct and hostile classes: 'The convict is exposed to the scorn of the freed convict; he in turn to the insults of his own son born free; and all to the haughtiness of the settler whose origin is without blemish'. In general, 'what Australian society essentially lacks is morals. And how could it be otherwise?' In 1828, with about two-thirds of the population convicts, Australia's position was unique: 'vice obtained the support of the majority'. The women in the colony had not raised the moral tone: 'they had lost those traditions of modesty and virtue which characterise their sex in the mother country and in most of its free colonies . . . bastards still made up a quarter of the children'. And yet the lack of women among the convicts, inevitable since they committed fewer crimes than men, encouraged the degradation; obviously, 'for the morals of a nation to be unsullied, the two sexes must be in fairly equal proportions'. It was not just the lack of morality that was obvious in Australia, it was the abundance of crime; Australia, with its tiny population, had between one-quarter and one-third as many executions as England.

For Tocqueville, the final telling point was that Australia was the only English colony deprived 'of those precious civil liberties that have brought about the glory of England and the strength of her offspring in all parts of the world'. How was it possible to give the functions of jury service and the direction of public affairs to a vice-ridden and divided population? Deportation could certainly increase the population rapidly, but it could not make a successful colony:

> It can fashion free colonies, but not strong and peaceful societies. The vices that we so remove from Europe are not destroyed; they are only transported to another soil, and England unburdens itself of part of its miseries only to bequeath them to its offspring in the southern lands.[13]

In the final chapter of the appendix Tocqueville turned to the particular difficulties that France would face with a penal colony. He asserted that supporters of penal colonies ignore these difficulties: they tended to make generally favourable points, adding some details about Australia. But where could a satisfactory place be found for a French colony? 'The world no longer seems to us to be unoccupied, all the sites appear to us to be taken.' Fortune had favoured England fifty years earlier: 'A vast continent and consequently unlimited prospects, spacious ports, assured ports-of-call, fertile and uninhabited land, European climate, all were brought together there, and this privileged place was set in the antipodes'. Some now suggested that France might settle part of Australia. They did not know England; the American experience had warned it of problems from neighbours:

> [England] has declared several times that it would not tolerate a single European settlement being established in Australia. Certainly we are as much aware as anyone what arrogance and insolence are contained in such a declaration, but do the supporters of deportation want a naval war with England in order to found a penal colony?

Even if a suitable site could be found, Tocqueville argued, the 'character' of France meant that it was less suited for maritime ventures than England:

> France, by its geographic position, its size and its fertility, has always been destined to be in the forefront of the continental powers. It is the land that is the natural theatre for its power and its glory; maritime commerce is only an appendage of its existence. The sea has never prompted, and doubtless will never prompt in us those deep sympathies, that sort of filial respect, that seafaring and trading people feel for it.

As a result, private capital for colonial enterprise was found only with difficulty, and the men who offered themselves were second-raters with little future at home. When England conceived the idea of transportation to New South Wales in 1785, it had then almost established its great commercial development and its maritime dominance. It was thus well-placed to establish a penal colony. Even so, the early days of Botany Bay were very painful and costly. Tocqueville contrasted the English position then with the current position of France, and concluded that French success would require great financial sacrifices.

But what would the future hold for a French penal colony? In Tocqueville's view France had to face the fact of England's 'indisputable superiority on the seas'. In a war with England, France could probably defend effectively its possessions near home, 'but history teaches us that its distant colonies have nearly always finished by succumbing to the blows of its rival'. If a penal colony were strong enough to survive, England could isolate it and it would not be able to receive convicts. Was a war with England

HISTOIRE
DE BOTANY-BAY,

ETAT PRESENT DES COLONIES PÉNALES DE L'ANGLETERRE.
DANS L'AUSTRALIE,

OU

EXAMEN

DES EFFETS DE LA DÉPORTATION,

CONSIDÉRÉE COMME PEINE ET COMME MOYEN DE COLONISATION;

PAR M. JULES DE LA PILORGERIE.

> I have no high opinion of the efficacy of transportation, either for reformation or example.
>
> (SIR J. MACKINTOSH.)

PARIS,

PAULIN, LIBRAIRE-ÉDITEUR,
RUE DE SEINE, 33.

1836.

The *Histoire de Botany-Bay* (1836), of which this is the title page, was Jules de la Pilorgerie's reply to Blosseville's 1831 history.

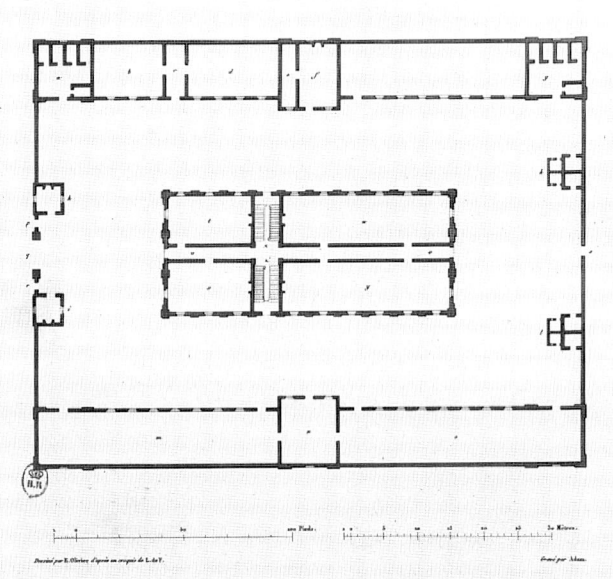

Plan and elevation of the convict barracks, Sydney, in 1819, from a sketch by Louis de Freycinet [L. de Freycinet, *Voyage autour du monde* . . . *Atlas historique*, 1825, Plate 106]

sufficiently likely that this consideration should be taken into account? 'If the annals of our history are examined, it is clear that the peace that at present survives is one of the longest to exist between the English and ourselves for four hundred years.'[14]

In this appendix Tocqueville's method was to analyse the British penal experience with transportation to Australia, and then to draw conclusions for France. He argued that Australia had attributes that made it almost ideal as a penal colony, and that these particular qualities could not be found elsewhere. But the Australian experience had demonstrated that crime was not discouraged by deportation and that determined deportees were able to return home, that a penal colony was not significantly cheaper than a prison, that hostility to the motherland developed and that an immoral and unworkable society was created. Moreover, in relation to penal colonies, France was less favourably placed than England.

The thrust of these arguments was not new in France: as has been shown, criticisms of Botany Bay were not uncommon, and a sustained case concerning its penal failure had been made by Lucas in 1827, and especially by Barbé-Marbois in 1828.[15] These critics had drawn on a number of English and French sources, and had made particular use of the Bigge report of 1822 for a picture of Australian society. Tocqueville had access to this earlier writing and the source material on which it was based; but by 1833 he was able to exploit two new publications. One was the general history of Australia written by his friend, Ernest de Blosseville. This work provided him with information, but not a viewpoint that he could accept. Near the beginning of the appendix he wrote:

> In all the following, we have often had occasion to resort to the book by M. de Blosseville. This work, whose author appears moreover in favour of the deportation system, is full of interesting facts and intriguing research. It constitutes the most complete document that has been published in our language on the English settlements in Australia.[16]

The other publication was more congenial to Tocqueville's taste, and he used it extensively and directly. This was the 1832 House of Commons report on secondary punishment; it was most critical of the failings of transportation and especially of what it saw as the lenient treatment of convicts in Australia.*

French critics of Botany Bay were able to draw on arguments produced in Britain over the previous fifty years—arguments which had their origin in the main in the hostility of Jeremy Bentham to transportation to Australia. What Tocqueville did was to marshal his case in a systematic and logical way, while at the same time drawing attention to aspects which seemed especially relevant for France. In particular, he emphasised that in relation to the establishment and operation of a penal colony, France was in an inferior position to Britain. The main penal objection to 'transportation was, of course, that it did not discourage crime in the homeland, but it is interesting to see how much importance Tocqueville gave to the detrimental effects on the recipient society. His general analysis is, however, one-sided, and although combined with acute observations his use of evidence is selective. Perhaps the only mention of a favourable penal outcome was his grudging remark that 'sometimes' an ex-convict becomes a 'useful and respected citizen'. While noting that Blosseville, his main general source on Australia, favoured deportation, he gave no indication of Blosseville's reasons. Other critical accounts in France of the penal aspects of Botany Bay did acknowledge and attempt to account for its apparent economic success; Tocqueville hardly mentioned it. The contrast in the approach between the appendix and the body of the report is striking. The report is a scholarly, balanced description of two rival penitentiary systems in the United States, which both bring favourable comment. Not so with Tocqueville's discussion of penal colonies, which fits easily into the mainstream of English criticism of the transportation system: penal colonies are damned entirely.

---

*Tocqueville was careful to state that this was a majority report: 'At least this is what we have been assured by a very distiguished member of the British parliament, who was a member of it'. (*OC*, vol. 1, p. 275) He also referred to several other parliamentary papers for recent information on transportation, prison costs and convict employment.

How effective was Tocqueville's attack on deportation? It is impossible to separate its impact from that of the book as a whole. While the appendix criticised deportation, the main text offered a credible and penally attractive alternative in the form of a transformation of the prison system. One direct result of its publication was a widespread stimulation of interest in, and support for, the new American penal systems. In Britain the book was received enthusiastically.* Reviews were most favourable;[17] and Tocqueville was delighted that his reputation had gone before him when he visited England briefly only seven months after the book first appeared.† In 1834 the Home Secretary sent William Crawford, the penal reformer, on an official mission to examine prisons in America, and he returned to Britain with the strongest recommendation in favour of the Philadelphia system.[18] It has been suggested that in the Western world from this period, 'separate confinement was . . . regarded as the penal panacea, and the Western Penitentiary near Philadelphia as the penal Mecca'.[19] Certainly, in France the influence of the deportationists began to wane. Nevertheless, within a few years Tocqueville felt it necessary to return to the topic of penal colonies.

In 1836 a new edition of *Système pénitentiaire* was published with a number of additions, the principal of which was a long introduction of some 25 000 words. It can be presumed that demand for the work warranted the new publication, a demand which may have been encouraged by an increased interest in

---

*A long and very favourable review (unsigned) was given by the Benthamite, Henry Southern, in the journal devoted to foreign works not translated into English, *Foreign Quarterly Review*, pp. 49–79. Southern damned the existing English penal arrangements: 'A criminal may be said in this country to take his degrees by imprisonment. The gaols are the schools, the hulks the universities of crime. The man who has served four or five years at Chatham or Portsmouth comes out a master of arts. His doctor's degree he gets *per saltum*, that is to say, by a broad leap across the seas to the Antipodes, in the classic land of Australia'. (p. 50)

†In August 1833 Tocqueville wrote to his father from London: 'This work has caused a greater stir . . . in the political and scholarly world than I imagined and I have noticed with great pleasure that I found in it the best passport that I could desire'. (*OC*, vol. 1, p. 24)

Tocqueville following the publication of his book on American democracy the year before. But wishing, as they did, to establish political careers and to maintain their claim to expertise in penology, the authors would no doubt have welcomed in a general way, and encouraged, a new edition.* It also met a more specific need. In 1833, with no status in the field, they had reported favourably on the American penitentiary system and had cautiously recommended its gradual introduction into France. Now, having established their names, they were in a position to write with authority and participate in the mainstream of the penal debate. The new introduction provided the means.

Almost immediately the subject matter of the introduction is set out: all writers on the penitentiary system are agreed that some degree of silence and isolation is required of the prisoner; this system has grown in the United States in the last few years and there have been encouraging developments in some countries in Europe. How then is the following situation to be explained?

> In England and in France there are two odd facts. In these two countries it can be fairly said that public opinion fervently desires a penitentiary regime founded principally on the rules just spelt out: and nevertheless, in Great Britain this system is only incompletely organised; and, in France, the question is hardly on the agenda.[20]

Tocqueville's intention in the remainder of the introduction was to research 'the causes of these phenomena whose existence we might question were they not placed under our eyes', and he gave roughly equal space to each country.† In writing about France, Tocqueville was responding to defenders of the existing French

---

*They would also have welcomed it as an opportunity to reprint a number of favourable reviews of the first edition, and to answer criticisms made by the prison bureaucracy.

†The introduction was actually written by Beaumont, but represents the joint ideas of both men. Given Tocqueville's authorship of the appendix to the first edition, it seems probable that his input on the same topic in the second edition would have been substantial. In the following discussion it is convenient to continue to refer to Tocqueville as the author.

penal system as well as attempting to increase pressure for a change along American lines. It is not so obvious why he should have continued to give so much attention to Great Britain and to transportation. Three reasons can, however, be suggested. First, he may have felt that supporters of penal colonies in France remained strong enough to be a threat to prison reform. Second, developments in Britain designed to make transportation a more severe penalty and more of a deterrent to crime might be used to strengthen the French case for penal colonies. Finally, the new introduction could provide an opportunity, not taken up in the first edition, to contrast more directly the virtues of the penitentiary system with the shortcomings of deportation. In what follows attention will be confined to the introduction's discussion of transportation to Australia.

Tocqueville began by praising the parliamentary legislation of 1835 which committed England to a cellular system of imprisonment based on silence and isolation, and under the direction of the central government. However, he continued, the overwhelming majority of those sentenced to prison in England were imprisoned for a very short period, while more serious crimes brought the sentence of deportation. Yet it was precisely the long-term prisoners whose reform might be obtained by the penitentiary regime. Why then, Tocqueville asked, did England, in the face of public opinion and accepted penal theory, persist with its system of deportation? Three principal reasons were advanced. Tocqueville began with the bureaucracy:

> Let us first observe that the foundation of the penal colonies of Australia and the activation of the system on which they are based are one of the rare judicial matters which is entrusted to the central government in England, for which it has a general administration, permanent employees, a special budget. This is already a reason for the existing state of affairs to be maintained: for a large number of civil servants owe their whole existence to its preservation.[21]

It was possible, then, for government employees to frustrate public opinion; nevertheless, Tocqueville asked, how strongly did public opinion favour imprisonment as against deportation? Some of those favouring penitentiaries did not have the interests of society or the convicts at heart; they simply supported a new and fashionable theory, and 'this system prospers in the United States, and England does not wish on any account to be left behind America'. There were also those who simply felt that old lags could not be reformed. But by far the greater number of the supporters of penitentiaries were 'so eminently religious, pious and enlightened men who favour this new theory because it offers hope of regeneration to the worst criminals, and still gives society a guarantee of order'. They put their case well, but there was a second reason for the protection of the Australian penal colonies:

> ... it is their very existence and the huge size of the expenditure that their establishment has cost. As we have said previously, England is set on a course from which it no longer knows how to depart; when it thinks of renouncing deportation, it is immediately held back by the recollection of the immense sacrifices that it has already made in order to set it up.[22]

It was not as though there were not recognised weaknesses in the deportation system, such as those Tocqueville believed he raised in the appendix to his book in 1833. There it was pointed out that the principal defect of that punishment was in 'not inspiring in the guilty and those tempted by crime that salutary terror that should be the first aim of all penal regulations'. Indeed, it had been accepted in England that many criminals chose the type of crime that carried the penalty of deportation. Overall convictions for attacks on both person and property had increased disproportionately to population growth, and various explanations had been offered: alcohol, new and unsatisfied wants, unemployment from the increasing use of machines or perhaps simply a more efficient police force. 'Would it not be more natural' asked Tocqueville, 'to see in this increase the logical consequence of an ineffectual punishment?' And, he noted, it was precisely since the establishment of the penal colonies in Australia that this increase of crime had been observed.[23]

A parliamentary inquiry in 1832 recognised the inadequacy of deportation. Eloquent in his support of the penitentiary regime was Archbishop Whately, and everything pointed to the end of deportation.[24] Again Tocqueville asked why it survived. He repeated the second of the two reasons he had already advanced, and suggested a third: 'it is still a view shared by a large number of those in power in England, that it is necessary at any cost to get rid of the population of criminals'. They readily admitted that a population nucleus provided by the courts was a bad seed; but if it drained England of poison,'what matters the fate of Van Diemen's Land?'

> They will concede to you that for these colonies, from which a half century has already removed the original flaw, it is a terrible misfortune to receive new seeds of corruption each day, and to see thus renewing itself the contamination from which they work ceaselessly to cleanse themselves.

For his part, Tocqueville 'will never allow the iniquitous maxims of this selfish policy', but undoubtedly those in power in England would continue with their self-interested view. However, they had reacted to the failure of deportation to discourage crime:

> They have said: 'Deportation is a sentence that does not frighten; we shall make it a terrible punishment. The lot of the convict exiled to Australia will cease to be envied by criminals . . . it will soon be known that the penal colony is founded on a code of blood; that all deportees are subjected there to an arbitrary and pitiless discipline; that the happiest are the exiles, whose condition is like that of slaves; that in short the deportee can hope for neither indulgence nor mercy.'[25]

Tocqueville drew on correspondence between the Colonial Office and Governor Bourke in New South Wales in which the British government acted on this resolve by ordering that convicts be divided into three classes: the first to be isolated in a penal settlement, the second allocated to road gangs and the third assigned to private employers.* The governor replied with details

---

*The correspondence between the Colonial Office and Governor Bourke and the associated documents were Tocqueville's principal new sources on Australia for this second edition. He saw the material in *PP* 82, 1834 (Secondary Punishments).

of the severity of the treatment given the first two classes, but strongly emphasised that no English worker could envy an assignee, because any misbehaviour by the latter made him liable to the most drastic punishment. Attached to the governor's letter was a document, which, in Tocqueville's words, 'we could not pass over in silence'. It was a petition from settlers to the governor, dated before the Colonial Office instructions, claiming that existing punishment of convicts was not severe enough to be effective. The governor's response was to call for reports from police superintendants in each district with details of corporal punishment inflicted on convicts during the month of September 1833. These reports were included in the despatch, and from them Tocqueville set out 'a passage that we take at random'. It consisted of the first eleven of 247 cases reported by the Maitland police. An example is No. 6: 'James Hull.—Threats to an overseer. 50 lashes. Back lacerated and bled much. Appeared to suffer much'. Two examples from Sydney follow. One is No. 4, James Clayton:

> Absent without leave and neglecting his duty, 50 lashes. The skin was lacerated at the fifth lash, and there was a slight effusion of blood; the prisoner subdued his sense of pain by biting his lips. The skin of this man was thick to an uncommon degree, and both his body and mind have been hardened by former punishments, and he is also known to be what is termed 'flash' or 'game'; nevertheless, I am of opinion, that if all his former (or perhaps only his first) punishments had been as vigorously administered as this last, his indomitable spirit would have been subdued.[26] *

Tocqueville gave details from some of the reports of suggestions as to how the lash could be made more painful,[†] and he commented:

---

*This quotation is not a translation from Tocqueville, but is taken from the original English document. Tocqueville does not appear to have been able to catch the meaning of 'flash' and 'game', apparently taking the latter to mean hunted animals. He referred in italics to a *'vrai gibier de police'*.

†Tocqueville made a point of quoting in a footnote a passage in English: 'The cord may be sufficiently heavy, but of too soft a twist; although it bruises, bleeding but seldom is caused: consequently the offender escapes that acute pain and smarting to the extent so desirable should be experienced under the lash'.

'We do not have the courage to continue these horrible details'. What this meant was that 'the insolent, the lazy, the drunken and the insubordinate' received 9934 lashes in the month, which multiplied by the number of months 'leads to the total of 119, 208 lashes given each year in the penal colonies of Australia'—for 40 000 deportees. And this did not include punishments on Norfolk Island.*

> Let us pause here a moment: let us rest a little from the sad feelings that we have just experienced. Can it be that in the nineteenth century, and in a nation in the van of civilisation, men are made to submit to treatment worthy of savage countries and barbarous times?[27]

In Tocqueville's view, such a penal system was not excused by saying that treatment was quite similar in the English army, the French navy and American prisons. Any penal code 'based on blood and torture' should be rejected out of hand.

Having emphasised the savage aspect of convict discipline in Australia, Tocqueville then did at least a partial about-face: he qualified his description of the convicts' treatment and raised doubts about its effectiveness in discouraging crime: 'in a great number of cases criminals fear imprisonment more than deportation, whose excessive harshness brings with it certain advantages and privileges always denied to convicts in prison'. The huge majority of convicts in New South Wales—class three prisoners—were well fed and their families provided for. Even on Norfolk Island, convicts were 'sometimes permitted to communicate freely with their wives' and, for good conduct, to keep a small garden. It may be, Tocqueville surmised, that the convicts were so degraded that, like domestic animals, they were 'resigned to being whipped provided that the hand that beats them fattens them'.

But there remained an important question: were the punishments ordered in England necessarily carried out in the colony? The interests of the two were different. England wanted severity: the

---

*Horrified though Tocqueville was, he appears to have severely underestimated the amount of flogging in Australia. In 1833, according to A. G. L. Shaw, in New South Wales and Van Diemen's Land (excluding penal settlements) 36 000 male convicts (females were not flogged) were given 323 000 lashes. (*Convicts and the Colonies*, p. 202)

colony's natural interest 'is to turn to account the labour sent to it, and to deal severely with deportees only to the extent required for it to have nothing to fear from them'. Moreover, it would not be surprising if the governor's report darkened the picture of punishment and only incompletely described the concessions. To govern men, especially corrupt men, rewards must be offered as well as punishments, otherwise 'the certainty of misfortune with no remedy casts the convict into despair and the acts of violence that stem from it'. Excessive punishment would 'ruin the colonies', so that 'whatever instructions England gives its agents, it will not get a society situated 4,000 leagues away to commit suicide for the greater good of the motherland'. To put it another way, 'England will send them [convicts] to it to punish them; the colony will accept them to make use of them'. Of course, ultimately, when it was strong enough, the colony would refuse to accept convicts, and then the enormous sums invested in the system by England would 'be entirely lost'. Thus England's attempt to increase the deterrent effect of transportation by ordering more severe punishment in New South Wales had to fail. In any case, the favourable view of transportation then held by criminals would have to change, but the opinions of the masses, especially in England, did not change easily.[28] *

Concluding his case, Tocqueville touched on two points he had made earlier. The first related to criminals' preference for deportation rather than imprisonment. What would be the effect, he wondered, of the spread of the cellular system in English penitentiaries?

> It can be seen that if imprisonment is already more feared in England than transportation, it will inspire comparatively yet greater fear,

---

*The views expressed here by Tocqueville had been put by Archbishop Whately in 1832: 'To govern in the best manner, with a view to the *convicts*, so as to make the penalty of transportation answer the end proposed [deterrence] (which is the most *important* point), and to govern in the best manner, with a view to the prosperity of the *colony* (which is the point a governor is naturally the most likely to *aim* at), are two objects each, separately, difficult of attainment, but together inconsistent and opposed to each other'. (L. Radzinowicz and R. Hood, *History of English Criminal Law*, pp. 476–7)

once the new discipline, founded on silence and solitude, is established everywhere. There will be advantage in committing the worst crimes, since they are punished with a penalty that is little feared, while the lesser ones incur a sentence that is greatly feared.

The second point bears on Tocqueville's distress with corporal punishment: 'Penal legislation of all modern nations is clearly tending to become milder'. As evidence, he produced figures for the decline in the number of executions in France, some American states and Belgium. Even England, 'so prodigal with sanguinary sentences, is temperate with executions'. Given these developments, he asked rhetorically:

> Is it possible that this movement will stop? That England, sparing of blood on its own territory, will be prodigal with it on Australian soil; that it will add fresh torments to a penal system for whose maintenance a yearly allotment of 120,000 lashes is already necessary?*

On the basis of his survey of the Australian experience, Tocqueville felt he could now draw some 'incontestable' conclusions concerning the efficacy of transportation, all of which cautioned France against this penal policy:

1. That the founding of a similar colony (supposing that a distant land is available to establish it in) is a long and very expensive undertaking;
2. That the assembling of criminals, chosen from among the most perverse and corrupt that prison and society holds, is a very sad nucleus for a society;
3. That if, in the course of time, a colony thus formed is purified and manages to cast off its scum, it must naturally spurn with horror the new seeds of vice and corruption that the motherland sends it each year;

---

*Tocqueville's abhorrence of corporal punishment was widely shared in France, and this may partly explain the prominence given by Tocqueville to flogging in Australia. The use of the whip in American penitentiaries under the Auburn system to maintain silence during communal work was a telling argument against that system's introduction into France.

4. That any such system is defective in that it is temporary and ceases to be operative the day the colony has an interest in rejecting the deportees who are sent to it, and is strong enough to resist the motherland;
5. That moreover deportation does not produce the effects that should be expected from a penal system, to wit punishing the guilty and intimidating all possible offenders. It is true that the deportee is punished and deportation made a terrible penalty by combining imprisonment with exile and the whip with bondage; but then one goes to extremes worse than the disease for which the cure is sought; indeed if prisons are built in the colony, there are both the expenses of transportation and of imprisonment; two punishments, whose combining is cruel, are imposed; finally, transportation is made an effective punishment only by means of torments that are sufficient to make it rejected.[29]

The thrust of Tocqueville's discussion of penal colonies in the introduction to the second edition was different from that in the appendix to the first. In the earlier work he argued simply that the history of transportation to Australia had shown that this was not a path that France should follow. In the later one, he asserted that the case for penitentiaries was proven, and asked why Britain persisted with transportation. The answer turned on the vested interest of part of the bureaucracy, the investment made in the penal settlements in Australia and an overwhelming desire to expel criminals irrespective of the type of society being created in Australia. But he also wanted to show that the British attempt to make transportation a credible deterrent by increasing the ferocity of the corporal punishment associated with it must fail. In theory it could succeed, but in practice it was not in Australia's interest to impose such penalties, and in any case it was absolutely morally unacceptable. For Tocqueville, Australia's history had shown transportation to be irredeemable.

In 1839 Tocqueville was elected to parliament. He threw himself into penal reform and became a fervent supporter of the Philadelphia system. His opposition to the use of corporal punishment would have been a factor in his rejection of the Auburn system. In 1844, when the parliamentary committee, for which he was the spokesman, proposed the introduction of the cellular system for France, the transportationists rallied and forcefully introduced the Australian example into the debate. Tocqueville spoke relatively briefly and more moderately than he had done in the past. He admitted the 'immense benefits' from deportation: criminals were completely removed from society; whereas one way or another some life prisoners got out of prison, 'experience has proven' that it was rare for even term prisoners to return to the motherland from deportation. Moreover, he conceded, it was possible to exaggerate the financial costs of deportation: an English report showed the cost per prisoner in Australia to be well below that in prisons at home. However, for Tocqueville, the case for deportation was outweighed by two arguments of 'extreme gravity'. First, if large numbers were deported, a society was created, 'composed of vicious elements which sooner or later form a people difficult to govern and dangerous to free'. Second, again 'experience has proven' that unless the system of deportation were preceded by lengthy imprisonment, it was not a deterrent and actually encouraged criminality. Tocqueville spoke with the intention of reaching a compromise with the transportationists. In fact, he had to give little away. The Chamber agreed on deportation for small numbers, and then only after a significant confinement in 'silence and solitude'.[30]

Tocqueville came to the study of transportation and of the Australian penal colonies indirectly. From his own philosophy and reflections, and from personal observation of the American penal system, he was convinced that a cellular penitentiary system based on silence and solitude was appropriate for France. This conclusion appears to have been reached before he gave close consideration to transportation as an alternative and, given his commitment, it might seem that he had no alternative but to reject transportation as a complete failure. This would be too harsh a view. Tocqueville's criticisms of transportation are consistent with his whole penal philosophy, they are rationally argued and he is able to make a powerful case. Tocqueville viewed crime as an attack on society, an attack made by the free decision of the criminal. He had little sympathy with social theories of crime. Society had to be protected from crime, and this would be assisted by penalties sufficiently severe to act as a deterrent. Equally important, criminals deserved to be punished. For Tocqueville, the cellular prison system was the most effective punishment. It was a punishment that was feared. Since criminals could not communicate with each other, imprisonment did not make them worse. Indeed, some degree of reform was possible. Finally, work had a desirable moral and disciplinary effect, helped meet the cost of the prisons, and American experience had shown that it was necessary to prevent mental deterioration.[31] Transportation did not meet these conditions.

In contrast to his study of the American penal system, Tocqueville was not able to base his examination of conditions in Australia on first-hand observation, but he read widely and used primary sources. Yet in making his case against transportation, Tocqueville presented an account which was all black. The outstanding example of this lack of objectivity was his failure to consider more closely the behaviour of the emancipists and the positive aspects of the emerging Australian society. At the same time, it must be remembered that for Tocqueville the primary requirement of a penal system was that its punishments be so effective as to ensure that the crime rate would be contained.* Moreover, Tocqueville was engaged in a fierce polemic over penal policy, and it would be asking too much to expect him to give any encouragement to his opponents. It would seem that by the late 1830s Tocqueville had discarded scholarly detachment concerning prison reform in France, and that after 1838, when he declared himself for the Philadelphia system, he closed his ears to any criticism of it. He did not, for example, accept evidence concerning the devastating effects on prisoners of solitary confinement over an extended period; and it is interesting that while he emphasised

---

*When criticising transportation, Tocqueville also emphasised the additional reason of the effects on the recipient society. It was on these two grounds that the British government stopped transportation to New South Wales in 1840. (J. Hirst, *Convict Society*, p. 9)

how much criminals feared cellular imprisonment, he did not conclude that it was necessarily 'cruel'. Of the effects on the prisoner of the Philadelphia system, he wrote:

> The wholly mental punishment that is inflicted on him, casts deep down in his soul a terror more profound than chains and blows. Is it not thus that an enlightened and humane society should wish to punish? Here the punishment is at the same time the most gentle and the most terrible that has ever been invented.[32]

The contrast with his attitude to corporal punishment is marked. While Tocqueville's criticism of transportation is equally partial, he nevertheless was able to draw on mature political reflection and make penetrating observations concerning the penal system, government and society in England and Australia. Some points stand out: the weakness of transportation as a deterrent unless it was accompanied by some other form of punishment; the clash of interests over punishment between the authorities in England and Australia; the ubiquity of the lash for discipline and punishment; the importance for the continuance of transportation of the vested interest of its bureaucracy; the ruinous effect on the recipient society of sustained and large-scale transportation, but the inevitable rejection of transportation as soon as that society was strong enough. Inasmuch as Tocqueville argued that transportation failed in Australia where conditions were ideal but also unique, he was arguing that it was a penal system whose costs must outweigh any benefits.

6
Histoire de Botany Bay

The second French history of Australia, *Histoire de Botany-Bay* ... by Jules de la Pilorgerie was published in Paris in 1836.* Its publication was clearly prompted by the preoccupation of those involved in the French penal debate with the Australian settlement. In his introduction Pilorgerie set out the background to his work. There were, he wrote, two rival systems competing as models for the reform of the French penal system: one was a penitentiary system similar to that which had evolved in the United States; the other was based on the use of penal colonies such as Britain had established in Australia. Pilorgerie briefly outlined the history of French policy and attitudes on deportation, which had culminated in the 1820s in widespread enthusiasm for the establishment of a penal colony. In turn, it was this support that had prompted Barbé-Marbois to make his attack on deportation in 1828, an attack which Pilorgerie regarded as eloquent and authoritative. But it was a writer who took a view contrary to that of Barbé-Marbois on whom Pilorgerie wished to concentrate:

> Such was the state of the question when M. Ernest de Blosseville undertook with a book to refute the brochure of M. de Barbé-Marbois; his work, written with real talent is a vigorous plea in favour of the punishment of deportation and of penal colonies. According to the author, what one has dared to call the romance of Botany-Bay, is a true history, and in his enthusiasm it very nearly is, he has made an epic of it. This book, destined to supply excellent

---

*Jules Luette de la Pilorgerie (1804–1881) continued to publish in a number of fields, but this is his only recorded publication on penology.

arguments to the defenders of a system which had counted until then more zealous partisans than enlightened appraisers, includes the only extensive documents that we possessed on the intriguing English settlements in the southern lands.[1]

This work, Pilorgerie continued, doubly dangerous because of the talent and good faith of the author, called for a reply, but other events had turned public attention temporarily aside. Now he thought it appropriate to respond and, declaring himself to be a supporter of the penitentiary system, he stated the policy implication of his book: 'the bent of this study, is, I confess, negative. Its conclusions are summed up in the counsel of not doing, of not imitating England, and of profiting from its experience so as to refrain'. Pilorgerie saw his role as fleshing out the criticisms already made by Beaumont and Tocqueville in *Du système pénitentiaire*, 'corroborated by the authority of the facts, supported by the most authentic and latest documents'.[2] Pilorgerie's viewpoint was, in fact, immediately indicated by the epigraph on the title page; it is attributed to 'Sir J. Mackintosh'* and is in English: 'I have no high opinion of the efficacy of transportation, either for reformation or example'.

In Pilorgerie's opinion the supporters of deportation fell into two groups: those who saw it as a model form of punishment, and those 'more numerous and powerful' who put more emphasis on their belief that through the development of a penal colony criminals could be used to the advantage of the mother country:

> I have tried to refute with facts these two errors. It was necessary to apply myself first to investigate if these kinds of colonies are advantageous for the motherland, and if it is true that it is easy to found prosperous societies with the refuse of old societies. The history of Botany-Bay and the investigation of the causes which have produced the beginning of prosperity which the English penal colonies enjoy, were the only means to obtain the answer to this question.

---

*James Mackintosh was a member of the House of Commons and prominent opponent of transportation. Charles Lucas also found support in his views (see p. 46)

In the second place, the analysis of official documents, of parliamentary inquiries, of the better accounts of voyages and journals published over the last fifteen years, in England and even in Australia, by the numerous migrants who the hope of making a fortune drew to the other hemisphere, have supplied me with observations that I have believed appropriate to throw new light on the issue of deportation considered as a punishment.[3]

Pilorgerie's history is a substantial work. It consists of an introduction of 14 pages, a text of 378 pages and an appendix of 17 pages. There is no formal bibliography, but references in some footnotes and in the text suggest a familiarity with a wide range of sources. The content is set out roughly in chronological order and chapters are given to the periods of successive governors. The four concluding chapters adopt a slightly different approach. The work has something of the air of a general history, but it is, in fact, narrower than that. The unifying aspect is Pilorgerie's use of Australian history in an attempt to answer the penological questions that he has posed. It is basic to his interpretation, as will be shown later, that there is a dividing line in Australian history in 1821.

After two preliminary chapters, Pilorgerie began his study of the first period with a comment on the sources relating to the early years of the settlement. He noted the 'scarcity' and 'dryness' of the available information; there was only 'the journal of judge advocate Collins, a few fragments due to some officers employed in the first expeditions and some recollections dispersed in some later publications'. This was in contrast with the large number of publications that dealt with the present prosperous state of the colony; but these recent studies

... do not take into any account the obstacles that the founders of the penal colony had to overcome. Convinced that it is impossible to give any fair idea of the task that a nation undertakes, in attempting to found a similar settlement, without studying the history of the first years of Sydney, I have dwelt, at the risk of tiring the reader, on some facts undoubtedly not very interesting by themselves, but, in my opinion, full of useful information. By itself, this strong reason is able to persuade me to continue, while trying nevertheless to give more pace to the narrative, and by neglecting some particulars whose repetition would become tedious.[4]

The result was that the next three chapters covered the period up to Governor Hunter's departure in 1800, and they relied heavily on, indeed significantly paraphrased, two principal sources: David Collins' account and John Dunmore Lang's recently published history of New South Wales. The two following chapters on the periods of Governors King and Bligh were based on Lang, as was the beginning of the next chapter on the early years of Macquarie; this chapter subsequently summarised and quoted extensively from the report of the British inquiry into transportation in 1812.[5] This is probably the first time that this important source had been referred to in any detail in the French literature, and Pilorgerie noted that it 'is to be found in the precious collection sent by the parliament to the chamber of deputies'. The final chapter in this section, which was designed to examine Macquarie's regime (1810–21), again began by relying on Lang but subsequently made extensive use of the Bigge report. Throughout this part of his history it was Pilorgerie's intention to emphasise the problems of the early period of settlement; he therefore felt it necessary to disparage the adulatory view of penal aspects of the settlement at Sydney, which François Péron, the most famous and influential of the early French observers, had made:

> His account scarcely offers us more than a scientific and topographical picture of the colony. It is true to say that he was employed neither in the commission nor the narrator's job of ascertaining the degree of prosperity of the settlement considered as a penal colony, and of examining if the goal that England proposed by creating it had been attained or not. So, apart from the very natural astonishment that the officers of the expedition experienced at the view of Sydney which was beginning to have the appearance of a European city, the astonishment that Péron shows in high-flown terms, apart from again a small number of statistical details and also a few notes on the various stages of the settlement since its

beginning, the reader should look there only for some excellent observations on natural history, the geological make-up, meteorological phenomena and the geography of the parts of New-Holland visited by the French expedition.[6]

At the beginning of chapter X Pilorgerie believed he was now in a position to reflect on the main characteristics of Australian history up to 1821, and on the lessons that the French could learn from them. Macquarie's departure 'really ends the history of Sydney Ponérople,* of Botany-Bay, as a colony of *forçats* and freed convicts'. In Pilorgerie's view, it had not been sufficiently recognised that this was a dividing line; after it a new and prosperous period opened:

> The emigration of free people, belonging to the middle classes of England, and possessors of capital borrowed from Great Britain's mass of riches, will come in the future to give a greater value to the work of these slaves, while supplying them with masters more honest, and at the same time more industrious, than were able to be those former accomplices, for whom the pompous title of emancipist was too often only a diploma for a teacher of vice.[7]

Those in France who still wished to found a penal colony, Pilorgerie argued, would have to examine those first thirty years of the Australian settlement, which he regarded as a 'complete test' of the viability of such a scheme. What would they discover?

> They will learn what energy is required of a government and its principal agents to lay the foundations of similar settlements; what terrible risks of famine, of revolt, what dangers arising all together from the components that must be employed, from the unyielding soil that has to be turned to use, threaten the infancy of these societies which some utopians say are so easy to create. They will see there that the choice of the men who agree to work for the realisation of the wishes of the mother country, is necessarily very limited; that supervision by the central government is impossible,

---

*'Ponérople' was a term taken from Blosseville, who defined it as 'the name that Phillip, father of Alexander, wanted to give to a city where he would have brought together all the *wicked men* in Greece'. (*Histoire des colonies pénales*, p. 63)

that some mistakes are inevitable; that the honestly calculated expenditure greatly exceeds the estimates that the partisans of this system do not fail to produce in support of their programmes; and finally, if they are of good faith, it seems to us that they will be obliged to acknowledge that the chances of success are infinitely less numerous than the chances of breaking up, of abandonment, of complete failure.

What results had been achieved in the first thirty years of Australian settlement when many of the conditions for an ideal penal colony were met and such great efforts had been made?

> A few thousand acres of mediocre soil cleared, but the produce of which still remains below consumption, some villages whose principal buildings are a tavern and a prison and where most often the school and the church are missing; some freed deportees as corrupt as those of their accomplices to whom they have been entrusted as slaves, and who, very far from accepting the title of landowner as a sufficient compensation for exile, think only of ways of selling their land, in order to acquire the means to return and exercise in Europe their detestable trade; some women of unequalled depravity, a new generation two-thirds made up of bastards raised at public expense, or of unhappy children torn by order of authority from the disastrous traditions of the family; above this lowly mass, a few more artful rogues, exploiting the vices of the crowd; crime, debauchery, immorality everywhere, repentance nowhere. I am mistaken. Bring together at great expense twenty-five thousand deportees five thousand leagues from the society that they have offended, preach to them for thirty years, through the mouths of highly-paid moral professors, the benefits of order and industry, two hundred and a few chosen ones will reply to your voice, and yet how few in this minority, already so small, will have shed the precious tears of atonement!
>
> I say no more. The facts that I have chosen for the task of explanation speak sufficiently on their own.[8]

In chapter X Pilorgerie again made use of Lang's work to move quickly through the history of the colony during the governorships of Brisbane and Darling (1821–31). He concluded it by disagreeing with the view of Beaumont and Tocqueville that there was little goodwill in Australia for England; in his opinion the flow of free migrants and convicts for slave labour would maintain harmony. The next chapter contained a more or less contemporary description of Sydney and New South Wales; it covered natural history, society, the economy and Aborigines. Pilorgerie emphasised that the settlement was prosperous and thriving and asserted that, although the most important reasons for this state of affairs were 'independent of administrative action',[9] Governor Bourke should be given some credit for it. Van Diemen's Land then received similar contemporary treatment, and developments relating to Swan River and Port Lincoln were briefly surveyed.

In his last two chapters Pilorgerie adopted a more analytical approach. He began by claiming that he had succeeded in showing that the penal colony before 1821 was a failure both in the economic sense and as a means to reform convicts; moreover that economic success had been achieved only since then because of free migrants. He now wished to examine two specifically penal questions. First, in the more recent period, since 1821, was convict reform taking place? Second, over the entire period since 1788, had the punishment of transportation intimidated and acted as a deterrent for crime in Britain?

To answer the first question, Pilorgerie, unconvinced of the impartiality of the published accounts of migrants and freed convicts, relied on the report of the House of Commons inquiry into secondary punishments:

> It is this important document which will supply facts in support of our conclusions, it is in the impressive evidence of honourable men called into the heart of the committee, that we will find the most complete justification for a judgement which, invested with this solemn approbation, thus loses its individual quality.[10]

Pilorgerie rejected the view put forward by some witnesses at the inquiry that no reform of criminals was ever possible. However the evidence of other witnesses, whom he cited, showed that the experience of transportation both on the voyage and in Australia was likely to make the convict morally worse. In addition, their evidence concerning recent social conditions in Australia also demonstrated to Pilorgerie that convicts at best remained unreformed.

What of intimidation? Deterrence? Severe punishment, according to Pilorgerie, was in the interests of the criminal so that he could atone for his crime but, more importantly from society's point of view, it would also be a deterrent. Such a punishment, he maintained, and one that was also not degrading, could be supplied by the penitentiary system. Indeed, at first the dangers, the misery, the permanent separation of transportation meant that it had influenced criminals in Britain. How different it had become!

> But as the colonies of New South Wales and Van Diemen have approximated to the economies of the societies of Europe, the rigorous aspects of deportation have gradually disappeared. Little by little this punishment has lost its severity, until it has finally become rather an encouragement to crime than a means of intimidation with regard to the depraved part of society. This observation that experience has put beyond doubt, would permit us to conclude in general that the prosperity of a penal colony and the maintenance of the efficacy of the punishment are two results which cannot co-exist, but which follow each other by being mutually incompatible.[11]

In order to support this argument, Pilorgerie made extensive use of evidence given at the inquiry. To deal with the problem of inadequate deterrence, he claimed that the committee wished to impose preliminary imprisonment in England before transportation, but for reasons of expediency recommended harsher discipline in Australia. In arguing that this was not a solution, Pilorgerie covered the same ground as Beaumont and Tocqueville: he drew on the same official correspondence and, like them, rejected the cruelty of the method, as well as doubting whether the Australian governors would be as severe as ordered and as they would claim to be.

For Pilorgerie 'the test is now complete'. His study of Australian history permitted him to reach two final conclusions on the penal effectiveness of transportation.

> Very far from offering possibilities of reforming the guilty, deportation entails the reciprocal corruption of morals.
>
> Very far from intimidating the malefactors of the metropolis, it quickly transforms itself, following the degree of prosperity of the penal colonies into a medium of enticement, of inducement to crime.[12]

Pilorgerie believed in the reform of the French penal system through the establishment of penitentiaries in France. He wrote his history of Australia to counter Blosseville's favourable interpretation of the penal and economic results obtained by transportation to Australia. His book appeared five years after Blosseville's, and during that time there had been a shift of support in France away from penal colonies and in favour of penitentiaries. This shift, as we have seen, reflected both the general reformatory views of the new government after 1830 and the rising prestige of the penitentiary system which had, in turn, been encouraged by Beaumont and Tocqueville's report on the American prison system.

Pilorgerie was able to draw on critical sources not available to Blosseville. He was able to find support in the authority of Beaumont and Tocqueville, but made greater use of the 1832 inquiry report and Lang's history. All were very important in supplying him with the ammunition for his onslaught on transportation. In fact, it is a very strong criticism of Pilorgerie that he so closely follows such a limited range of sources. This dependence, surprising though it is given the awareness he shows of other material, severely detracts from his work as a scholarly history.* It should also be noted that the dividing line that he set

---

*This view of the use of sources was not necessarily felt by contemporaries. When Hyacinthe de Bougainville was preparing his own study of Australia he inserted as a footnote a 'PS.' dated July 1836; here he stated that Pilorgerie's book had just appeared, and in giving the title he inserted in parenthesis the word '*consciencieux*', thus making it in his view a conscientious examination. He then continued: 'This history, moreover, recommends itself by new insights into the English colony, drawn in great part from a work published in London in 1834 under the title: [then in English] Dunmore Lang's statistical account of New South Wales'. (see H. de Bougainville, *Journal de la navigation*, p. 469)

for Australian history at about the year 1821—between economic failure based on convict settlement and economic success based on free migration—was not as novel to French ears as he implied; the same case had been made firmly, if not as coherently, by Barbé-Marbois in 1828.

The real focus of Pilorgerie's study of Australian history is suggested by the sub-title of his book: 'An examination of the effects of deportation, considered as a punishment and as a means of colonisation'. It should therefore be viewed primarily as a polemic against transportation. Certainly Pilorgerie was not interested in any contrary evidence, but he was able to find plenty of authoritative support for his point of view in the reports of the British official inquiries of 1812, 1822 and 1832. The result was that he succeeded in consistently using the Australian experience for his own particular interpretive purposes, while at the same time imparting a good deal of more general information. In his own terms it was an effective document, and it was widely acknowledged in the penal debate as one of the two authoritative studies, Blosseville's being the other, of Australia's historical experience as a penal colony.* In 1836 Pilorgerie's view on the desirability of a penitentiary system for France was in line with the emerging government policy, and he was rewarded by being sent to Belgium by the Minister of the Interior in 1837 to study the prison system there.[13]

---

*As late as 1872 Charles Lucas wrote: 'the history of English transportation known for so long through the works of M. de Blosseville and M. de la Pilorgerie'. (La transportation pénale, p. 4)

7
Penal Colonies and Parliament

The 1831 debate in parliament had settled nothing in relation to the manner of detention of criminals; the government had simply been urged to pursue the early establishment of a penal colony. During the debate opponents of penal colonies had claimed that a better alternative would be the replacement of the existing prison system with the more modern penitentiaries. Support for this course of action was growing rapidly: it had received considerable impetus from Beaumont and Tocqueville's analysis of the American system, and it was in accord with modern penological thinking.

In their report Beaumont and Tocqueville had described the two rival American systems of penitentiaries. Under the Auburn (New York) model prisoners were isolated during the night and worked communally in absolute silence during the day. In contrast, the Philadelphia (Pennsylvania) model stipulated the complete isolation of the prisoner with work provided in his cell. Reformers in France were divided between these two models; the most prominent supporter of the Auburn system was Charles Lucas, while from the late 1830s Tocqueville favoured the Philadelphia form. It has been claimed that debate beween the two groups 'occupied much of the time and the attention of the French political elite from 1832 until 1848'. In 1836 the government despatched a second investigating party to the United States and its report in general confirmed Beaumont and Tocqueville's earlier findings, but it came down strongly in favour of complete isolation as practised in Philadelphia. Responding to the reform movement, the government began tentative steps towards setting up a penitentiary system. From 1836 all new and reconstructed departmental prisons had to be designed on the cell principle,* and in the following year the Paris juvenile prison was converted to a cellular structure. Discipline in prisons was also tightened, and from 1839 attempts were made to impose the rule of silence in the *maisons centrales*.[1]

In the 1830s the desire to change the method of prisoner detention expressed itself mainly through the improvement of the existing prison structure, but two issues in particular drew parliamentary attention to the need for penal colonies. One was the seemingly intractable problem of the *bagnes*. The navy remained most unhappy with its responsibility for maintaining them, and their regime was criticised both for being too harsh and for not being harsh enough. There was almost general agreement on the incorrigible nature of the *forçats*, yet there did not seem to be any practical way they could be fitted into an emerging penitentiary structure. Departmental governments continued to pass resolutions about the problems caused by freed *forçats*.† Perhaps a penal colony was still the answer to their recidivism, and indeed it appears that the French government had been quietly obtaining information concerning transportation from the British goverment.‡

The other issue that drew attention to penal colonies was the failure of parliament in 1831 to find a satisfactory solution to the problem of detainment for political prisoners. It had simply decided to retain the sentence of deportation, but to keep deportees in a prison in France until a penal colony became available. Mont Saint-Michel was used but was unsuitable for the regime required

---

*In theory these prisons held only short-term and pre-trial prisoners who, it was claimed, would be corrupted by hardened criminals.

†A recommendation to establish a penal colony was often included. Publicity was given to these views by the annual publication of lists in the *AMC* (see, e.g., 2, 1836, pp. 173–7).

‡In 1837 the House of Commons select committee on transportation requested the return from France of the 'Reports and other Documents which have lately been prepared on the subject of the Punishment of Transportation with reference to the question of introducing that punishment into the Criminal Code of France'. (FO, 27/535).

for these political prisoners, and in 1835 a more suitable centre for detention was designated at Doullens. Continued and violent political unrest within France led to more repressive legislation; in particular, in 1835 a law was introduced to enable political deportees to be detained forever, not just at a centre in France but also in a fortress in one of the French possessions. The rider remained that this course of action would be pursued only until a more suitable penal settlement was established. But in what French possession could such a confining fortress be built? At first Pondicherry was favoured, but finally the Isle de Bourbon was fixed upon. To finance the construction of a fortress there, a draft Bill was presented to parliament; the parliamentary committee reported back—endorsing the Bill—in March 1837.

In outlining the Bill to the Chamber of Deputies, the spokesman for the committee, Baron Tupinier,* could not avoid involving himself in the long-running controversy concerning the alternative course of action of establishing a specifically penal colony. After stating that the use of the fortress would be only until a colony for deportation was set up, Tupinier agreed that the expense was justified only if there 'remained no probability of being able, in a few years, to resolve the problem relating to the formation of a penal colony in the manner of those that the English have founded in Australia'. With this point in mind, the committee had therefore asked itself two initial questions:

> Have sufficient searches been made to find a place outside the realm where individuals condemned to deportation may be sent?
>
> If these searches have not led to a definite result, do they at least leave hope that they will be crowned by success in a more or less distant future?

In its search for answers, Tupinier continued, the committee discussed locations that in the past had had some support. The Falklands? France's claims to these islands would be difficult to sustain. French Guiana? Most of it had a terrible mortality record for Europeans. The same applied to the shores of Senegal.

---

*A Councillor of State and Director of Ports.

7 Penal Colonies and Parliament 131

Obviously a temperate area was required and here 'the example of England seemed to be conclusive: why, as was repeated on all sides, did not France succeed in doing what that power had done? Why did it not choose to form a penal colony on the banks of the Swan river, which had been explored by Baudin's ships at the beginning of the century?' For two reasons this argument had been found to be 'very specious'. First, Baudin's exploration had been followed by eleven years of war with England. Second, the fifteen years of the Restoration saw 'the birth and death of many projects, among which the occupation of the Swan river was sometimes indicated; but no negotiation took place on this subject, and while we were deliberating, the English indeed occupied the place in question'. Any current French—or Dutch—claim to parts of the west coast of New Holland, based on prior discovery, was opposed by the English with 'effective occupation', and the English also found legitimacy in the work of Flinders. What then of New Zealand, which had been endorsed in the reports of several French voyages as 'a perfectly suitable place in which to establish a penal colony', and where some land had recently been offered to France by speculators? The problem, Tupinier declared, would be the reception given by the inhabitants: however guilty the political deportees, 'the law wishes neither to condemn them to death, nor to impose on them the necessity to defend their existence every day against the ferocity of the cannibal tribes'.

These difficulties, Tupinier continued, did not disabuse the supporters of penal colonies, and they still pressed the question: 'Why would France not succeed in doing in this manner what England has done?' The answer turned in part on lines of communication, ports of call, to settlements in Australia and New Zealand, which England had but France did not:

> And moreover, gentlemen, let us not deceive ourselves on what these colonies now are. For some years yet they will be able to keep the appearances and the name of penal colonies; but henceforth their own logic and their regimen lead to quite another end.

This consideration led Tupinier into a brief history of Botany Bay: established purely for penal reasons, the 'modest project' faced enormous difficulties in its early years, but had expanded to cover the whole continent. The lesson for France was that 'a colony of deportees would be able to prosper only in the condition of constant expansion . . . it is certain that the colony of Sydney would have failed in the face of difficulties of all sorts if it had been necessary for it to remain confined in territory of small extent'. Also, who could say with confidence that the English government had not been alarmed by the great cost, and that it did not recognise that far from reducing crime, the prospect of deportation to Australia, 'depicted as a place of happiness', encouraged it?

Tupinier then summarised quickly the current situation in Australia, the manner by which it was achieved, and the reasons why it was now impossible for France to achieve similar results:

> It is clear therefore that England, which at first wished only to establish a reformatory settlement, will have prepared for Australia the most astonishing of revolutions, by covering it with civilised populations who will probably escape one day from their motherland by making themselves independent; but these new nations will keep the manners and customs of the English; from their midst sooner or later will depart travellers, traders or missionaries, who will bear into the numerous archipelagos of the Pacific the civilisation which most of the scattered races of men in that part of the world still lack; and this result will certainly be more advantageous to humanity and to England itself than the one which it wished to obtain and that it will have lost by going beyond the objective.
>
> Your committee, gentlemen, believes it sees, in this faithful account of the complete facts, the most complete proof of the impossibility of France doing now what England did in 1787.
>
> With favourable circumstances, great perseverance and the firm will to be discouraged neither by the huge cost nor any other obstacle, the English government was able to succeed in an undertaking, the results of which, in some degree unforeseen, appear to be something of a marvel. But now if France wished to attempt something similar, it would not succeed, unless it has at its disposal a second continent like Australia, a limitless budget, and as much facility as our neighbours in finding adventurous speculators, always

ready to come to the help of the government by supporting its projects with their capital and their industry.

It is also necessary to recognise that if France still has no settlement where persons sentenced to deportation can be sent, it is neither for want of attempts vainly repeated in French Guiana, nor for want of searches to discover elsewhere a place in which it could be carried out.

To round off his survey of possible sites, Tupinier considered it necessary to canvass the possibility of Madagascar, but although it was very conveniently located he ruled it out on the grounds of health and the vigorous opposition of the indigenous people.

With the completion of his presentation of the committee's case, Tupinier believed that he had succeeded in his main objective of justifying expenditure on the construction of a fortress in a French possession for the confinement of deportees. These outlays, he said:

> ... will not be rendered useless by the discovery of a suitable place to receive, for the benefit of France, a colony of deportees in the manner of that of Australia, since this discovery, if ever it takes place, can only be very distant.

Discussion of the committee's report was immediately adjourned, but then several weeks later it was removed altogether from the legislative programme and the government took no further action. Apparently it felt that it had failed to gain sufficient support in the Chamber for the project.[2]

The government's case for an overseas site for a prison for deportees makes it plain that, in spite of the dominance of the philosophy of the penitentiary, the strength of the push for a penal colony had to be reckoned with. In part this shows up in a negative way through the attacks on penal colonies by Tocqueville and by Pilorgerie. As will be shown in a later section on the navy, there was positive support for a penal colony from some government circles and from the King himself.

At the end of the decade, a resurgence in support for such a colony was apparent in a variety of published works, four examples of which are surveyed below.

In May 1839 *a petition from a former magistrate, Castéra*, in favour of establishing a penal colony was presented to the Chamber of Peers. The member who presented and endorsed the petition was Baron Pelet (de la Lozère), who had been secretary of the 1819 committee. After briefly summarising Castéra's argument, he stated that under the Restoration there had been a real intention to establish a penal colony:

> It was stopped by the difficulty in finding a suitable place, and perhaps also by considerations of cost. But we believe that, either in Guyana, or in some still uninhabited part of New Holland, or in that part occupied by the English, by making an agreement with them, it would not be impossible to establish a place for deportation similar to theirs. The cost should not stop an object of this importance. It is certain that the existing state of affairs is intolerable and calls for a prompt remedy. Society is frightened all the time by the crimes committed by the wretches from the *bagnes*, which are often prepared and planned in the *bagnes* themselves. These are dens of depravity more dangerous than useful. Their reform or their replacement by deportation is the most urgent part of this improvement of the prisons, the need for which has occupied public opinion for some time.[3]

The Chamber endorsed the sending of the petition to the Ministers for the Interior, Justice and the Navy.

Castéra's petition, which was printed in *Annales maritimes et coloniales*, was written in lurid language. It emphasised the dreadful crimes committed by the men released from the *bagnes* and the impossibility of their re-absorption by society.

> To sum up, the freed *forçat* is morally and perhaps inevitably what he was on the day of his sentencing; either a thief, or a murderer, or a corrupter, supposing even that in the interval he has not become all of these by accumulation; and this is the man to whom one gives freedom.

Castéra went on to argue that while France was still discussing penitentiaries, England had made the right decision to transport its convicts. England was peopling its colonies with

Fort Macquarie on the eastern point of Sydney Cove in 1825, with *L'Espérance* at anchor, from a drawing by Edmond de la Touanne, a member of Hyacinthe de Bougainville's expedition [E. de la Touanne (ed.), *Album pittoresque de la frégate* La Thétis *et de la corvette* L'Espérance. *Collection de dessins relatifs à leur voyage autour du monde en 1824, 1825 et 1826*, Paris, 1828, Plate 29]

The government gardens in Sydney in 1825 with the Government House stables in the background, from a drawing by Edmond de la Touanne [H. de Bougainville, *Journal de la navigation . . . Atlas*, 1837, Plate 12]

View of the Macquarie Lighthouse, Sydney, in 1826

The entrance to Sydney Cove in 1826

Both are from paintings by Louis de Sainson, artist with Dumont d'Urville's expedition of 1826–29 [J. S. C. Dumont d'Urville, *Voyage de la corvette* L'Astrolabe *exécuté par ordre du Roi, pendant les années 1826, 1827, 1828, 1829 . . . Atlas historique*, 1833, Plates 26 and 28]

7 Penal Colonies and Parliament

... its worst subjects, and yet historians have noted with satisfaction that, from the second and even the first generation, an honourable population had been obtained, whilst their fathers, the banished, the outlawed that their frightened country had spewed on to the unknown land, have generally improved their principles and their conduct, and that, among those who had lived out their life there, there are some who, in their last days, have been regarded as honest folk, transformed by the attraction of that pastoral life which had given them a conscience and would have placed happiness in it, if it had not prompted remorse there.[4]

In bringing about this moral change, Castéra emphasised aspects of the new environment—simplicity, farming, equality, 'a new world'.[5]

An influential *memoir by a Captain Rigodit* also appeared in 1839.[6] He saw deportation as the only way to deal with men who were 'utterly depraved'. He pointed out that many petitions had favoured this course of action, but the problem was to find an appropriate place. He admitted that there was disagreement in England over the success of transportation, but he maintained that customs duties on new trade with the colony had compensated for the cost of transportation; that even if convicts did not reform, England nevertheless had got rid of them; and that any growth in crime in England was partly the result of 'excessive gentleness' in Australia. Indeed so easy were conditions in Australia that English convicts claimed transportation 'as a right'. Rigodit commented also that the penal settlements had been the birthplace of 'those fine colonies that we envy England'. However, by far the greater part of Rigodit's memoir was given over to an examination of possible places for a penal settlement. Such a place had to be healthy, fertile and isolated, but 'also of such a nature that the convicts did not have an existence there happier than in the homeland'. He then surveyed the Falklands, Port Famine near the Straits of Magellan, the western coast of Patagonia and New Zealand, and concluded that they all 'brought together the greatest part of the conditions for looking again into the establishment of a colony of deportation'.

Another influential document, in which there are several references to Rigodit, was that of the *Count de Mauny*.[7] Mauny began by emphasising the preoccupation, confusion and disagreements in society over the fundamental matter of the treatment of criminals. However, he quickly stated that he regarded colonies of deportation as 'a necessity . . . to fill the double goal of punishment and reformation of the condemned while thoroughly preparing a maritime and commercial future; it remains only to determine the most favourable place for the protection of the French flag'. In fact, moving on to what he saw as France's problem of over-population, he found the solution in three words: 'Shipping, Trade, Colonisation'. To make his case, Mauny spent over half his essay examining the Australian situation. In his view Blosseville was 'almost alone' in his 'remarkable work' in claiming success. There were many critics. Pilorgerie was one, but the most important was Tocqueville. Such was the 'talent' of that writer on democracy in America that Mauny claimed he would not have put forward his own views had he not had such strong convictions. After listing the main criticisms of the Australian penal colony, he attempted to provide a systematic rebuttal, and it is obvious that he was more interested in the colony as an economic centre than as a penal colony. He admitted that convicts were a 'sad nucleus' for a colony, but penal colonies all differed, and Sydney had 'responded successfully'. As for the criticism that the first thirty years were very difficult, this was not surprising: 'a part of the world then nearly unknown; [England] didn't even take the precaution of making an exploratory voyage . . . [it acted] on the vague information given by Cook'. In any case France could learn from the Australian experience. Mauny's conclusion was an exhortation:

> When Major Philipp [sic] founded the colony of Sidney [sic], the English had no great resources in Australia, but the isolation did not stop them, and today they gather to our detriment the fruits of their foresight, and of their boldness. We cannot make too much haste in planting our flag on several of the places indicated by Captain Rigodit . . .

7 Penal Colonies and Parliament

It was mentioned earlier that one of the responses to Barbé-Marbois in 1828 was *a memoir from Mortemart de Boisse to the Navy Minister*. His argument was unusual in that, while accepting all Barbé-Marbois' criticisms of Botany Bay, he claimed that France could learn from the mistakes there and should proceed with a penal settlement on the Falklands. This memoir was published without alteration in Le Havre in 1840,* and was commented on in an article on transportation in the *Journal du Havre* which was in turn republished in *Annales maritimes et coloniales*.[8]

The writer of the article, 'V. B.', agreed with Mortemart de Boisse's views on Australia: 'far from copying the course followed by England, it is precisely that which must be carefully avoided'. Writing from an additional twelve years' perspective, he argued that England had not obtained its goal because the place of deportation had become a flourishing colony. The cost was that crime had increased and immorality had become more flagrant and audacious: 'it has worsened the evil which it wished to remedy, and it is now beyond doubt that the prosperity of Sydney has developed only in spite of the presence of the *convicts* and not because of it'. So what should France do? In V.B.'s view it should not renounce the idea of a penal colony, but more consideration was needed. Several writers were engaged on this, but he particularly wished to mention Mortemart de Boisse's work. This article was not the place to judge it, but it caused 'the reader to reflect, and shows him that this important question is still far from being thoroughly examined'.

In spite of the views of the Auburnists and the transportationists, the Philadelphia method was given priority by the government, and in 1840 a Bill was introduced into parliament to establish

---

*Le Havre was the port to which Mortemart de Boisse, a naval officer, was attached, and it was from there that an expedition set out in 1840 to establish a settlement in New Zealand. The editor of *AMC* introduced the article saying that his journal 'would hardly be able to collect carefully all the appropriate documents to inform on the question which is current at this time on the best penitentiary system, especially when included in them is the punishment of deportation, because the department of navy and colonies is particularly interested in its solution'.

this system in France.* 'From that moment (May 1840) until the revolution of 1848, the issue of penal reform was to remain the most persistent and contentious item on the parliamentary agenda.'[9] But the government's Bill put forward only cautious and tentative proposals, and the Chamber took the issue into its own hands and called for a report from a committee headed by Tocqueville. That report was prompt and much more decisive, but various delays saw four years elapse before, in April 1844, a full parliamentary debate took place. It occupied much of the Chamber's time for the next month. Just as the 1831 parliamentary debate was a culmination of the widespread disputation of the previous ten years, so it was in 1844. But now the debate was even more wide-ranging and could draw on a greater range of specialist literature. The government had a specific proposal to change the penal system, but this necessarily involved discussion of the familiar themes of rising crime rates, of recidivism, of all the problems associated with imprisonment, thus opening the doors for a resurgence of the argument in favour of transportation.

Because of the deleterious effects on prisoners' health, the Bill proposed a maximum of twelve years' solitary confinement; after that longer-term prisoners would be transferred to a general prison. In introducing the Bill, the Interior Minister pointed out that such a transfer would mix these prisoners with ordinary criminals, and might undo the moral benefits of their solitary confinement. He therefore cautiously approached the subject of deportation. It was, in his view, no substitute for solitary confinement:

> I am convinced that deportation does not have sufficient penal force to stop the progress of crime.
>
> In England, deportation does not have an effect on the minds of criminals, they confuse it with emigration.

Moreover, it would be very costly as each year some 6000 to 7000 would require deportation, this being the number sent to

---

*In the early 1840s the French government was still formally seeking information in London 'respecting Prisons and Prison Discipline in this country, and respecting the British Penal settlements in Australia'. (FO, 27/680)

the *bagnes* and the *maisons centrales*. In certain circumstances, however, it could be of value:

> ... after a cellular imprisonment of a certain length, it can be useful for long punishments to have recourse to deportation; when the mind of the criminal has been influenced, when his baleful connections have been broken, when one has exerted sufficient repressive influences, then recourse can be had to deportation.[10]

Under these conditions, the minister continued, deportation would apply to only the relatively small number of individuals who had long sentences, of which they had already spent some years in solitary confinement. This initial type of imprisonment would make them better settlers.

When the debate in parliament began, action along the lines suggested by the minister was argued with passion by Alphonse de Lamartine.[11] Poet and politician, he was possibly the Chamber's most eloquent and effective speaker. He would not, he said, agree to very long terms of imprisonment:

> This system that I shall propose, and I shall say it whatever may be the grumbles that greet it; (No! No! No!); this system is deportation, it is a deportation, after a certain number of years spent in prisons, to a foreign land, to a penal land, which then becomes a land of rehabilitation. (Hear hear! Hear hear!—Prolonged uproar.)

In Lamartine's view, crime abounded in France. Recidivism was a major source of crime, and on his estimate there were 110 000 ex-prisoners. England tackled the problem by sending its criminals to New South Wales. For his part, he had 'read all that has been written for ten years, all the journals, all the English publications on these deportations'. They were very critical of the system, but 'to all that I reply with the official inquiries of parliament'. They showed that it was cheaper to send convicts to Sydney than to imprison them in England. What of the claim that these colonies were 'the shame of European civilisation ... a place of disorder and abomination'? Lamartine scorned such views, and described the situation in the Australian colonies in terms that portrayed them as a triumph both morally and economically. Even the criticism that as it developed Australia would eventually refuse to accept convicts was, in Lamartine's opinion, the ultimate in praise of deportation: 'let us accept this censure as the most splendid praise of the deportation of prisoners. (Hear hear! Hear hear!)' He concluded his stirring oration with a call for decisive action:

> I would say especially to the speaker to whom I have responded for so long . . . What is this talk of adjournment? What is this talk of waiting? Crime doesn't wait; the dangers for society do not wait; the corruption of each other by the condemned does not wait! Why then should morality, society, the country, law-abiding citizens be the only ones to wait? No. Let us resolve the question by deportation for long punishments, by imprisonment isolated but solaced for short detentions. That's the only solution. (Hear hear! Hear hear!)

Lamartine's rhetoric brought enthusiastic applause, but not all members agreed with him. As one member (Daguenet) put it: 'The honourable M. de Lamartine . . . has presented a magnificent picture of deportation; the chamber was properly moved and like everybody I was impressed. I was impressed, but I was not convinced'.[12]

Time and again in the debate, members worked over the history of Botany Bay and of French attempts to establish a penal colony. Some members wanted deportation without any preliminary imprisonment, others were entirely opposed to any form of deportation. The latter argued that no matter how successful economically the Australian colonies now were, they had been a penal disaster; a strong counter to this criticism was that it was no longer relevant, because of the recent provision in the English law requiring prior imprisonment. One speaker, D'Haussonville, made a telling point:

> I do not believe that it should often be necessary to go and take examples from other countries. Nevertheless it is intriguing to see two great countries, which are not acting in concert, which have not sought to copy each other, setting out from two opposite extremes, from two completely different systems, and arriving at this middle course of a preliminary detention followed by

7 Penal Colonies and Parliament

deportation. I am able to say, gentlemen, that here the advantage would be entirely on our side; for intimidation would be much stronger in the system that we propose than in the English system.[13]

With the support of the Minister of the Interior and of the Chamber's committee on the Bill headed by Tocqueville, the majority of members favoured deportation after imprisonment, but the important question remained of how long the period of imprisonment should be. The minister accepted that the period could be reduced from twelve years to ten and, surprisingly, stated that after consulting the Ministers for Justice and for the Navy, he would not 'hesitate to say in their names that it is easy to determine a place of deportation which brings together all the desirable conditions'.[14] Moreover, since the new sentence could not be applied retrospectively, there would be ten years in which to find such a place, and that even then the numbers to be deported would be small.* Tocqueville, for his part, was prepared to give the courts the right to reduce the period of solitary confinement to eight years, but speakers more committed to transportation favoured periods as low as two years.† Clearly, the shorter the period of confinement the more the French system would appear to be a system of transportation with initial imprisonment; the longer the period of confinement the more it would duplicate the Philadelphia example, merely capped by transportation. It was, of course, recognised that the choice of method would greatly affect the numbers transported and thus the site and nature of a penal colony.

When the vote was taken, the winning amendment gave the courts discretion to set the period of confinement at the low figure of five years. Several times during the debate it had been stated

---

*Five years later the government was firmly reminded of the optimistic claim by A. Lacoudrais, a prominent supporter of transportation. Lacoudrais went on to argue for the general adoption of transportation, 'or else, our unhappy France will become inevitably and before long, assisted by the railways, the Botany-Bay of the whole of Europe'. (*Lettres sur la transportation*, p. 2)

†During the debate the minister emphasised that the subject matter was 'transportation', not 'deportation', which applied only to political prisoners. (*Moniteur*, 15 May 1844, p. 1381)

that members were not influenced in their views by party affiliation but, given the government's position and the general tenor of the debate, this was a very surprising result and it may be that some members misunderstood the motion when casting their votes. Certainly the vote was followed by a disturbance in the Chamber which was both prolonged and tumultuous, and a member interjected: 'Gentlemen, listen then, if you want to vote with full knowledge of the facts'.[15]

Far from settling the matter, the decision in the Chamber of Deputies turned out to be simply a prologue to a further three years of investigation and argument. First the Bill was referred to the Chamber of Peers and, in its turn, this Chamber required reports from two committees. The thrust of their recommendations was strongly in favour of long-term solitary confinement; the only compromise offered to the transportation cause was the possibility of the replacement of the *bagnes* by cellular prisons in Algeria or islands off the coast of France. Such was the position, with the proposals about to come back to the Chamber of Peers for perhaps some definitive resolution, when the revolution of February 1848 put paid to this formal attempt to remodel the French penal system.

8
The Role of the Navy

Before 1831 members of the crews of naval ships, such as Péron, Arago and Jules de Blosseville, had been authoritative sources of information on the circumstances of the Australian penal colony. This role was maintained by the commanders of two other official voyages, who had set out before Louis-Philippe's successful revolution. One was Dumont d'Urville. He returned to France in March 1829 after a voyage of almost three years, which included stays of several weeks, first in Sydney in December 1826 and then in Hobart a year later. Soon after his arrival home he began to write an account of his voyage, and this began to appear in published form in 1830. His writings and his personal views concerning the degree of success of the penal colony were eagerly sought and were in fact used by both sides in the parliamentary debate of 1831. His full historical account was completed by 1833, and included three chapters on New South Wales and two on Van Diemen's Land—in all some 420 pages. The work was based in part on his own observations, but there were extensive quotations from a small range of secondary sources, including Sydney newspapers. He was particularly critical of what he saw as the bitter feuds and the unworkable society created from the mixture of free settlers, emancipists and convicts.[1]

The other influential voyager was Cyrille Laplace, who spent two months in Sydney and Hobart in 1831. His 236-page examination of Australia, published in 1835, opened with a long reflective essay on whether the English system of colonisation suited the needs of France.[2] He argued that English migration was driven principally by a surplus of population and the amassing of land into the hands of 'a small number of lords'. This population pressure had led to destitution and crime—a situation which did not apply in France. Moreover transportation was not successful. The convicts were 'rarely capable of a true repentence', and they 'generally show the hideous picture of the same perverseness, of the same vices, which in our *bagnes* . . . make mankind grieve'. England's draconian law meant that the deportees' unhappy state 'springs from misery rather than depravity', and there was encouragement to crime in Britain because the deportees enjoyed 'a condition much happier than that of peasants or workers in England'. The economic success of New South Wales was the result of free settlers: 'I observed everywhere an order, an activity unknown in the richest provinces of France'. Throughout his published work there was the exhortation not to follow the example of England.

Laplace's account of his voyage was summarised in *Annales maritimes et coloniales*, and in 1836 the reviewer commented on his views about the Australian penal colony:

> He has had to judge this system, not from the numerous articles borrowed with too blind a confidence by our reviews from those published on the other side of the channel . . . but from its effects and the testimony of the most educated and better informed men, of whom there, as everywhere, he has sought the society and consulted the knowledge. This part of the voyage of M. Laplace is of the greatest interest. It deserves to attract the attention particularly of those, and we confess that we are of the number, who would be seen more preoccupied with the necessity for France to seek in colonisation an outlet and a food supply for its population, clearly too large or too congregated.[3]

A few years later, in 1839, Laplace felt that he could claim that his critical report on the penal aspects of Australia could have influenced the attitude of the French government.*

---

*While on a second visit to Hobart in 1839, Laplace wrote to his minister saying that the English had now judged the penal system there to be a failure. He continued: 'It is therefore fortunate that France has renounced copying England in this respect and I myself am pleased to have perhaps contributed a little to persuade our government to take this latest resolution'. (AM, BB4, 1008)

Dumont d'Urville and Laplace had published their impressions of Australia with some despatch. The publication in the 1830s of the views of two other naval commanders had their origins in much earlier voyages. It took an order from the Department of the Navy to force Hyacinthe de Bougainville to publish his account of his 1824–26 voyage in 1837.[4] He admitted that his information had lost its 'principal merit, that of newness', and that there were other, more recent accounts. He would, therefore, confine himself to 'some simple sketches'. The relatively short 82-page Australian section of his work was based on a three-month stay in Sydney in 1825. Bougainville noted that universally Botany Bay and deportation were 'almost synonyms', and his observations paid particular attention to social conflict within the population. Of particular interest are two general comments, the first of which introduces his Australian chapter.

> How has this creation, still so recent, taken on such a life, nearly unknown to Europe, so to speak. And how has it become suddenly the object of general curiosity, the subject of such a large number of publications, that New South Wales or rather Australia, to baptise it with the name recently imposed on New Holland (as it will end up, God willing and our carelessness, by taking over entirely), is at present as well-known to many people in France as most of our provinces.
>
> What country, moreover, deserves more to attract the attention of the observer, of becoming the objective of investigations by the naturalist and the philosopher! Without speaking of its strange natural products, of the almost inexplicable phenomena that it shows, and of the quite natural singularites which have earnt it the name of *Continent sans pareil*, are not the various elements of the population, now widespread on its soil, a valuable subject for studies and observations: a land of true liberty and independence, suddenly transformed by a turn of fortune into a place of slavery and servitude.

The other general point made by Bougainville, which is worthy of note, is a variation on a common French sentiment. He asked himself what genius had created Sydney:

> This genius, it is that of Great Britain, that of the one nation of our epoch which has mastered the science of colonisation to the highest degree; that hand, that of an active and resolute government, whose plans once resolved upon suffer no delay in the execution, and never meet with any obstacles from successive persons in power; the full explanation finally of all these marvels is the spirit of continuance and foresight, completely backed up indeed by the adventurous character of our overseas neighbours, their cosmopolitan practices and the facility that they find in taking them over in the prodigous extension of their commerce.[5]

The other naval commander who published on Australia in the 1830s after a long delay was Louis de Freycinet. He had visited Sydney for a little over a month in 1819 but, although he began publishing the account of his voyage in 1827, he did not publish the Australian section until 1839.[6] Freycinet devoted a massive 584 pages to Australia, and it was overwhelmingly a social and economic study. Like Bougainville, he thought that his own observations would have lost their impact, so he wrote his account largely from other sources. His problem, as he saw it, was how to draw the truth from such conflicting accounts:

> Among the divergent opinions of their authors, I have had to employ great circumspection in order to distinguish those which had as a basis reason and fairness: thus some, driven by a thoughtless enthusiasm, have drawn a picture flattering beyond measure of the convicts and their descendants; others, on the contrary, have painted them with gloomy colours and frightful traits.
>
> It is between these extremes that the truth existed, but I felt how difficult it would be for me to tear away entirely the veil which hid it from my eyes, if a serious and well-informed man, uniting an intimate knowledge of the facts to that rectitude of principles which withstands the temptation of passion, did not come to enlighten me with his advice. The return to Europe of my excellent friend Mr Barron Field,* procured this advantage for me; he has truly

---

*Barron Field was in New South Wales as a a judge of the Supreme Court between 1817 and 1824.

wished, as much through love for science as through affection for me, to examine and explain all that appears to me to be subject to controversy.

Freycinet went on to enlarge on the role played by Field, and he also acknowledged his indebtedness to Mrs Macquarie, the widow of the former governor of New South Wales, and 'the protectress of the school for aborigines at Parramatta'. She replied to his questions on Aborigines so that he knew 'in precise detail various intriguing facts which bring out their character'. More generally, Freycinet drew on a large and diverse array of source material, which was almost entirely in English. It included, for example, 'the complete collection of the Sydney Gazette, from its beginning [1803] up to 1826'.*

A considerable part of Freycinet's survey was given over to aspects of the convict system. This subject seemed so important to him that within the Australian section of his account he included a 44-page digression on *bagnes* and on the prison system in France generally. Included were some practical suggestions for obtaining a better penal outcome from the *bagnes*. As for transportation:

> Several people, both well-informed and well-disposed, have expressed many times the wish that France had a settlement for deportation *analogous* (I insist on this word *analogous*, because I am far from believing that one cannot propose notable improvements to the plan that the English followed in the founding of their southern colonies) to that of Port-Jackson. This project is perhaps not impracticable, but it presents difficulties of various kinds, of which beyond a doubt the most serious are the choice of a suitable locality, the great expense that it would require, and especially a constancy maintained long enough with the same views, to have sufficient chance of success. (Our admirable courage on the battlefield, says M. de Villeneuve Bargemont, wavers before enterprises which call for time and patience.) Without this last condition, any project in which time is a necessary condition could not be crowned with success.[7]

---

*The one French source cited was Ernest de Blosseville

This was as close as Freycinet came to recommending that France follow the Australian example. Concluding his survey of the colony, he made some general observations on its penal aspects. He thought that if the morals of the convicts had not improved, at least they had not become obviously worse. There were in fact many examples of reform, but this was made difficult by the congregation of prisoners, the imbalance of the sexes and inadequate religious instruction. Moreover, deportation to Botany Bay was not a real punishment, and therefore had little effect on crime in England. Finally, Freycinet noted the harmful social divisions in the colony, and expressed a hope that the future purification of the population would take care of them.

The writings of the commanders of the official voyages added significantly to the knowledge in France about developments in the Australian colonies. At the same time, popular accounts of the same naval voyages were also published. Three, in particular, should be mentioned. *Voyage pittoresque autour du monde* ... (1834) was published 'under the direction of M. Dumont d'Urville'. This was an account by a fictional traveller visiting the places seen by the great voyagers. Australia was given 68 pages. Jacques Arago, who had become blind in the 1830s, wrote up his 1822 account as *Souvenirs d'un aveugle* (1839). It was very popular and ran into numerous editions. He maintained his earlier view of Sydney: 'You are in Paris, you live in London, you have not left Europe'.[8] R. P. Lesson, the surgeon on Duperrey's 1822–25 expedition, published *Voyage autour du monde* ... (1838) in which Australia was given 83 pages. Despite the hospitality shown to the French voyagers in Sydney and the friendships established, there remained an uneasy undercurrent of rivalry and of tension from the recent war. Lesson wrote:

> The name of Waterloo has been over-used by the English with such profusion that it will become synonymous with *false glory*. How a nation as civilised as is the English people can disfigure its trophies (if trophies there are, for Blücher has as much right to claim them) with tinsel and tawdry finery which denote poverty and bad taste! A multitude of places in New South Wales carry this name and that of Wellington. The day when the Russians will

attack India and take an uncontested preponderence in Europe, the English, driven from their vast possessions, will appreciate what is the value to them of the battle of Waterloo about which they have been made so dizzy as to lose their heads—although already the sane part of the nation may be able to judge its results with maturity.[9]

All these accounts looked back to French voyages of the Restoration period, and indeed there was a pause in French voyaging to the Pacific in the first half of the 1830s, when the new government was involved in affairs closer to home. Later in the decade, however, official expeditions began again, and their commanders were normally asked to investigate the availability of a penal site. Their reports yielded further material on Australian penal arrangements, but by the 1840s this type of first-hand observation was less influential than the mass of information coming from England. Throughout this period there was a growing French presence in the Pacific with the expansion of whaling, commerce and missionary activities, and these required naval protection which, in turn, demanded provisioning ports. But France did not forcefully pursue colonial expansion in the region. Its principal colonial interests were in Africa, and British attitudes also had to be considered. It was not just the strength of the British navy on the world's oceans; perhaps of greater importance was the French desire to remain on cordial terms with Britain. Something of a minor confrontation took place over New Zealand, and here French penal interests were involved.

When the French realised by the mid-1820s that there was little chance of their making a successful claim to the south-west region of Australia, their attention had turned to New Zealand, and it has already been shown that Dumont d'Urville (1826–29) was ordered to search there for a place which would be suitable for the transportation of common criminals. Towards the end of the 1830s a number of factors came together to concentrate French attention on New Zealand again; more specifically, their interest turned to the South Island, since from the late 1830s British possession of the North Island had been accepted.[10] French whaling activities in the area had suddenly expanded in a marked fashion.

There were encouraging reports from Captain Dupetit-Thouars, who had made an assessment of the region, and in general there seemed to be trade and development possibilities. This was also the last extensive temperate land mass in the Pacific unclaimed by a colonial power, and it offered possibilities for a penal settlement—the lack of such a site in the French colonies had recently been underlined by Tupinier when introducing the draft Bill on deportation in 1837. In this situation the French government decided in 1839 to further its colonial aims by acting through a private organisation—the Nanto-Bordelaise Company—which was being established to form a settlement on lands 'bought' from the Maoris at Akaroa by a French whaleman. Clearly it saw this as a first step in obtaining French sovereignty.

Why did the French government not act directly to establish a colony? Undoubtedly it was influenced by the complex situation in the South Island in relation to British interests and to land ownership by the Maoris. It wished to avoid giving provocation to Britain. Léonce Jore suggests an additional reason: 'The only plausible motive is that the Government feared the disapproval of Parliament and of public opinion and preferred to present them with a fait accompli'.[11] In the event, the extent of the support by the government for the company was kept secret, as were the company's concessions to the government in terms of land and control.

In the miscellany of reasons for the French government's involvement in Akaroa, the penal aspect appears to have been very important.* In the middle of the negotiations with the company, attention switched temporarily to the Chatham Islands, some 900 kilometres to the east of New Zealand, as a site for a penitentiary. Decazes, president of the Chamber of Peers, stated that the King himself was greatly interested in the project: 'The King is still very preoccupied with the idea and need of a place for deportation. He strongly recommended that I should not give his

---

*In his study of the French settlement, Peter Tremewan argues that the submissions of the Nanto-Bordelaise Company to the government show that it 'believed that the creation of a penal institution was a primary consideration for the Government'. (*French Akaroa*, p. 43)

'Vooloo-Moloo', Port Jackson, in 1831

Sydney, the 'principal settlement of New South Wales', in 1831, showing the Rocks area and Fort Macquarie

Both aquatints are from drawings by Barthélemy Lauvergne, official artist of the Laplace expedition of 1830–32 [C. P. T. Laplace, *Voyage autour du monde . . . exécuté sur la corvette de l'état* La Favorite *pendant les années 1830, 1831, et 1832, Album pittoresque*, Paris, 1835, Plates 64 (top of page) and 63]

The penitentiary at Port Arthur, Van Diemen's Land, in 1839, painted by F.-E. Pâris, a member of Laplace's expedition of 1837–40

Ministers any peace until they have presented a bill for the Chatham Island expedition. The Minister of the Interior, whose particular concern this is, is very well disposed to it'.[12] However, in the view of Lavaud, the commander of the naval ship being sent to protect French interests in the area, the Chathams were too remote and lacked a suitable anchorage.[13]

Rumours concerning the penal intentions of the French had already circulated in New South Wales and England, and had caused considerable alarm. Substance for the rumours appeared to be found in 1840 in the *Journal du Havre* when it commented on the departure of the Nanto-Bordelaise ship for New Zealand: the aim was not just to establish a colony; 'it has, it is said, received from the government a commission to investigate whether the nature of the locality would be able, if such should be the case, to lend itself to the realisation of a project concerning *forçats* and *réclusionnaires*, in which case the company would be able to cede to the government some part of its land which would be suitable for it'.[14] When the British Ambassador pursued this issue with the French Foreign Minister, he replied that there was nothing in it; Jore comments that this 'was not contrary to the truth, the eventual founding of a penitentiary in that country being simply foreseen in the agreement passed between the state and the Nanto-Bordelaise Company'.[15]

The attempt to establish a French outpost in New Zealand failed, the British having formally taken possession of the South Island shortly before the arrival of the French expedition. While this was a very serious colonising enterprise of the French, it nevertheless seems to have lacked some final resolve. It is interesting that the French company was apparently unable to recruit enough suitable French settlers,[16] and Dumont d'Urville revealed some of the ambiguities and doubts in the French attitude:

> But supposing even that France had been able to remain in charge of colonising New Zealand, I strongly doubt that it would have been able to create there a lasting and profitable settlement. It is not that I believe our nation incapable of extending itself and of creating colonies, but it lacks intermediary points capable of connecting through continual exchanges countries so distant. It is

necessary to add also that the character of the French nation is far from showing, as does the English character, some quite specific facility for colonisation. Each day there can be seen arriving from England in the ports of Australia free men possessing considerable capital, who, encumbered with large families, come to establish themselves in these distant lands in order to increase their fortune and often without retaining the thought of returning to the motherland after a voluntary exile. In France, emigration brings to our colonies only men who possess nothing.[17]

Rebuffed in New Zealand, France took possession of the Marquesas and established a protectorate in Tahiti in 1842. In the case of the Marquesas, although it was intended that possession should lead to the founding of a penal colony,[18] the islands' potential as a destination for convicts proved to be very limited.

At the end of the reign of Louis-Philippe, French penal policy was in a state of flux. Parliamentary opinion tended to favour the development of a cellular system of solitary confinement and work on the Philadelphia model. But strong support had been maintained for transportation, especially because of the introduction in England of imprisonment before consignment to Australia. One factor which still inhibited the case for transportation was the inability of its supporters to name a site for a penal colony which was demonstrably satisfactory. Although the navy had ranged the world, it had been unsuccessful; and as time passed its chance of success was diminished.

III

The Triumph of Transportation, 1848–1854

9
Napoleon III and French Guiana

The revolution of February 1848, which forced Louis-Philippe to flee France, began a four-year period of political instability. Political groups formed and re-formed, the composition of the legislature changed and the quasi-democratic republic which began in 1848 became, via a *coup d'état* in December 1851, the Second Empire of Napoleon III in December 1852. These political changes were associated with marked changes both in the demands made on the penal system and in its philosophy and practice. The dominant penal theme during this period was the drive to expel overseas both political and common-law prisoners. The main problem common to the ejection of both types of prisoner remained the long-standing one of finding a suitable location.

Construction of prisons of cellular design continued during 1848 irrespective of parliamentary discussion, but one of the early acts of the new Constituent Assembly was to establish a committee to inquire into, as Barbaroux put it, 'the urgent need to find an answer to the issue of recidivists'.[1] It was a distinguished committee, chaired by Adolphe Thiers, with Léon Faucher as secretary and *rapporteur*.* Because of the wide range of interests involved, the members, seventeen in number, were drawn from parliamentary committees on the interior, finance, legislation, Algeria and the navy. The presentation of its report, dated December 1848, was first delayed as a result of Faucher joining the ministry, but was then permanently put aside by the turmoil of political events. Its

---

*Thiers played a leading role in French political life between the 1820s and the 1870s; he became the first president of the Third Republic in 1871. Faucher was especially noted for his writings on public affairs.

broad findings were, of course, widely known and they marked a pronounced swing in parliamentary opinion towards transportation. The committee unanimously condemned the existing prison system, and it also felt that solitary confinement had serious penological disadvantages as well as being too costly. It recommended that common criminals should be transported, beginning with *forçats* then extending to *réclusionnaires* and finally including those with more than a two-year sentence.

Although the committee's report was not submitted to the Assembly, it was claimed there that it 'left to the Government's care the formulation of the mass of legislative measures'. Moreover, since the committee was convinced of the urgency of the need to transport *forçats*, it stated that 'it would present on this part of the scheme a draft decree indicating a precise date for its accomplishment, and with the formal injunction to follow it up with a government regulation'.[2]

Normal parliamentary proceedings had initially been interrupted by the insurrection in Paris in June 1848. In turn, the arrest of some 15 000 insurgents created a new penal crisis. The government's response was embodied in a decree which introduced the term 'transportation' into French legislation for the first time. It applied to specific categories of insurgents and was differentiated from deportation: 'it is a political measure, it is a special measure'. The decree had specified that transportation should be to 'French possessions overseas, other than those of the Mediterranean',[3] but this posed real problems. In July 1849 Tocqueville, as Foreign Minister, consulted the British Ambassador in Paris concerning the British views on the establishment of a prison for the leaders of the insurrection on the protectorate of Tahiti. The ambassador was not impressed by the choice but, as he said, 'we went . . . over the names of many possible destinations for these convicts and Mon. de Tocqueville certainly gave very sufficient reasons against the adoption of any'. In the event, the British government opposed the proposal, and the lack of suitable sites meant that from January 1850 Algeria had to be used.[4]

Three months later the government moved to make the deportation of political prisoners a more general and a more active part of penal policy. From a restricted range of choices it had selected the Marquesas as the site for a penal colony for this type of prisoner. When the Bill was introduced to the Assembly it encountered strong opposition. The first speaker, Farconet, took up themes which continued to be used throughout the long debate. He pointed out that deportation had long been in the penal code, but only in a nominal way. It normally meant imprisonment in France, so that to actually apply it literally would be quite new: 'It must be concluded that deportation is not our way, that it does not fit in with our ideas'. As for the location:

> ... under a tropical sun, on a volcanic land, in a country half wild, half inhabited by savage tribes, by cannibal hordes, a trans-Atlantic Siberia [Interjection: 'If it is a Siberia, it is not tropical.'] ... this will be the punishment of indirect death, this will be the death penalty with longer agony; this will be more than the tomb, this will be hell. (Some noise.)

Farconet claimed that deportation would effectively mean serving the sentence in a prison in the Marquesas and, in particular, he attacked the retroactive clause in the legislation.[5]

Victor Hugo used equally emotional language: 'The death penalty is re-established in political matters'. Alphonse de Lamartine, on the other hand, said that while he opposed particular aspects of this Bill, he supported deportation in general; and he cited the English example: 'in New Holland, where is founded today under a gentle and moderate system of exile, a colony at the same time penal and agricultural'.[6] Opponents made a strong showing against the Bill, but the government, although it failed to gain support for the retroactive clause, carried the day in a close vote of 329 to 313. Such a limited area as was provided by the Marquesas could not accommodate a large penal establishment and only a small number of political deportees was sent there between 1851 and 1853.[7]

In the two years following the 1848 revolution significant steps had been taken to remove prisoners from France and place them in a penal establishment overseas. Legislation had been introduced only for political prisoners, but support for the transportation of common criminals was given a formal and decisive impetus by the President of France, Louis-Napoleon Bonaparte. In his message to parliament in November 1850, he indicated the direction which penal policy should take:

> Six thousand convicts, imprisoned in our *bagnes* at Toulon, Brest and Rochefort burden our budget with their great cost, become more and more corrupted and ceaselessly threaten our society. It seems possible to make the punishment of hard labour more effective, more morally-improving, less expensive, and, at the same time, more humane, by using it in the development of French colonisation. A draft bill will be presented on the question. (Murmurs of approval.)

In justification of the proposed change in penal policy, Louis-Napoleon emphasised the growth of crime and the necessity to deal with recidivism.[8]

The slowness of the government in drafting the legislation brought impatience from its supporters in parliament. In May 1851 two distinguished members, Boinvilliers and Dupetit-Thouars,* put forward their own proposal for penal change; it included 'suppression of the *bagnes*; the founding of a place of deportation for common law crimes; colonies for freed prisoners'. This proposal was referred to a parliamentary *commission d'initiative*, which reported back through a member, Grelier-Dufougeroux. In a lengthy survey of the subject he asserted that penal reform had been discussed for more than thirty years in France and that the existing system had not reduced crime, had not reformed prisoners and had not made society safer; moreover, two and a half years had elapsed, with nothing done, since the Thiers committee completed its report. Grelier-Dufougeroux continued by pointing out that since the system outlined in the

---

*Admiral Dupetit-Thouars, a member of the Admiralty Council, made an important Pacific voyage between 1836 and 1839. His official history of the voyage included a long examination of the convict system in New South Wales, and he recommended that France replace the *bagnes* with deportation. (see *Voyage autour du monde*, vol. 3, pp. 167–301) E.-E. Boinvilliers was a member of the Council of State.

current proposal provided for prisons for the deportees in the place of deportation, it would 'thus keep a character of intimidation that it has not always sufficiently had in England'. Although Grelier-Dufougeroux reminded members that the purpose of the *commission d'initiative* was ' to explain; it should not judge', it is clear that it had responded very sympathetically to the penal proposal.[9]

When, in July, the proposal came to the Assembly for discussion, the Minister for Justice, over some opposition, was able to obtain the agreement of the Assembly to refer it to the Council of State. The reason he advanced was that the government had the matter firmly in hand, and that this would be the quickest way to proceed. In fact, Louis-Napoleon's message of 1850 had been followed up most promptly in the same month with the preparation of draft legislation in the Justice ministry but, as the minister put it: 'This draft bill would have been submitted to you [but] problems were raised on the designation of the sites'. The Minister of the Navy felt he needed further advice on the selection of a site, so a committee was set up in his department. This committee's report, said the Justice Minister, had very recently been sent to himself and to the ministers of the Interior and the Navy. The three of them then 'joined together to submit on this matter a draft Bill to the assembly', but first the Bill had to be examined by the Council of State. The minister also said that he wanted to emphasise to his political opponents in the Assembly the 'enormous difficulties' in getting the project running:

> I have studied in depth in England the system of transportation to Botany-Bay; I have read the numerous debates which have been set in motion there, and I declare that from the point of view of retroactivity in penal matters, from the penitentiary point of view, there are some very great difficulties, independent of all questions of party, for there are no questions of party there.[10]

The committee to recommend on a penal site had been set up in February 1851, and was composed of naval officers and colonial officials. The scanty reports on New Caledonia, which was not claimed by any European power, were sufficient for some of the naval members to recommend that site, but they were opposed by the Director of Colonies, Mestro, and the officials. Arguments against New Caledonia included its tropical climate and its proximity to Australia, which would ensure the colony's loss in time of war with England. It would also be more costly than the alternative of Guiana: since it had not been settled it offered no supporting infrastructure, and the long voyage meant high transport costs. It has also been claimed that Mestro did not believe that a penal colony was viable, but since there had to be one to satisfy public opinion—and Louis-Napoleon—it was wiser to choose the cheaper alternative.[11] In its report to the government, the committee by a close vote (6 to 4) recommended Guiana. It had been able to conclude that, contrary to its history and reputation, Guiana was in fact very healthy and its resources were ideal for development. At the same time, the committee recommended that the government take action to ensure a French presence in New Caledonia.

It appeared that all the groundwork had been done to permit decisive action. But before any parliamentary steps could be taken on these recommendations, the political scene was again transformed by Louis-Napoleon's *coup d'état* of December 1851. What happened then in penal terms was almost a replay of the situation in 1848. There had been considerable popular resistance to the coup, and about 27 000 opponents of the regime were sentenced by special courts. Of these almost 12 000 were sent under varying conditions to Algeria, and 239, considered the most dangerous, to a specially created penal colony in Guiana.[12]

Following the coup, the Legislative Assembly became the 'Corps législatif', its powers were substantially reduced and it became subservient to the wishes of Napoleon.* Even before its first meeting in March 1852, action was taken to carry out his wish, as expressed in his message of November 1850, for the commencement of transportation of *forçats*. In a formal report to Napoleon, Théodore Ducos, the Minister of the Navy and Colonies, first

---

*Its proceedings could not be published verbatim, but only in the form of minutes approved by its president. At the same time an upper house, the Senate, was also created.

outlined the findings of the 1851 committee; then, after admitting there was no legal provision to deport *forçats*, he went on to state how this problem had been overcome, what had subsequently been done and the results obtained:

> Under the constitution you have the right to show mercy. It has therefore been lawful for you to mitigate the required measures which apply to the *forçats* in the *bagnes* and to outline the circumstances by which this alleviation would be obtained.
>
> By your order, I have had some registers opened in the *bagnes* of Brest, Rochefort and Toulon, in which the convicts, after having been acquainted with the new regime to which they must be subjected in French Guiana, have been invited freely and voluntarily to enter their names.
>
> There are about three thousand of them who, in the first hours, have asked spontaneously to leave the *bagnes* and to be deported. This number, undoubtedly destined to grow, is already more than sufficient to satisfy all the needs of the moment.[13]

To obtain this enthusiastic response the *forçats* had been promised a dramatic change in the conditions of their imprisonment. No longer would they be attached in pairs, subject to the ball and chain, and chained at night; more positively, good behaviour would bring the grant of significant freedom.[14]

In his report Ducos appears to have emphasised colonial development rather than punishment and reformation. In his 1850 message Napoleon had said that transportation would 'make the punishment of "hard labour" more efficacious, more morally improving, less expensive and at the same time more humane, by using it for the advancement of French colonisation'. When Ducos repeated this statement—and it was italicised in *Moniteur*—the words 'more morally improving' and 'more humane' were omitted.* All that was now required was a decree by Napoleon. This was issued on 27 March 1852, the first article stating:

---

*A member of the 1851 committee quite explicitly stated that the purpose of the transportation was to provide a workforce to replace the slaves who had been freed in 1848. (C.-O Barbaroux, *De la transportation*, pp. 202–4)

> Hard labour convicts, now detained in the *bagnes* and who will be sent to French Guiana to undergo their punishment, will be employed there in the work of colonisation, of cultivation, of exploitation of the forests and in any other works of public utility.[15]

The dispatch of the transportees took place immediately.

Although transportation had begun, it was by decree and on a voluntary basis. Its full accomplishment required more general legislation and the removal of choice from the convicts. In the event, the Corps législatif set up a committee to examine the draft Bill in relation to the execution of the punishment of hard labour, and it reported back its deliberations through its spokesman, Rudel du Miral, in May 1853. Naturally, the committee favoured transportation, but it is clear that it felt such a striking change in penal legislation required extensive justification.[16]

Du Miral began by asserting that crime, especially by recidivists, was increasing; indeed the return to an honest life by freed convicts was not made easy in France because of their identification and supervision. Some method of dealing with crime, other than simply the harshness of the punishment, had to be found. He then examined the history of the attempts in France to introduce transportation, before turning to the new draft Bill:

> Two principal ideas dominate it: the performance of forced labour outside the continental territory: the requirement of permanent residence in the penal colonies, even after the punishment has been completed, for all those condemned to more than eight years, and, for those with less than eight years, of a residence equal to the length of their punishment.[17]

It was this limitation on the return of transportees that du Miral underlined as 'the truly new arrangement of the project, it is without precedents in our legislation, and we do not know of any example of it in foreign legislation'. In his view, 'the new punishment is a mixed punishment, which, without losing its original character of hard labour, draws at the same time on French deportation and on British transportation'.[18] Opponents he said, criticised this legislation as an 'ill-timed' borrowing from England,

and drew for their own purposes on the history of English transportation. But in this history, du Miral went on, 'we ourselves will find there useful information, important evidence'. With this in mind, he proceeded to make a lengthy survey of the subject. It was true that there had been considerable problems in Australia in the early years, but this was principally because convicts made up too large a proportion of the population. Moreover, a solution had been provided by free migration, so that the period 1820–34 was one of 'remarkable prosperity'; then, the convict system was based on '*assignment* . . . It was, in reality, for the convicts, a type of *compulsory domestic service*, or mitigated slavery'. Du Miral reiterated that this system was not entirely satisfactory, partly because of the power over the convicts that was given to their masters, but also because it was not sufficiently intimidatory: 'Nothing would better show these serious difficulties than the inconsistency and variety of the measures which were then successively proposed, tried, abandoned'.[19] He then outlined the British legislation and the Australian experience up to 1849 when the existing system had been introduced. This consisted, he said, first of the solitary cellular regime at Pentonville, then of severe discipline with work in common at Portland, and finally of transportation to Australia until the expiration of the sentence. How had this system turned out?

> The results obtained up to the present by this new method are excellent. They are the result of an ingenious and expert combination of the various elements through which humanity is able to arrange with the most success for the improvement of the guilty: isolation, work, discipline, professional and moral education, and above all religious instruction.[20]

It was true that as colonies developed they rejected the convict system with distaste, as had happened in the United States and later in New South Wales. It was now the turn of Van Diemen's Land. But the new Australian colonies in the west were asking for convicts, and this succession of demands was not an 'insuperable obstacle'. In du Miral's view the English system did now succeed in intimidating, but the new French system would be 'incontestably superior, by reason of the element of perpetuity that it includes and that the English law does not possess'. What of the criticism that convicts were bad colonising material? Du Miral's reply was that colonising was only a secondary objective of transportation. In any case:

> In what way have several of the most flourishing colonies of the English realm begun? Through transportation ... It can be said, with truth, that, since the beginning of the last century, the transportees have been the pioneers of civilisation; it will be able to be said again more strongly, now that the transportee will be given over to colonising only after an improving atonement.[21]

As far as the location of the French penal colony was concerned, du Miral pointed out that the government had already chosen French Guiana, and that some members of his committee thought it ideal for both colonisation and intimidation; they also thought that the mortality rate there was not exceptionally high. He, however, was more cautious:

> The majority of your committee, without gainsaying any of these appreciations or hopes, has thought that we should confine ourselves with greater reserve; that the question was not put to us, and that it would be inopportune to give so firm an opinion without being asked.[22]

Given the composition and powers of the Corps législatif, discussion of the draft Bill when it was introduced in May 1854 was inevitably largely formal. Only one member, Louis-François Lélut, who was also the first speaker, put forward any opposing arguments. He believed that on all counts the project was misguided: the punishment aspect could be dealt with by making the regime in the *bagnes* more severe. As for the claim that transportation had the benefit of excluding freed *forçats* from France, Lélut felt that their number was so small in relation to the total number of criminals as to be of little significance. Referring to the question of colonisation, Lélut thought it 'the biggest mistake of the project'. Convicts alone were unsatisfactory material for establishing a society: 'There is no need, to demonstrate this, by citing the example of England, the evidence of common sense is sufficient'.[23] Finally, he drew attention to the 'dangerous climate' of Guiana.

Lélut's opposition elicited two official replies. Du Miral emphasised the severity of transportation as a punishment and stated that *forçats* were the most dangerous of all convicts. He also said that although colonisation was not the principal aim of the project, nevertheless:

> ... one is strongly forced to recognise that England has created colonies by means of transportation; the same result will be obtained by France, provided that honest settlers come to take the place of the *forçats*.[24]

The second response was from Mestro, now *commissaire du gouvernement*. He believed it his duty to report on what had happened in Guiana in the two years since the convict volunteers had been sent there. His response was, in fact, somewhat muted: mortality was not as high as claimed, 'but still too high'; some material progress had been made, and there was some evidence of moral improvement. Moreover, successful colonisation would not depend entirely on *forçats* or on white settlers:

> But there are blacks in Guiana, and immigration, which has become today the hope of all colonies, especially Indian and Chinese immigration, will introduce there some varied elements of population to supplement the white race.

When Mestro also mentioned that the government had New Caledonia in reserve as a site for a penal colony, Lélut commented: 'This latter locality is not yet well known, but Guiana is only too well known'.[25]

Five more speakers followed. All supported the Bill and the government's view on such matters as the deterrent effect of transportation, the healthiness of the climate in Guiana and the success of English transportation. With a massive majority—225 votes to 3—the legislation was passed which ensured the introduction of transportation into French law.

10
The Navy and New Caledonia

During this whole period, the navy continued to promote the cause of penal colonies. As in the past, it was driven by two main motives: the removal of its responsibilities for the *bagnes*, and the enhancement of the naval role that colonies would make necessary. In 1846, for instance, the Minister of the Navy, Portal, observed:

> The *forçats* now number almost 12,000. It is a frightful burden for the navy. Not only do they cost a lot, but they corrupt the population of our arsenals. And it takes whatever there is of morality and action in the administration of the navy to avoid the ruin of our stores and dockyards. A committee has been appointed to see if there would not be some means of employing them in the interior or of deporting them, where they could be given the hope of a better future. Up till now, a suitable place for deportation has not been found. Whatever may come of these plans, I have had the position of these wretches examined and it appears by comparing it with that of these workmen that their condition has been made too pleasant.[1]

In July 1851, Pariset, Controller in Chief of the Navy combined an attack on the *bagnes* with vigorous advocacy for a penal colony in a 77-page monograph. He began, very diplomatically, with a quotation from Napoleon I as the epigraph:

> It is impossible that this punishment [deportation] be not allowed, since it is at the same time useful and humane: between it and prison, there is no difference, other than that it opens a more spacious and commodious prison to the condemned. There should be no hesitation in peopling a new world by purging the old.

His first footnote then quoted the statement on the necessity for transportation made by Napoleon III in November 1850 (see p. 158).

Having identified such important support, Pariset devoted the first 37 pages of his work to the problems of imprisonment in *bagnes* and also under the Philadelphia system. The remaining section was given over to an examination of transportation to Australia. In it he first reviewed carefully the problems found in Australia in the early period, and suggested that France could meet them by such methods as ensuring the administration was in the hands of civilians, rotating the military garrison, establishing a police force, maintaining equality in the numbers of men and women, and transporting smaller numbers of convicts. But would transportation intimidate? In reply, Pariset, like many others, catalogued the increasingly stern measures introduced in Australia and the pre-transportation gaol sentence adopted in England. He believed these measures had been successful, but in contrast to the position in England there would be an additional deterrent in France:

> Everyone is aware of how little is known in our provinces about the sea and colonies. There just the fact of deportation, with the prohibition on return to the continental territory for a set period would, in my opinion, be a great incentive to stop criminals.[2]

As for finding a suitable site, Pariset criticised the strict criteria that the opponents of transportation had attempted to impose. All that was needed was somewhere reasonable enough for convicts to continue to reside there when their sentences were complete.

Throughout, Pariset showed his awareness of, and drew on, a wide range of sources. His evidence for the economic success of New South Wales, and for the reformation of convicts that had taken place, was obtained mainly from the 1836 work of Montgomery Martin. He concluded with the wish that his notes would help to 'show that with the example of England, we can succeed, by bringing to the accomplishment the same resolve and the same determination'.[3]

Naval exploration in the Pacific had resulted in official visits to New Caledonia and, with a missionary presence temporarily established there, France flirted with the possibility of taking possession in the early 1840s. However, only limited and often contradictory information was available to the committees on transportation at the end of the decade on the island's suitability as a site for a penal colony. The 1848 committee which met again in 1849 was able to recommend the Marquesas for political deportees but, because it believed that a larger site was needed for common criminals, it urged further exploratory voyages. The Navy Minister decided that New Caledonia warranted further attention and, acting on secret orders, d'Harcourt on the *Alcmène* began a careful investigation of the island in September 1850. It is a measure of French desperation that even without more information the Mackau committee in 1851 only narrowly decided against New Caledonia as a penal site, although it made clear it felt a French presence was required there. Very encouraging reports from the *Alcmène* arrived in April 1852 and, judging that in the current international situation Britain would not respond unfavourably, the navy was ordered to take possession.[4] When, in 1853, the French flag was raised in New Caledonia, the act was officially justified solely on penal grounds:

> The government had long wished to possess overseas some places which could, if needed, receive its penal settlements.
> New Caledonia met all the desired conditions.[5]

A contemporary French historian caught the mood of the times when he wrote that New Caledonia was 'destined to become, as a maritime station or a penal colony, the Sydney of France in Oceania.[6]

It should be said that Sydney did not welcome this emulation. One of a number of editorials in the *Sydney Morning Herald* on this subject complained:

> No sooner, therefore, have we got rid of British convictism, than we are threatened with French convictism. An unlimited collection of Parisian brigands within a short and easy voyage from our northern coasts, will tend as little to the security and happiness of the colonists as a similar collection of English outcasts in Van Diemen's Land.
> This, at least, ought not to be permitted.[7]

10 The Navy and New Caledonia

The manner in which transportation began at the beginning of 1852 suggests that it resulted from the personal decision of Louis-Napoleon. He strongly favoured colonial expansion and his belief in the use of convicts for development was part of a Bonaparte heritage. He made his views plain in his message to parliament in November 1850, and the action on transportation was one of his earliest acts following his coup of December 1851. Moreover, at that time his personal authority was at its height. But in a more general way, events following the insurrection in Paris in 1848 had favoured transportation: conservative forces were strengthened and it was thought necessary to rid the country of a large number of dangerous insurgents. Crime remained a subject of great concern, and there was considerable doubt about the results obtained by penitentiaries, which were also very costly. The obsession with the role of recidivists and the depraved nature of the *forçats* continued. The navy and colonial expansionists endorsed the action. In other words, it was a popular measure and, as it was presented, it was even popular with the *forçats*. Louis-Napoleon was thus able to tap a sentiment, widespread in the general public, endorsed by many penologists and supported by the military. This sentiment had been developed as a coherent argument over the years by its supporters, who depended heavily on their assessment of the success of Botany Bay. The particular difficulty that they had faced was the lack of a suitable location for a penal colony. Louis-Napoleon broke this log-jam and, using the endorsement by his committee of French Guiana, nominated a site which had so often been considered inappropriate for this purpose.

Epilogue

There had been general acceptance in French discussions of Botany Bay that the early years had been disastrous. Along with admiration for the dash and daring behind the original landing went strong criticism of the lack of planning and foresight. It was agreed that France could learn from Britain's mistakes and could do better. The opportunity came in French Guiana early in the 1850s. This country had been the site of a large-scale attempt at colonisation by France in 1763, but such was the onslaught of disease that the survivors had to be rescued and repatriated: of the 12 000 settlers only 3000 survived. Since then, development had been slight, and it retained a sinister reputation for its effect on the health of native Frenchmen. Blosseville commented on the deaths of many political deportees there in the 1790s: 'For a long time the name of Sinamary will recall only unhappy memories'.* Given the very restricted choice facing France, it was inevitable that French Guiana's name should keep recurring as a possible site for a penal colony; equally there were as many warnings against its use. Nevertheless, it was the first choice of the committee set up in 1851 to recommend on the location of a penal colony, and volunteer *forçats* were rushed there in 1852. They were welcomed by the new governor:

> My friends, there is not under the sun any more beautiful, any richer country than this. It is yours. Prince Louis-Napoleon has sent me to ensure you share it. You are going to go ashore, work, prepare the ground, erect some huts. During that time, I shall survey

---

*Sinamary was a location in French Guiana where the political deportees were held. (E. de Blosseville, *Histoire des colonies pénales*, p. 25)

Epilogue

the colony. I shall select in the most charming sites, the most fertile districts; then these lands cultivated in common will be shared between the most worthy.[1]

In the event, the transportation of convicts to Guiana was a tragedy. To begin with, the navy was not ready. Looking back in 1867, the Minister of the Navy and Colonies wrote:

> When transportation took place, fifteen years ago, under French public law, it was to the department of the navy that the care of applying this new penal regime fell. The department was not prepared for this mission; hesitations, tentative procedures were therefore inevitable, and during the initial period the Administration was obliged, in the very interest of the work entrusted to it by fate, to refrain from any appreciation which could give rise to thoughtless fears or premature hopes. Although all the obstacles are not yet overcome, it can now desist from this caution.[2]

The *forçats* were first located on the Salut (Salvation!) islands off Guiana's coast,* and there dysentry and typhoid swept though them. Attempts to begin the development of sites on the mainland were defeated by a high death rate, which averaged 12 per cent per annum between 1853 and 1860; peaks of 24 per cent in 1855 and 26 per cent in 1856 were the result of yellow fever.[3] Two years after the dispatch of the first convicts Mestro, *commissaire du gouvernement*, admitted that mortality was 'still too high', but he went on to claim that people had been too optimistic, and that now convoys of convicts were being sent less frequently and a stricter discipline had been imposed. Moreover, he felt that there were hopeful signs of moral improvement:

> The transportees, even those who sometimes appeared to regret having preferred transportation to the *bagnes*, declare, in their letters to their families, letters which are sent open, that they find, in order to bear their sufferings, new strengths in this thought that they have before them a future that they could not hope for in France.[4]

---

*The three islands of the group include the notorious Devil's Island.

At the same time Mestro felt it necessary to spell out that New Caledonia was there as an alternative if needed. And although investment and prestige were committed in Guiana, this option was soon being closely considered. As we have seen, a major problem was the lack of knowledge about New Caledonia and the absence of any infrastructure there. In 1855 the governor of French possessions in Oceania was not prepared to forecast a date when the island would be ready to receive convicts:

> I believe it is my duty to express the hope that there is not too much haste in beginning [deportation]; we need time to study the country more thoroughly, to clear the land, to obtain some influence over the miserable tribes who inhabit it; without that, we would risk compromising the success of this great operation.[5]

In 1857, at the opening of parliament, the Emperor himself formally recognised the extent of the failure in Guiana:

> A wholly philanthropic thought induced the government to transfer the *bagnes* to Guiana. Unhappily, yellow fever, foreign to that country for fifty years, has come to halt the progress of colonisation. A plan designed to transfer these establishments to Africa or elsewhere is being worked out.

The Emperor mentioned Africa, but the committee he had set up to report on the question recommended New Caledonia. In the ultimate analysis no other place was satisfactory, and New Caledonia had to be the choice.* Even the Empress threw her weight behind it. She wrote to the naval minister:

> Would it not be possible to send the convicts . . . to New Caledonia where the climate is magnificent, the soil fertile, and which lacks population. There they could be employed on public works and in other labour from which they could keep the produce.[6]

Little had changed in New Caledonia since the 1855 assessment, and it was not until 1863 that it was formally declared a site for transportation and the systematic shipments of convicts began. In

---

* One group that favoured the transfer to New Caledonia was the convicts in Guiana.

1867 it became the only destination for transported hard-labour prisoners from continental France; Guiana was reserved for convicts from the French colonies who, it was claimed, could cope better with the climate.

During this period French legislators remained very conscious of the Australian example. One historian wrote of the legislation in 1854 that introduced transportation: 'One should however object to it, as a system employed at the beginning in Australia, by which it is too inspired since it has followed it even in its flaws'. The legislation specified that convicts were to be employed 'in the most laborious work of colonisation and in all other works of public utility'. Good conduct and repentance could bring assignment to private employment or even a grant of land. Indeed, it was claimed that the use of the term *assignation* (assignment) was a borrowing from the Australian experience.[7]

More generally, in 1856 a semi-official article drew attention to the recent Australian experience. It began:

> The following references, extracts from official correspondence relating to transportation to Australia and submitted to the English parliament in May 1854, have an opportuneness that we do not need to point out.*

Publications discussing the example of the Australian penal experience continued to appear. Perhaps the most interesting was that of Ernest de Blosseville who, in 1859, brought out a new edition of his 1831 history of Australia, which extended the terminating date of his original work to 1857. Faivre reports that he was congratulated by Napoleon III for having 'prepared opinion for the organisation of transportation to New Caledonia'.[8]

European interest in the usefulness of penal colonies continued, even extending into the twentieth century. A number of international conferences on penology examined the results achieved by Britain and France. When Germany obtained colonies there

---

*It is interesting that one of the main subjects of the official correspondence referred to was the discontinuance of transportation to Van Diemen's Land. ('De la transportation et de la discipline des convicts dans les colonies de l'Australie', *Revue coloniale*, vol. 15, pp. 141–54)

was strong support for their penal use.⁹ Proposals in Britain to resume large-scale transportation were defeated. The *Economist* in 1862 poured scorn on the idea, arguing that, to be a punishment, transportation would have to be to a most unattractive destination—like French Guiana:

> Finally, the proposed penal settlement *might* be so located that the convicts would be frozen in winter and broiled in summer; for Great Britain has possessions both in the Tropics and in the Arctic Circle. They might be placed where life itself would be necessarily short, and necessarily wretched while it lasted,—at the Mouth of the Niger, or on the ice-bound coast of Greenland or Labrador. We *might* thus quietly slay our convicted ruffians as France is said to slay her's at Cayenne. But what Minister would venture to recommend the establishment of such a colony? What Parliament would sanction it? What decent governor or gaolers, or soldiers would go out to manage it?—for they must die as well as the convicts, and nearly as fast,—and be nearly as miserable while they lived. Lastly, how much would such a settlement cost in comparison with the establishments at Dartmoor, Portland, or Chatham? And why not face the facts, and hang our desperate criminals at once? It would be more honest, more merciful, as decent and far cheaper.¹⁰

Although the experience of the first years in New Caledonia was not nearly as bad as that in Guiana, in 1867 the Minister of the Navy and Colonies still had to draw what solace he could from Australian history:

> To sum up, if the goal assigned to the efforts of the French administration has not been completely attained, if we have gone through some painful trials, if the distance which separates us from success still seems great, one finds at least, in the history of English transportation, compared to that of the first years of French transportation, more of an argument to justify the past of the latter and more of a reason to conjecture favourably about its future.¹¹

In fact the future turned out badly. Transportation to New Caledonia ceased in 1896 but continued to French Guiana until 1938. In all some 104 000 prisoners were consigned to these two colonies—a little less than two-thirds of the Australian number. For those French supporters of transportation whose principal aim was to rid France of criminals, the venture could be judged a success. To the extent that there was a brutal regime in the penal colonies for the entire period, the system maintained one important aspect of the Australian experience. Whether it succeeded as a deterrent to crime in France is another matter. But many of those who had argued for transportation had done so in the hope that a penal colony would develop along the lines of their vision of Botany Bay—a place where freed convicts lived reformed lives in a community expanding with free migration and becoming a centre of trade and of strategic importance. Their hopes were dashed entirely. For one thing, the French convicts did not provide a demographic base for an increasing population. A leading French criticism of the Australian experience was the lack of gender balance—only some 15 per cent of the convicts were female. But under French law women convicted of certain crimes were given a choice of where to spend their sentence; only a small number, 2 per cent of all transportees, chose to leave France. There were other factors that limited the development of any significant or viable convict-based community, but in one major respect the whole operation was doomed from the start: it had proved impossible to find a penal site with anything like the economic potential of the Australian settlements. A French Botany Bay proved to be a mirage, a false lure.

Transportation from France finally ended in 1938, 150 years after the original stimulus to this French penal enterprise—the landing of the first convicts at Botany Bay. France turned its back on this aspect of its penal past, and in the same year Australia took a similar step. Official celebrations in Sydney for the sesquicentenary of the beginning of the British settlement of Australia eschewed any reference to the presence of those same convicts, who had figured so prominently in French thinking on crime and punishment for so long.

Abbreviations

AJCP	Australian Joint Copying Project
AM	Archives de la marine
AMC	*Annales maritimes et coloniales*
AN	Archives nationales
AN, SO-M	Archives nationales, section d'outre-mer
AP	*Archives parlementaires*
BN	Bibliothèque nationale
BN, MNAF	Bibliothèque nationale, manuscrits, nouvelles acquisitions françaises
CO	Colonial Office
FO	Foreign Office
HRA	*Historical Records of Australia*
Moniteur	*Le Moniteur universel*
OC	*Œuvres complètes* (Alexis de Tocqueville)
PP	*Parliamentary Papers*

Notes

1 SUPPORT FOR A PENAL COLONY

[1] L.-A. de Bougainville, *Voyage autour du monde, par la frégate du Roi La Boudeuse*. See also J.-E. Martin-Allanic, *Bougainville navigateur et les découvertes de son temps*, vol. 2, chs 35 and 37, for Bougainville's reception in Paris.

[2] See C. Gaziello, *L'expédition de Lapérouse 1785–1788*, esp. pp. 38–41 and 51–4; also Alan Frost, *Convicts and Empire*, esp. p. 96.

[3] J. White, *Voyage à la Nouvelle Galles du Sud, à Botany Bay, au Port Jackson, en 1787, 1788, 1789*, pp. x–xi.

[4] P.-E. Lémontey, *Éloge de Jacques Cook* . . ., p. 42.

[5] F. Péron, *Voyage de découvertes aux terres australes*, vol. 1, pp. 368, 375–6.

[6] Ibid., vol. 2, pp. 393–427.

[7] See, for example, P. O'Brien, *The Promise of Punishment*, pp. 13–20.

[8] A. Zysberg, 'Politiques du bagne (1820–1850)', p. 277.

[9] G. Wright, *Between the Guillotine and Liberty*, p. 6.

[10] *AP*, 23 May 1791, p. 330; 3 June 1791, p. 724.

[11] A. C. Thibadeau, *Bonaparte and the Consulate*, p. 180.

[12] G. Wright, *Between the Guillotine and Liberty*, p. 6.

[13] J. Valette, 'Le bagne de Rochefort, 1815–52', esp. pp. 206–15.

[14] G. Wright, *Between the Guillotine and Liberty*, p. 6. Also A. Zysberg, 'Politiques du bagne', pp. 270–8.

[15] C. Duprat, 'Punir et guérir', esp. pp. 66–71.

[16] *AP*, 11 Nov. 1831, p. 481.

[17] Forestier, 'Mémoire sur le choix d'un lieu de déportation', 14 Oct. 1816.

[18] AN, SO-M, H1, pièces 2, 3, 5, 6, 7.

[19] Hyde de Neuville (Minister of the Navy and Colonies), 'Rapport au Roi', p. 692.

[20] E. de Blosseville, *Histoire de la colonisation pénale*, vol. 2, p. 231.

[21] AN, SO-M, H1, 'Déportation des condamnés: Question générale'; this file holds a forty-page translation from the English by M. Roux of the Report of the Select Committee on Transportation, November 1817; separately in H1 is a several-hundred-page translation from the minutes of the 1812 committee on transportation.

[22] AN, SO-M, H1, pièce 3.

[23] Hyde de Neuville, 'Rapport au Roi', p. 692 (he says the committee was inclined to favour deportation for those sentenced in the future to ten or more years hard labour).
[24] AN, SO-M, H1, 'Déportation des condamnés: Question générale'; Forestier, '1er rapport à la Commission', 10 Feb. 1819.
[25] AN, SO-M, H1, pièce 3.
[26] Forestier, '1er rapport à la Commission', 10 Feb. 1819.
[27] L. R. Marchant, *France Australe*, p. 229 (for a discussion of the committee's meeting, see pp. 227–9).
[28] AN, SO-M, H1, letter, 30 Dec. 1819, from the Administrator to the Minister of the Navy and Colonies; H2, B. de Basterot, 'Observations sur la déportation', 24 Jan. 1830.
[29] AN, SO-M, H1. Forestier, memorandum to the Minister of the Navy and Colonies, 21 July 1821 (he may have been referring to the dramatic change in government in February 1820 as the cause for the deflection of interest).
[30] See, for example, his autobiographical account, *Journal d'un déporté non-jugé*.
[31] *AP*, 30 Mar. 1819, p. 488; 6 Apr. 1819, pp. 521–2.
[32] Ibid., 22 Apr. 1819, pp. 752, 753.
[33] Ibid., p. 754.
[34] Ibid., p. 755.
[35] Ibid., 27 Apr. 1819, pp. 57–8.
[36] Ibid., pp. 58–9.
[37] Ibid., p. 59.
[38] Ibid., p. 60.
[39] Ibid.
[40] Ibid., 1 May 1819, pp. 139, 141. The minister, Decazes, commanded considerable power.
[41] H. G. Bennet, *Letter to Viscount Sidmouth*. A. G. L. Shaw describes Bennet's writing as 'vitriolic' and based on Collin's *Account* of some twenty years earlier. *Convicts and the Colonies*, p. 102.
[42] E. de Blosseville, *Histoire des colonies pénales*, pp. 36–7.
[43] *AMC*, part 2, vol.1, 1828, p. 169.
[44] F. Barbé-Marbois, *Observations sur les votes*, p. 4.
[45] M. Alhoy, *Les bagnes*, pp. 227, 228. He was drawing on the work of Charles Lucas. See pp. 44–5.
[46] See, for example, the discussion in F. Barbé-Marbois, *Observations sur les votes*, and in *AMC*, passim.
[47] J. Arago, *Promenade autour du monde*, vol. 2, pp. 262–3, 265, 292.
[48] Hyde de Neuville, 'Rapport au Roi', p. 693.
[49] J.-F.-T. Ginouvier, *Le Botany-Bey français*, pp. 9, 13, 17. Ginouvier published extensively on a variety of topics, including French prisons. See Quérard, *La France littéraire*, vol. 3, 1829, p. 360.
[50] Benoiston de Chateaneuf, *De la colonisation*, pp. 5, 10.
[51] W. C. Wentworth, *A Statistical Account of the British Settlements in Australasia*. The article in the *Revue britannique* (a journal devoted to translating English material), no. 6, Dec. 1825, pp. 285–325, was entitled 'Établissemens anglais dans les terres australes ou Australie'.

[52] Benoiston de Chateauneuf, *De la colonisation*, pp. 19, 54.
[53] Hyde de Neuville, 'Rapport au Roi', pp. 693–7.
[54] Quentin, *Mémoire*, pp. 6, 8–9, 10.
[55] *AP*, 9 May 1821, pp. 324–5; 26 June 1821, pp. 376, 377.
[56] Ibid., 27 Apr. 1825, p. 196.
[57] Ibid., 1 May 1826, p. 567.
[58] Ibid.
[59] Du Hamel was described as a 'naval authority' by G. Wright, *Between the Guillotine and Liberty*, p. 232, n. 69.
[60] *AP*, 6 June, 1826, pp. 459–60.
[61] Ibid., p. 460.
[62] Ibid.
[63] Ibid., 6 June, 1826, p. 464.
[64] L. R. Marchant, *France Australe*, p. 245.
[65] Governor Darling to Major Lockyer, 4 Nov. 1826, *HRA*, ser. 1, vol. 12, p. 701.
[66] R. P. Lesson, *Notice historique sur l'amiral Dumont d'Urville*, p. 120, quoted in J. Dunmore, *French Explorers in the Pacific*, vol. 2, p. 111.
[67] J. de Blosseville, 'Projet d'une colonie pénale', 'Suite', 1 July 1829.
[68] E. de Blosseville, *Jules de Blosseville*, p. 52.
[69] J. de Blosseville, 'Projet d'une colonie pénale', 30 Jan. 1826.
[70] Ibid.
[71] Ibid.
[72] Ibid.
[73] J. Dunmore, *French Explorers*, vol. 2, pp. 178–80.
[74] AM, BB4, 1002. 'Voyage de l'Astrolabe—Minutes, No. 83, Instructions', 8 April 1826 to Dumont d'Urville, pp. 7–8, 9.
[75] AN, SO-M, H2, pièce 19. Confidential letter to 'Le Ministre de la Marine et des Colonies' from 'Le Directeur de la Police, Franchet d'Esperey', 8 May 1827.
[76] Ibid., 'Rapport'.

2 EMERGING OPPOSITION IN THE 1820S

[1] C. Duprat, 'Punir et guérir', pp. 65, 74. See also G. Wright, *Between the Guillotine and Liberty*, p. 57.
[2] 'Souvenirs d'un déporté à la Nouvelle-Galles du sud'. The author's name was given simply as 'Mellish'. The English source was the *London Magazine*, vol. 2, 1825, where the article was entitled 'A Convict's Recollections of New South Wales. Written by himself'. The author's manuscript was entitled 'Mellish's Book of Botany Bay'.
[3] *Du système pénitentiaire en Europe et aux États-Unis*, vol. 2, p. 268.
[4] Cited in A. Lepelletier de la Sarthe, *Système pénitentiaire*, p. 280.
[5] *AP*, Chambre des Pairs, 6 Apr. 1819, p. 524.
[6] F. Barbé-Marbois, *Observations sur les votes*, pp. 9, 13.
[7] Ibid., pp. 25, 27.
[8] Ibid., pp. 32, 33.

[9] Ibid., pp. 49, 53.
[10] Ibid., pp. 62, 63.
[11] AN, SO-M, H57; *AMC*, vol. 1, 1828, p. 169.
[12] Mortemart de Boisse, *Mémoire sur la déportation des forçats* ... There are several references in naval files identifying the author.
[13] Ibid., pp. 13–14, 16.
[14] 'Observations sur la déportation'. A letter from Basterot on the files accompanying this document thanks Baron d'Haussez, Ministre Secrétaire d'État in the Department of the Navy and Colonies for sending it to the Dauphin.

3 THE GREAT PARLIAMENTARY DEBATE, 1831

[1] Hyde de Neuville, *Rapport au Roi*, pp. 690–7.
[2] *AP*, 11 Nov. 1831. The relevant section, from which detailed quotation is made, is pp. 481–3.
[3] *AP*, 23 Nov. 1831, p. 10.
[4] Ibid., 24 Nov. 1831. The relevant section of the debate, from which detailed quotation is made, is on pp. 25–39.
[5] For a discussion of the political situation in 1830–31, see H. A. C. Collingham, *The July Monarchy*, esp. chs 1–7.

4 THE FIRST HISTORY OF AUSTRALIA

[1] S. Macintyre, 'The writing of Australian history', ch. 1 in D. H. Borchardt (ed.), *Australians: A Guide to Sources*.
[2] W. C. Wentworth, *A Statistical, Historical, and Political Description of the Colony of New South Wales*. J. West, *The History of Tasmania*.
[3] S. Macintyre, 'The writing of Australian history', p. 8.
[4] Ibid., p. 9.
[5] Blosseville, *Histoire des colonies pénales*, pp. 537–8. He is referring to David Collins, *An Account of the English Colony in New South Wales*; in Blosseville's bibliography only the abridged edition (London, 1804) is cited.
[6] Ibid., p. 570.
[7] This publication is mentioned by M. G. Dubosc in his obituary of Blosseville, *Rouen en 1886, l'année rouennaise*, p. 175.
[8] L. Passy, *Le marquis de Blosseville*, p. 161; Blosseville, *Histoire de la colonisation pénale*, pp. iii–iv.
[9] Blosseville, *Histoire des colonies pénales*, p. 3. He noted that the public used the term 'Botany Bay'.
[10] Ibid., p. 19.
[11] The quotation is from a submission made by G. de Beaumont and A. de Tocqueville to the French government for permission to inspect and report on American penitentiaries. See their '*Note sur le système pénitentiaire*' in *OC*, vol. 1, p. 51.

[12] Blosseville, *Histoire des colonies pénales*, pp. 5–6, 65.
[13] Ibid., pp. 6–7, 8.
[14] Ibid., p. 125.
[15] Ibid., p. 138.
[16] Ibid., p. 157.
[17] Ibid., p. 186.
[18] Ibid., p. 316.
[19] Ibid., pp. 427–8. 'Sentimental' is used in the early nineteenth-century sense of promoting agreeable feelings.
[20] Ibid., p. 409.
[21] Ibid., pp. 411–12.
[22] Ibid., pp. 430, 431.
[23] Ibid., pp. 422, 423–4.
[24] M. G. Dubosc, *Rouen en 1886*, p. 175.
[25] Blosseville, *Histoire de la colonisation pénale*, pp. iv–v.
[26] Quoted in M. G. Dubosc, *Rouen en 1886*, p. 175.
[27] *AMC*, vol. 2, 1837, pp. 589, 594, 595.
[28] For a discussion of this journal, see W. E. Houghton (ed.), *The Wellesley Index to Victorian Periodicals 1824–1900*, p. 129ff.
[29] *Foreign Quarterly Review*, pp. 423–4.
[30] Blosseville, *Histoire de la colonisation pénale*, pp. iv–v.
[31] Blosseville, *Histoire des colonies pénales*, pp. 510–11. Blosseville believed that even reformed ex-prisoners were not accepted by society, so that almost inevitably they finished up in the poor house.
[32] L. Passy, *Le marquis de Blosseville*, p. 160.
[33] *OC*, vol.1, p. 21. The comment is made by the editor of the work, Michelle Perrot.
[34] Ibid., vol. 2, pp. 62–3.
[35] Ibid., vol. 1, p. 269. The original work is *Système pénitentiaire aux États-Unis*.
[36] Arthur Marwick, *The Nature of History*, p. 19.
[37] Blosseville, *Histoire des colonies pénales*, pp. 11–13.

5 TOCQUEVILLE AND AUSTRALIA

[1] *OC*, vol. 1, p. 7. I wish to acknowledge my debt to the scholarly introduction of Michelle Perrot.
[2] *On the Penitentiary System in the United States* (1833).
[3] *OC*, vol. 1, p. 64.
[4] Blosseville, *Histoire des colonies pénales*.
[5] *OC*, vol. 2, p. 63.
[6] *On the Penitentiary System* (1964), p. 181.
[7] *OC*, vol. 1, p. 153, n. 3.
[8] Ibid., p. 267.
[9] Ibid., pp. 268–9.
[10] Ibid., pp. 270–1.
[11] Ibid., pp. 271–2.

182   Notes to pages 99–127

[12] Ibid., pp. 273–5. Tocqueville provided details of estimates of costs in a separate note (pp. 307–8).
[13] Ibid., pp. 277–80.
[14] Ibid., pp. 281, 282, 284–5.
[15] C. Lucas, *Du système pénal*; F. Barbé-Marbois, *Observations sur les votes*.
[16] OC, vol. 1, p. 269, n.12.
[17] For extracts from reviews in the *Monthly Review*, *Edinburgh Review* and *Law Magazine*, see OC, vol. 1, pp. 441–3.
[18] See, for example, M. Ignatieff, *A Just Measure of Pain*, pp. 195–6. Prussia and Canada also sent missions, and in 1837 France sent a second mission. See G. W. Pierson, *Tocqueville and Beaumont in America*, pp. 707–8.
[19] L. Radzinowicz and R. Hood, *History of English Criminal Law*, p. 491.
[20] OC, vol. 1, p. 89.
[21] Ibid., p. 94.
[22] Ibid., p. 95.
[23] Ibid., pp. 95, 96–7.
[24] Tocqueville cited Richard Whately's *Thoughts on Secondary Punishments . . .* (London, 1832).
[25] OC, vol. 1, pp. 98, 99.
[26] Ibid., pp. 101, 102, 103.
[27] Ibid., pp. 103, 104.
[28] Ibid., pp. 104–7.
[29] Ibid., pp. 108, 111.
[30] Ibid., vol. 2, pp. 278–81.
[31] These issues are discussed by A. Peyrefitte, 'Tocqueville et les illusions pénitentiaires', pp. 47–60. See also, M. Perrot, 'Criminalité et le système pénitentiaire au XIXe siècle', pp. 3–20.
[32] OC, vol. 1, p. 40.

6 HISTOIRE DE BOTANY BAY

[1] Pilorgerie, *Histoire de Botany-Bay*, pp. x–xi.
[2] Ibid., pp. xi, xii.
[3] Ibid., pp. xii, xiii.
[4] Ibid., pp. 49, 50.
[5] *Report from Select Committee on Transportation*.
[6] Pilorgerie, *Histoire de Botany-Bay*, pp. 172, 126; Bigge, *Report of the Commissioner of Inquiry* (this report was also cited by Pilorgerie as being in the parliamentary collection).
[7] Pilorgerie, *Histoire de Botany-Bay*, pp. 220–1.
[8] Ibid., pp. 221–3.
[9] Ibid., p. 243.
[10] *Report from the Select Committee on Secondary Punishments*; ibid., pp. 323–4.
[11] Ibid., p. 344.
[12] Ibid., pp. 376–7.
[13] F. Bourquelot and A. Maury, *La littérature française contemporaine, 1827–1849*, p. 606.

7 PENAL COLONIES AND PARLIAMENT

1. G. Wright, *Between the Guillotine and Liberty*, pp. 63, 67, 68.
2. All references to Tupinier's address are from *Moniteur*, 7 Mar. 1837, pp. 484–5. Tupinier's report was summarised in *AMC*, 2, 1837, pp. 26–39. Later, the comment was made that the reception of the report by the deputies was 'very bad'. See *Moniteur*, 15 May 1844, p. 1367.
3. *Moniteur*, 9 May 1839, p. 669.
4. *AMC*, 1, 1839, pp. 413–22.
5. His petition was also published separately as a pamphlet by the Imprimerie Royale in May 1839: *Proposition de déporter désormais hors de la France continentale tous les forçats libérés et quelques repris de justice*.
6. 'De la nécessité d'une colonie de déportation', pp. 1–18. In a letter to *Amiral* (Admiral) on 2 July 1839, after writing his memoir, Rigodit urged the choice of New Zealand. (AM, BB4, Campagne 1012)
7. 'Essai sur la fondation de colonies de déportation', 1840, pp. 1–36. De Mauny was the author of several publications on French colonies.
8. Mortemart de Boisse, 'De la déportation—extrait du Journal du Havre', pp. 175–8.
9. G. Wright, *Between the Guillotine and Liberty*, p. 72.
10. *Moniteur*, 25 Apr. 1844, p. 1084.
11. Ibid., 7 May 1844, pp. 1247–8.
12. Ibid., 15 May 1844, p. 1369.
13. Ibid., p. 1368.
14. Ibid., p. 1370.
15. Ibid., p. 1382.

8 THE ROLE OF THE NAVY

1. J. S. C. Dumont d'Urville, *Voyage de la corvette L'Astrolabe*, vol. 5.
2. C. P. T. Laplace, *Voyage autour du monde*, vol. 3, pp. 147, 165, 166, 169, 352.
3. F. Chassériau, p. 61.
4. H. de Bougainville, *Journal de la navigation autour du globe*. The Australian section is in vol. 1.
5. Ibid., pp. vii, 460, 455–6, 460.
6. L. de Freycinet, *Voyage autour du monde*, vol. 2, pts 2 and 3.
7. Ibid., vol. 2, pp. 649, 650, 1181.
8. J. Arago, *Promenade autour du monde*, vol. 4, p. 34.
9. R. P. Lesson, *Voyage autour du monde*, vol. 2, p. 266.
10. L. Jore, *L'océan Pacifique*, p. 193.
11. Ibid., p.194.
12. P. Tremewan, *French Akaroa*, pp. 27–8. Decazes was also a promoter of the expedition.
13. C. R. Straubel in J. Hight and C. R. Straubel (eds), *A History of Canterbury*, p. 64.
14. *AMC*, 1, 1840, p. 175.

[15] L. Jore, *L' océan Pacifique*, p. 199.
[16] P. Tremewan, *French Akaroa*, pp. 44–5.
[17] J. S. C. Dumont d'Urville, *Voyage au Pôle sud*, vol. 9, pp. 11–12.
[18] J.-P. Faivre, *L'expansion française dans le Pacifique*, p. 499.

9 NAPOLEON III AND FRENCH GUIANA

[1] C.-O. Barbaroux, *De la transportation*, p. 10.
[2] *Moniteur*, 17 June 1851, p. XI.
[3] *Gazette des tribunaux*, 29 June 1848. Quoted by M. Perrot, '1848: révolution et prisons', p. 306.
[4] FO, 27/846; C.-O. Barbaroux, *De la transportation*, p. 12.
[5] *Moniteur*, 5 Apr. 1850, p. 1104.
[6] Ibid., 6 Apr. 1850, p. 1112; 20 Apr. 1850, p. 1283.
[7] Y. Person, *La Nouvelle-Calédonie et l'Europe*, p. 168.
[8] *Moniteur*, 13 Nov. 1850, p. 3246.
[9] Ibid., 4 May 1851, p. 1266; 17 June 1851, p. XII.
[10] Ibid., 2 July 1851, p. 1869.
[11] For a discussion of the report, see Y. Person, *La Nouvelle-Calédonie*, pp. 178–80.
[12] V. Wright, 'The *coup d'état* of December 1851', p. 308. A flow of pardons and commutations was maintained in the 1850s, and there was a general amnesty in August 1859 (pp. 325–6).
[13] *Moniteur*, 21 Feb. 1852, p. 293.
[14] C. Rigault de Genouilly, *Notice sur la transportation*, p. 4.
[15] *Moniteur*, 29 Mar. 1852, p. 510.
[16] Corps législatif, *Procès-verbaux*, 4, 1853, 'Rapport fait au nom de la Commission chargée d'examiner le projet de loi relatif de l'exécution de la peine des travaux forcés, par M. du Miral'.
[17] Ibid., p. 19.
[18] Ibid., pp. 19–20.
[19] Ibid., pp. 22, 23.
[20] Ibid., pp. 26–7.
[21] Ibid., pp. 33, 34.
[22] Ibid., p. 45.
[23] *Moniteur*, 4 May 1854, p. 490.
[24] Ibid.
[25] Ibid., 5 May 1854, p. 494.

10 THE NAVY AND NEW CALEDONIA

[1] Quoted in G. Lacourrège and P. Alibert, *La Nouvelle-Calédonie*, pp. 19–20.
[2] Pariset, *Sur la déportation des condamnés aux travaux forcés*, p. 56.
[3] Pariset's views were noted most favourably by A. Molineau, attaché to the Navy Ministry, in a long article in the *Revue coloniale*, pp. 243–69.
[4] See Y. Person, *La Nouvelle-Calédonie*, pp. 178–81.

Notes to pages 168–175

[5] *Moniteur*, 14 Feb. 1854, p. 177.
[6] C. Brainne, *La Nouvelle-Calédonie*, p. i.
[7] *Sydney Morning Herald*, 3 Nov. 1853, p. 4.

EPILOGUE

[1] Centre des Archives d'Outre-Mer, *Terres de bagne*, p. 19.
[2] C. Rigault de Genouilly, *Notice sur la transportation*, p. 1.
[3] Centre des Archives d'Outre-Mer, *Terres de bagne*, p. 31.
[4] *Moniteur*, 5 May 1854, p. 494.
[5] E. du Bouzet, *Documents relatifs à la Nouvelle-Calédonie*, p. 29.
[6] *Moniteur*, 17 Feb. 1857, p. 189; M. Pierre, *La terre de la grande punition*, p. 32.
[7] H. Cor, *Contribution à l'étude des questions coloniales*, pp. 58, 121; J.-B. Duvergier (ed.), *Collection complète des lois, décrets*, pp. 276, 278.
[8] J.-P. Faivre et al., *Géographie de la Nouvelle-Calédonie*, p. 92, n. 6.
[9] L. Radzinowicz and R. Hood, *English Criminal Law*, pp. 485–9. The longstanding Russian practice of transportation and exile to Siberia was generally considered as a special case and not relevant for other countries.
[10] *Economist*, vol. 20, 1862, p. 1405.
[11] C. Rigault de Genouilly, *Notice sur la transportation*, pp. 55–6.

Select Bibliography

I ARCHIVAL COLLECTIONS

FRANCE

Archives nationales—section d'outre-mer
  H1, H2, H57.
Archives de la marine
  BB4 1000, 1002, 1008, 1011, 1012, 1023.
Bibliothèque nationale
  Manuscrits: nouvelles acquisitions françaises 6785.

Signed Commentaries, Memorials and Reports

Basterot, B. de, 'Observations sur la déportation et sur la réforme des criminels en réponse à l'ouvrage de M. le Marquis de Barbé-Marbois intitulé "Observations . . . libérés"', Paris, 24 Jan. 1830. AN, SO-M, H2.
Blosseville, Jules de, 'Projet d'une colonie pénale sur la côte S.O. de la Nouvelle-Hollande', 30 Jan. 1826. BN, MNAF, 6785.
——, 'Projet d'une colonie pénale à la Nouvelle-Zélande', 'Suite', 1 July 1829. BN, MNAF, 6785.
Forestier, —, 'Mémoire sur le choix d'un lieu de déportation', 14 Oct. 1816. AN, SO-M, H1.
——, '1er rapport à la Commission, le 10 février 1819'. AN, SO-M, H1.
Mauny, — (comte de), 'Essai sur la fondation de colonies de déportation', 1840. AM, BB4, 1012.
Rigodit, — (capitaine), 'De la nécessité d'une colonie de déportation'. AM, BB4, 1012.

GREAT BRITAIN

Colonial Office (Public Record Office)

New South Wales: Original Correspondence
  CO 201/188, 1827 (AJCP 157–8).

Foreign Office (Public Record Office)

France: General Correspondence
  FO 27/535, 1837 (AJCP 3588); 27/680, 1843 (AJCP 3591); 27/846, 1849 (AJCP 3596).

II OFFICIAL PUBLICATIONS

FRANCE
Parliamentary Debates

Archives parlementaires de 1787 à 1860: recueil complèt des débats législatifs et politiques des chambres françaises, 1st ser. 1787–94, 2nd ser. 1814–39. Paris, 1879–.

Corps législatif, *Procès-verbaux du Corps législatif.* 1853–54.

Official Newspapers

Le Moniteur universel

Official Reports

Cour de cassation, *Avis et rapport sur la Projet de Loi concernant les prisons.* Paris, 1845.

Rigault de Genouilly, Charles (Ministre de la Marine et des Colonies), *Notice sur la transportation à la Guyane française et à la Nouvelle-Calédonie.* Paris, 1867.

GREAT BRITAIN AND IRELAND
Parliament (House of Commons), Parliamentary Papers

1812, PP 341, *Report from the Select Committee on Tranportation.*

1822, PP 448, Bigge, John Thomas, *Report of the Commissioner of Inquiry into the State of the Colony of New South Wales.*

1831–32, PP 547, *Report from the Select Committee on Secondary Punishments.*

1834, PP 82, *Secondary Punishments* [Australia].

III OTHER PRINTED RECORDS

Historical Records of Australia, Series 1, vol. X, Jan. 1819–Dec. 1822; vol. XII, June 1825–Dec. 1826; vol. XVII, 1833–June 1835. Sydney, 1917, 1919, 1923.

IV JOURNALS AND NEWSPAPERS

AUSTRALIA
Sydney Morning Herald

FRANCE
Annales maritimes et coloniales
Gazette des tribunaux
Journal des prisons, hospices, écoles primaires et établissements philanthropiques
Le Magasin pittoresque
Nouvelles annales de la marine et des colonies
Revue britannique
Revue coloniale
Revue des deux mondes

V BOOKS

Alhoy, Maurice, *Les bagnes: Rochefort*. Paris, 1830.

——, *Les bagnes: histoire, types, mœurs, mystères*. Paris, 1845.

Amat, Roman d', et al., *Dictionnaire de biographie française*, vols 1–17. Paris, 1933–94.

Arago, Jacques, *Promenade autour du monde pendant les années 1817, 1818, 1819 et 1820, sur les corvettes du Roi L'Uranie et La Physicienne, commandées par M. Freycinet*, 2 vols. Paris, 1822. Published in English as *Narrative of a Voyage Round the World* . . ., London, 1823.

——, *Souvenirs d'un aveugle: voyage autour du monde*, 4 vols. Paris, 1839.

Barbaroux, Charles-Ogé, *De la transportation. Aperçus législatifs, philosophiques et politiques sur la colonisation pénitentiaire*. Paris, 1857.

Barbé-Marbois, François, *Observations sur les votes de quarante-un conseils généraux de département, concernant la déportation des forçats libérés*. Paris, 1828.

——, *Journal d'un déporté non-jugé ou, Déportation en violation des lois* . . . Paris, 1834.

Beaumont, Gustave de and Alexis de Tocqueville, *Du système pénitentiare aux États-Unis, et de son application en France; suivi d'un appendice sur les colonies pénales et de notes statistiques*. Paris, 1833.

——, *On the Penitentiary System in the United States* . . ., trans. with introduction, notes and additions by Francis Lieber. Philadelphia, 1833 (reprinted New York, 1970); 2nd edn, 1868. Abridged edn, with introduction by Thorstein Sellin and foreword by Herman R. Lantz. Carbondale and Edwardsville, 1964.

Bennet, Henry Grey, *Letter to Viscount Sidmouth, Secretary of State for the Home Department, on the Transportation Laws, the State of the Hulks, and of the Colonies in New South Wales*. London, 1819.

Benoiston de Chateauneuf, Louis-François, *De la colonisation des condamnés, et de l'avantage qu'il y aurait pour la France à adopter cette mesure*. Paris, 1827.

Bérenger, Alphonse, *Le système pénitentiaire*. Paris, 1838.

——, *De la répression pénale, de ses formes et de ses effets*, 2 vols. Paris, 1855.

Blosseville, Ernest Poret de, *Histoire des colonies pénales de l'Angleterre dans l'Australie*. Paris, 1831.

——, *Jules de Blosseville*. Évreux, 1854.

——, *Histoire de la colonisation pénale et des établissements de l'Angleterre en Australie*, 2 vols. Évreux, 1859 (published in 1 vol. later in 1859).

Bonnemains, Jacqueline, Elliott Forsyth and Bernard Smith (eds), *Baudin in Australian Waters: The Artwork of the French Voyage of Discovery to the Southern Lands 1800–1804*. Melbourne, 1988.

Borchardt, D. H. (ed.), *Australians: A Guide to Sources*. Sydney, 1987.

Bougainville, Hyacinthe Yves Philippe Potentin de, *Journal de la navigation autour du globe de la frégate* La Thétis *et de la corvette* L'Espérance, *pendant les années 1824, 1825, et 1826* . . ., 2 vols. Paris, 1837.

Bougainville, Louis-Antoine de, *Voyage autour du monde, par la frégate du Roi* La Boudeuse, *et la flûte* L'Étoile; *en 1766, 1767, 1768 & 1769*. Paris, 1771; 2nd ed., 2 vols, Paris, 1772.

Select Bibliography 189

Bourquelot, Félix and Alfred Maury, *La littérature française contemporaine, 1827–1849* . . ., vol. 4. Paris, 1852. See also under J.-M. Quérard, below.

Brainne, Charles, *La Nouvelle-Calédonie: voyages—missions—moeurs—colonisation (1754–1854)*. Paris, 1854.

Brookes, Jean Ingram, *International Rivalry in the Pacific Islands 1800–75*. Berkeley Calif., 1941.

Brou, Bernard, *Mémento d'histoire de la Nouvelle-Calédonie: les temps modernes: 1774–1925*. Nouméa, 1973.

Brouilhet, Francis, *De la transportation: son organisation actuelle et ses résultats au double point de vue pénitentiaire et colonial*. Paris, 1899.

Centre des Archives d'Outre-Mer, *Terres de bagne: le bagne en Guyane et en Nouvelle-Calédonie, 1852–1953*. Aix-en-Provence, 1990. (Published to accompany an exhibition at the Centre des Archives d'Outre-Mer, Aix-en-Provence, 1 Oct.–30 Nov.1990.)

Collingham, H. A. C., with R. S. Alexander, *The July Monarchy: A Political History of France 1830–1848*. London and New York, 1988.

Collins, David, *An Account of the English Colony in New South Wales, from Its First Settlement, in January 1788, to August 1801: With Remarks on the Dispositions, Customs, Manners, &c. of the Native Inhabitants of that Country* . . ., vol. 2. London, 1802.

Cor, Henri, *Contribution à l'étude des questions coloniales*. Paris, 1895.

Cunningham, Peter, *Two Years in New South Wales: A Series of Letters, Comprising Sketches of the Actual State of Society in That Colony; of Its Peculiar Advantages to Emigrants, of Its Topography, Natural History, &c., &c.*, 2 vols. London, 1827.

Devèze, Michel, *Cayenne, déportés et bagnards*. Paris, 1965.

Dubosc, M. G., *Rouen en 1886, l'année rouennaise* . . . Rouen, 1887.

Du Bouzet, Eugène, *Documents relatifs à la Nouvelle-Calédonie: rapports adressés au Ministre de la Marine par M. le capitaine de vaisseau du Bouzet, gouverneur des établissements français dans l'Océanie* (15 March 1855). Paris, 1857.

Dumont d'Urville, Jules Sébastien César, *Voyage de la corvette* L'Astrolabe *exécuté par ordre du Roi, pendant les années 1826, 1827, 1828, 1829 . . . Histoire du voyage*, 5 vols. Paris, 1832–34.

——('sous la direction de'), *Voyage pittoresque autour du monde: résumé général des voyages de découvertes* . . ., 2 vols. Paris, 1834.

——, *Voyage au Pôle sud et dans l'Océanie sur les corvettes* L'Astrolabe et La Zélée, *exécuté par ordre du Roi pendant les années 1837–1838–1839–1840 . . . Publié par ordonnance de Sa Majesté . . . Histoire du voyage*, 10 vols. Paris, 1841–46.

Dunmore, John, *French Explorers in the Pacific*, 2 vols. Oxford, 1965, 1969.

Dupetit-Thouars, Abel, *Voyage autour du monde sur la frégate* La Vénus, *pendant les années 1836 à 1839 . . . Relation historique*, vol. 3. Paris, 1841.

Duvergier. J.-B., *Collection complète des lois, décrets* . . . Paris, 1854.

Echard, William E. (ed.), *Historical Dictionary of the French Second Empire 1852–1870*. Westport Conn., 1985.

Eddy, J. J., *Britain and the Australian Colonies 1818–1831: The Technique of Government*. Oxford, 1969.

Faivre, Jean-Paul, *L'expansion française dans le Pacifique de 1800 à 1842*. Paris, 1954.

———, et al., *Géographie de la Nouvelle-Calédonie: géographie et histoire—économie—démographie—ethnologie*. Paris, 1955.

Ferguson, John Alexander, *Bibliography of Australia*, vols 1–4 (1784–1850), facsimile edn. Canberra, 1975–76.

Foucault, Michel, *Surveiller et punir: naissance de la prison*. Paris, 1975.

Freycinet, Louis Claude de Saulces de, *Voyage autour du monde, entrepris par ordre du Roi . . . exécuté sur les corvettes de S. M. L'Uranie et La Physicienne, pendant les années 1817, 1818, 1819 et 1820. Historique*, 2 vols in 3. Paris, 1825, 1829, 1839.

Frost, Alan, *Convicts and Empire: A Naval Question, 1776–1811*. Melbourne, 1980.

Gaziello, Catherine, *L'expédition de Lapérouse, 1785–1788: réplique française aux voyages de Cook*. Paris, 1984.

Ginouvier, J.-F.-T., *Le Botany-Bey français ou, Colonisation des condamnés aux peines afflictives et infamantes, et des forçats libérés*. Paris, 1826.

Hight, James and C. R. Straubel (eds), *A History of Canterbury*. Christchurch, 1957.

Hirst, J. B., *Convict Society and Its Enemies: A History of Early New South Wales*. Sydney, 1983.

Horner, Frank, *The French Reconnaissance: Baudin in Australia 1801–1803*. Melbourne, 1987.

Houghton, Walter E. (ed.), *The Wellesley Index to Victorian Periodicals, 1824–1900*, vol. 2. Toronto, 1972.

Ignatieff, Michael, *A Just Measure of Pain: The Penitentiary in the Industrial Revolution, 1750–1850*. New York, 1980.

Jardin, André, trans. from the French by Lydia Davis with Robert Hemenway, *Tocqueville: A Biography*. New York, 1988.

Jore, Léonce, *L'océan Pacifique au temps de la Restauration et de la Monarchie de Juillet (1815–1848)*, vol. 1, *Politique française*. Paris, 1959.

Lacoudrais, A., *Vues pratiques sur la fondation immédiate de colonies pénales et de colonies libres*. Paris, 1848.

———, *Lettres sur la transportation*. Paris, 1849.

Lacourrège, Gérard and Pierre Alibert, *La Nouvelle-Calédonie aux temps des bagnes*. Paris, 1986.

Lang, J. D., *An Historical and Statistical Account of New South Wales, both as a Penal Settlement and as a British Colony*, 2 vols. London, 1834.

Laplace, Cyrille Pierre Théodore, *Voyage autour du monde par les Mers de l'Inde et de la Chine, exécuté sur la corvette de l'État 'La Favorite' pendant les années 1830, 1831 et 1832 . . . Histoire du voyage*, 4 vols. Paris, 1833–35.

Larousse, Pierre, *Le grand dictionnaire universel du XIXe siècle . . .*, 17 vols. Paris, 1866–90.

Lémontey, Pierre-Édouard, ('Citoyen de Lyon, membre du Corps législatif'), *Éloge de Jacques Cook, avec des notes, discours qui a remporté le Prix d'éloquence au jugement de l'Académie de Marseille, le 25 août 1789*. Paris, 1792.

Lepelletier de la Sarthe, Almire, *Système pénitentiaire: le bagne, la prison cellulaire, la déportation . . .* Paris, 1853.

Lesson, René Primavère, *Voyage autour du monde entrepris par ordre du gouvernment sur la corvette La Coquille*, 2 vols. Paris, 1838–39.

Lucas, Charles, *Du système pénal et du système répressif en général, de la peine de mort en particulier*. Paris, 1827.

——, *Du système pénitentiaire en Europe et aux États-Unis, ouvrage dédié aux Chambres, précédé d'une pétition qui leur est adressée, et orné de plusieurs plans de prisons et tableaux statistiques*, 2 vols. Paris, 1828–30.

——, *La transportation pénale, à l'occasion de l'ouvrage de M. Michaux, sur l'étude de la question des peines*. Orléans, n.d. [1872].

Lyon, E. Wilson, *The Man Who Sold Louisiana: The Career of François Barbé-Marbois*. Norman Okla., 1942.

McCormick, Anne and Derek McDonnell, *Pacific Voyages and Exploration: From the Carlsmith Collection and Other Sources*. Sydney, 1987.

McCormick, Tim, et al., *First Views of Australia, 1788–1825: A History of Early Sydney*. Sydney, 1987.

Marchant, Leslie R., *France Australe: A Study of French Exploration and Attempts to Found a Penal Colony, 1803–1826*. Perth, 1982.

——, trans. by Dominique de Saint-Ours with preface by Jean-François Deniau, *France australe*. Paris, 1988.

Martin, R. Montgomery, *History of Austral-Asia: Comprising New South Wales, Van Diemen's Island, Swan River, South Australia, etc.* London, 1836.

Martin-Allanic, Jean-Étienne, *Bougainville navigateur et les découvertes de son temps*, 2 vols. Paris, 1964.

Marwick, Arthur, *The Nature of History*. London, 1970.

Michelet, Jules, *Introduction à l'histoire universelle*. Paris, 1831.

Mortemart de Boisse, —, *Mémoire sur la déportation des forçats, présenté en 1828, à Son Excellence le Ministre de la Marine et des Colonies*. Le Havre, 1840.

Newman, Edgar Leon (ed.) with Edward Lawrence Simpson, *Historical Dictionary of France from the 1815 Restoration to the Second Empire*, 2 vols. New York and Westport Conn., 1987.

O'Brien, Patricia, *The Promise of Punishment: Prisons in Nineteenth Century France*. Princeton, 1982.

Pariset, — (controleur en chef de la marine), *Sur la déportation des condamnés aux travaux forcés*. Paris, 1851.

Passy, Louis, *Le marquis de Blosseville: souvenir*. Évreux, 1898.

Péron, François Auguste and Louis de Freycinet, *Voyage de découvertes aux terres australes, exécuté par ordre de Sa Majesté l'Empéreur et Roi, sur les corvettes 'La Géographe', 'Le Naturaliste' et la goëlette 'Le Casuarina' pendant les années 1800, 1801, 1802, 1803 et 1804 . . .*, 2 vols. Paris, 1807, 1816.

Perrot, Michelle (ed.), *L'impossible prison: recherches sur le système pénitentiaire au XIXe siècle*. Paris, 1980.

Person, Yves, *La Nouvelle-Calédonie et l'Europe*. Paris, 1953.

Petit, Jacques-Guy, et al., with preface by Michelle Perrot, *Histoire des galères, bagnes et prisons XIIIe–XXe siècles: introduction à l'histoire pénale de la France*. Paris, 1991.

Pierre, Michel, *La terre de la grande punition: histoire des bagnes de Guyane*. Paris, 1982.

——, *Le dernier exil: histoire des bagnes et des forçats*. Paris, 1989.

Pierson, George Wilson, *Tocqueville and Beaumont in America*. New York, 1938.

Pike, Douglas (ed.), *Australian Dictionary of Biography*, vols 1 and 2, 1788–1850. Melbourne, 1966, 1967.

Pilorgerie, Jules de la, *Histoire de Botany-Bay, état présent des colonies pénales de l'Angleterre, dans l'Australie, ou, Examen des effets de la déportation, considérée comme peine et comme moyen de colonisation*. Paris, 1836.

Portal, Pierre-Barthélemy d'Albarèdes de, *Mémoires de Baron Portal*. Paris, 1846.

Price, Roger (ed.), *Revolution and Reaction: 1848 and the Second French Republic*. London, 1975.

Quentin, — (lieutenant-colonel), *Mémoire sur la question suivante, mise au concours par la Société d'agriculture, sciences et belles-lettres de Mâcon: Indiquer en remplacement des travaux forcés une peine qui, sans cesser de satisfaire aux besoins de la justice, laisse moins de dégradation dans l'âme du condamné* (*'Mémoire sur les forçats'*). Paris, 1828.

Quérard, J.-M., *La France littéraire, ou Dictionnaire bibliographique*, 12 vols. Paris, 1827–59/64.

——, et al., *La littérature française contemporaine. Continuation de La France littéraire. Dictionnaire bibliographique* . . . (title varies), 6 vols. Paris, 1842–57.

Radzinowicz, Leon and Roger Hood, *A History of English Criminal Law and Its Administration from 1750*. Vol. 5, *The Emergence of Penal Policy*. London, 1986.

Schéfer, Charles, *La France moderne et le problème colonial: 1815–1830*. Paris, 1907.

Shaw, A. G. L., *Convicts and the Colonies: A Study of Penal Transportation from Great Britain and Ireland to Australia and Other Parts of the British Empire*, 3rd ed. Melbourne, 1981.

Sked, Alan (ed.), *Europe's Balance of Power 1815–1848*. London and Basingstoke, 1979.

Smith, Bernard, *Imagining the Pacific: In the Wake of the Cook Voyages*. Princeton, 1992.

Taillandier, A. H., *Réflexions sur les lois pénales de France et d'Angleterre*. Paris, 1824.

Thibadeau, A. C., trans. from the French and ed. by G. K. Fortescue, *Bonaparte and the Consulate*. London, 1908.

Thierry, Augustin, *Histoire de la conquête de l'Angleterre par les Normands, de ses causes et ses suites, jusqu'à nos jours* . . ., 3 vols. Paris, 1825.

Tocqueville, Alexis de, *De la démocratie en Amérique*. Paris, 1835.

——, trans. and ed. by J. P. Mayer and Max Lerner, *Democracy in America*. New York, 1966.

——, ed. by Michelle Perrot, *Alexis de Tocqueville: œuvres complètes: tome iv: écrits sur le système pénitentiaire en France et à l'étranger*, 2 vols. Paris, 1984.

Tremewan, Peter, *French Akaroa: An Attempt to Colonise Southern New Zealand*. Christchurch, 1990.

Turnbull, John, trans. by A. J. N. Lallemant, *Voyage fait autour du monde en 1800, 1801, 1802, 1803 et 1804* . . . Paris, 1807.

Wantrup, Jonathan, *Australian Rare Books: 1788–1900*. Sydney, 1987.

Wentworth, W. C., *A Statistical, Historical, and Political Description of the Colony of New South Wales and Its Dependent Settlements in Van Diemen's Land; With a Particular Enumeration of the Advantages Which These Colonies Offer for Emigration, and Their Superiority in Many Respects over Those Possessed by the United States of America.* London, 1819; 2nd edn, 1820.

——, *A Statistical Account of the British Settlements in Australasia: Including the Colonies of New South Wales and Van Diemen's Land* . . ., 2 vols (3rd edn of the above). London, 1824.

West, John, *The History of Tasmania*, 2 vols. Launceston, 1852.

White, John, trans. by Charles Pougens, *Voyage à la Nouvelle Galles du Sud, à Botany Bay, au Port Jackson, en 1787, 1788, 1789* . . . Paris, 1795.

Wright, Gordon, *Between the Guillotine and Liberty: Two Centuries of the Crime Problem in France.* New York, 1983.

VI ARTICLES, REVIEWS AND ESSAYS

UNSIGNED MATERIAL

'De la transportation et de la discipline des convicts dans les colonies de l'Australie', *Revue coloniale*, vol. 15, 1856, pp. 141–54.

[On transportation], *The Economist*, vol. 20, no. 1008, 20 December 1862, pp. 1404–5.

[Southern, Henry], Review of E. de Blosseville, *Histoire des colonies pénales de l'Angleterre dans l'Australie*, *Foreign Quarterly Review*, vol. 9, May 1832, pp. 422–37.

——, Review of G. de Beaumont and A. de Tocqueville, *Du système pénitentiaire aux États-Unis*, *Foreign Quarterly Review*, vol. 12, July 1833, pp. 49–79.

Two Years in New South Wales by P. Cunningham, review article, *Revue britannique*, no. 16, 1828, pp. 70–115.

'Y', Review of E. de Blosseville, *Histoire des colonies pénales de l'Angleterre dans l'Australie*, *Annales maritimes et coloniales*, pt 2, 1837, pp. 588–98

SIGNED MATERIAL

Bullen, Roger, 'France and Europe, 1815–1848: the problems of defeat and recovery', in Alan Sked (ed.), *Europe's Balance of Power 1815–1848*, pp. 122–44, 202–5.

Castéra, — (magistrat ancien), 'Proposition de déporter désormais hors de la France continentale tous les forçats libérés et quelques repris de justice, faites aux Chambres législatives', *Annales maritimes et coloniales*, pt 1, 1839, pp. 413–22. (Also published separately, Paris, 1839.)

Chassériau, F., Review of C. P. T. Laplace, *Voyage autour du monde*, *Annales maritimes et coloniales*, pt 1, 1836, p. 61.

Duprat, Catherine, 'Punir et guérir. En 1819, la prison des philanthropes', in Michelle Perrot (ed.), *L'impossible prison*, pp. 64–122.

Faucher, Léon, 'Les colonies pénales de l'Angleterre', *Revue des deux mondes*, no. 1, Feb. 1843, pp. 396–423.

——, 'Du projet de loi sur la réforme des prisons', *Revue des deux mondes*, no. 1, Feb. 1844, pp. 373–408.

Hutchinson, Mark, 'W. C. Wentworth and the sources of Australian historiography', *Journal of the Royal Australian Historical Society*, vol. 77, no. 4, 1992, pp. 62–85.

Hyde de Neuville, J. G. (baron), 'Rapport au Roi, sur la nécessité de répartir les forçats dans les ports du royaume, en raison de la durée de leur peine'. *Annales maritimes et coloniales*, pt 1, 1828, pp. 690–7.

Macintyre, Stuart, 'The writing of Australian history', in D. H. Borchardt (ed.), *Australians: A Guide to Sources*, pp. 1–29.

Mellish, —, 'Souvenirs d'un déporté à la Nouvelle-Galles du sud', *Revue britannique*, no. 8, 1826, pp. 108–53.

Molineau, Amédée, 'De la suppression des bagnes', *Revue coloniale*, vol. 8, 1852, pp. 243–69.

Mortemart de Boisse, —, 'De la déportation—extrait du Journal du Havre', *Annales maritimes et coloniales*, pt 1, 1840, pp. 175–8.

Perrot, Michelle, '1848: révolution et prisons', in Michelle Perrot (ed.), *L'impossible prison*, pp. 277–312.

——, 'Criminalité et système pénitentiaire au XIXe siècle: une histoire en développement', *Cahiers du centre de recherches historiques*, no. 1, Apr. 1988, pp. 3–20.

Peyrefitte, Alain, 'Tocqueville et les illusions pénitentiaires', *The Tocqueville Review/La Revue Tocqueville*, vol. 7, 1985–86, pp. 47–60.

Pinatel, Jean, 'La vie et l'œuvre de Charles Lucas', *Revue internationale de droit pénal*, vol. 2, 1947, pp. 121–54.

Valette, Jacques, 'Le bagne de Rochefort, 1815–1852', in Michelle Perrot (ed.), *L'impossible prison*, pp. 206–35.

Valserres, Jacques, 'Des colonies pénales de l'Australie', *Journal des économistes*, vol. 11, no. 2, July–Dec. 1852, pp. 173–200.

Wright, Vincent, 'The *coup d'état* of December 1851: repression and the limitations to repression', in Roger Price (ed.), *Revolution and Reaction: 1848 and the Second French Republic*, pp. 303–33.

Zysberg, André, 'Politiques du bagne (1820–1850)', *Annales historiques de la Révolution française*, no. 228, July–Sept. 1977, pp. 269–305. (Also in Michelle Perrot (ed.), *L'impossible prison*, pp. 165–205.)

Index

Aborigines, 124, 147; school for, Parramatta, 147
Académie française, 46n, 83
Africa, 13, 61, 149, 172
Akaroa, 150; *see also* New Zealand
Alcmène (corvette), 168
Algeria, 142, 155–6, 160
Alhoy, Maurice, 25
America, 9, 29, 39, 61, 82, 92, 99, 136; *see also* North America, United States of America
American Revolution, War of Independence, 7, 100
Annales maritimes et coloniales, 25, 36n, 51, 84, 129n, 134, 137, 137n, 144
Antilles, 65
Arago, Jacques, 26–7, 143, 148
Arctic Circle, 174
Asiatic Journal, 75
Auburn, Auburn system, 87, 94, 113n, 115, 128; *see also* United States of America (penal systems), France (penitentiaries)
Australia, history of and historiography, 4, 71–3, 74n, 76–83, 85, 88, 90–1, 98, 114, 118–27 *passim*, 174; *see also* Australian penal colonies, Botany Bay, New Holland, New South Wales, Van Diemen's Land
Australian Agricultural Company, 75
Australian colonies, western, 163
Australian penal colonies: convict system, 1–2, 9–11, 19, 45, 49, 59, 62–3, 65, 78–80, 99–100, 109–12, 123–4, 127, 137, 143–4, 147–8, 163, 167, (punishment) 49, 110–14, 117, (returned convicts) 50, 86, 96, 103, (women convicts) 11, 16, 49, 100–1, 123, 175; cost of, 49, 57–8, 62, 64, 98, 103, 108, 112, 132; emancipists, 39, 49, 59, 80–2, 86, 100, 116, 123, 143; emigrants, free settlers, 59, 62–3, 65, 81–2, 100, 110, 123, 127, 143–4, 163; governors, 125; governors' reports, 48n, 109–10, 112; *see also* Great Britain

Barbaroux, Charles-Ogé, 155, 161n
Barbé-Marbois, François, 13n, 18–19, 20, 22–5, 47–55 *passim*, 58, 61, 94, 103, 118, 127, 137; deportation to Guiana, 18
Barrington, George, 8n, 29, 48n, 80
Barrot, Odilon, 60, 62–3, 65–6
Barthe, Félix, 66n
Basterot, B. de, 53–4
Bathurst, Lord, 99n
Baudin, Nicolas Thomas, 9, 10n, 54, 131
Beaumont, Gustave de, 71, 76, 83, 87–8, 92–4, 96n, 106n, 119, 124–6, 128
Belgium, 113; prison system, 127
Bennet, Henry Grey, 24, 81
Benoiston de Chateauneuf, Louis-François, 28–9

Bentham, Jeremy, 22, 29, 50, 104; Benthamites, 85, 105n; panopticon, 22n
Bigge, J. T., 40n, 48n, 49, 75, 81, 99n; Bigge Reports, 40, 45, 80–1, 103, 121
Blackstone, William, 15
Bligh, William, 121
Blosseville, Ernest Poret de, 4, 24, 36n, 48n, 51n, 58, 72–91, 95, 103–4, 118, 122, 126–7, 136, 147n, 170, 173
Blosseville, Jules Poret de, 36, 40–1, 75, 143
Blücher, General, 148
Blue Mountains, 45
Boinvilliers, E.-E., 158
Bonaparte, Louis-Napoleon, 158–61, 169–70; *see also* Napoleon
Bonaparte, Napoleon, 13–14, 18n, 166; Napoleonic period, 42; Napoleonic war, 9; *see also* Napoleon
Botany Bay, 1, 3–4, 8–9, 11, 13n, 17, 19, 25–6, 28, 30–9 *passim*, 43–77 *passim*, 80–97 *passim*, 102–4, 118–19, 131, 137, 140–8 *passim*, 159, 169–70, 175; *see also* Australian penal colonies, New Holland, New South Wales
Bougainville, Hyacinthe de, 36, 74n, 126n, 145–6
Bougainville, Louis-Antoine de, 7
Bourbons, Bourbon Restoration, 3
Bourke, Richard, 109–10, 124
Brisbane, Thomas, 123
Britain, *see* Great Britain
Brougham, Henry, 81
Bulletin de la Société de Géographie, 84
bushrangers, 97

Castéra, —, 134–5
Cayenne, 61, 174; *see also* French Guiana
Chabrol de Crouzol, C.-A.-J., 28
Chalret-Durieu, —, 61–2
Charles X, *see* France
Chateaubriand, F.-A.-R., 72

Chatham, 105n, 174
Chatham Islands, 150–1
China, 9, 165
Clayton, James, 110
Collins, David, 29, 48n, 73, 120–1
Colombia, 82
colonies, 85, 96, 100
Cook, James, 7, 9, 136
corporal punishment, 2, 12, 113–15, 117
Crawford, William, 105
Crete, 16, 18
criminals, 1, 2, 9, 13, 16, 96–7, 116, 119, 125, 136; ex-criminals, 104; recidivism, 95–6, 98
Cunningham, Peter, 53, 63

Daguenet, —, 140
Darling, Ralph, 80, 123
Dartmoor, 174
death penalty, 8, 13, 15, 97
Decazes, Élie, 42, 150
Declaration of the Rights of Man, 13
Degérando, Baron, 16
Delille, Jacques, 44n
Delpon, —, 60–1, 63
deportation, 23, 50, 50n, 54, 89, 95–6, 99–101, 104, 114, 119–20, 126, 145
Devil's Island, 171n; *see also* French Guiana
Doullens, 130
Ducos, Théodore, 160–1
Du Hamel, —, 32–4
Du Miral, Rudel, 162–5
Dumon, Pierre-Sylvain, 56–7, 63
Dumont d'Urville, Jules-Sébastien-César, 36, 38–9, 50n, 55, 58–60, 63–4, 143, 145, 148–9, 151
Duperrey, Louis-Isidore, 35–8, 45, 75
Dupetit-Thouars, Abel-Aubert, 150, 158
Duprat, Catherine, 42

Economist, 174
Edinburgh Review, 75

Index

England, *see* Great Britain
Entrecasteaux, Antoine de Bruni d', 8
Eugénie, Empress, 172
Europe, 7–10, 18, 27, 38, 41, 43–4, 49, 82–3, 89, 96–7, 100–1, 106, 125, 130, 141n, 145–6, 148, 159; interest in penal colonies, 173–4; prisons in, 46, 99

Faivre, Jean-Paul, 173
Falkland Islands, 36n, 38, 52, 130, 136–7
Farconet, J.-F., 157
Faucher, Léon, 155
Field, Barron, 146–7
Flinders, Matthew, 131
Forbes, Charles, 81
Foreign Quarterly Review, 84, 105n
Forestier, —, 15–18
Foucault, Michel, 67n
France, 1–4, 9, 13–14, 32–44 *passim*, 51–2, 56, 61–2, 71, 75–8, 84, 92–106 *passim*, 113–14, 129–37 *passim*, 141–8 *passim*, 152–62 *passim*, 167–75 *passim*; Anglo–French relations, 17, 22n, 48n, 150, 151, 156, 160; Australia, French interest in settlement in, 17–18, 35–41 *passim*, 54, 131, 149; *bagnes*, 12–34 *passim*, 43–4, 53–5, 58–9, 62–3, 84, 129, 134, 142–7 *passim*, 158–67 *passim*, 171, (at Brest) 12, 158, 161, (at Lorient) 12, (at Rochefort) 12, 158, 161, (at Toulon) 12, 158, 161; civil code, 13; colonies, 14n, 33–4, 57, 60, 73, 86, 102, 130, 150–1, 156, 159–60, 161, 164, 166–9 *passim*, 172, 173; *Commissaire du gouvernement*, 165, 171; Council of State, 15, 158–9; *coup d'état* in 1851, 155, 160, 169; crime, 24, 28, 40, 43, 50, 129n, 138–9, 158, 162, 169, 175, (punishment) 12, 13, 20–1, 24, 40, 43, 61, 140, 157–8, 161–2, (recidivism) 24, 46, 55, 61, 76, 138, 155, 158, 162, 169; Dauphin, 47, 53; Departments, 25, 33, 47, 47n, 51, 56, 129; deportation, 8, 13–67 *passim*, 95, 103, 105, 115, 118, 129, 133–66 *passim*, (cost of) 40, 64, 115, 138; exploration, voyages, 7, 9, 17, 35, 131, 149, 167–8; finance, 155; fiscal problems, 7; *forçats*, 14–17, 20, 22–5, 27–34 *passim*, 38–40, 47, 55–9 *passim*, 66, 129, 151, 156, 160–70 *passim*, (*forçats libérés*) 14, 76, 129, 134, 164; foreign policy, 41, 151, 156; government, 1, 7, 10n, 12, 14, 16, 44, 59, 63, 66, 71, 73, 93–4, 126–9, 133, 137–8, 144, 150, 156–7; interest in Australia and the Pacific, 9, 72, 86, 91, 118; judiciary, 93; King of, 17, 20, 39, 42, 51n, 133, 150–1, (Charles X), 55, (Louis-Philippe), 55, 86, 143, 152, 155; ministers, 151, (Minister of the Interior) 23, 36–7, 42, 94, 127, 134, 138, 141, 151, 159, (Minister for Justice) 31n, 66, 134, 141, 159, (Minister of the Navy and Colonies) *see* navy; navy, 3, 17, 33–5, 38, 41, 44, 56, 111, 129, 143, 149, 151–2, 155, 159–60, 166–7, 169, 171, (Committee of the Navy and Colonies) 15, (Department of the Navy and Colonies) 17, 25, 27, 34, 40–1, 137n, 145, 159, 171, (Minister of the Navy and Colonies) 10n, 13, 15, 16, 27–8, 31–2, 34, 39, 51n, 55, 134, 136, 141, 144n, 159–60, 168, 171–4 *passim*; Parliament, 18, 20, 23, 94, 114, 128–30, 137–8, 150, 152, 158, 172, (Chamber of Deputies) 3, 18, 31, 56, 59, 63, 67, 71, 115, 121, 130, 133, 138–9, 142, (Chamber of Peers) 18–20, 23, 47, 66, 134, 142, 150, (*Commission d'initiative*) 158–9, (Constituent Assembly) 155–7, 159, (*corps législatif*) 160, 160n, 162, 164, (Legislative Assembly)

160, (Senate) 160n, (legislation) 59, 130, 133, 138, 142, 150, 155–9, 162, 164–5, 173, 175; penal code, 12–13, 19–20, 34, 84; penal colonies, 1, 9n, 13–16, 18, 25–6, 30–5, 37–40, 46–71 *passim*, 76, 86–95 *passim*, 101–2, 107, 118, 122–34 *passim*, 140, 150–2, 157–74 *passim*, (cost of) 19, 30–1, 50, 57, 64, 134, 160, (response by Great Britain) 39–41, 102–3, 149, 156, 168; penal debate, 3–4, 8, 14–15, 18–24 *passim*, 31, 39, 47, 61–9, 71, 83–93 *passim*, 106, 115, 118, 127–8, 138–43 *passim*, 157, 164–5; penal policy, system, 3, 12–14, 42, 47, 55, 87, 93, 106–7, 113, 116, 138, 152, 155–8 *passim*, (committees on) 16–17, 19, 56, 59, 61, 66n, 115, 138, 141–2, 162, 164, (1819 committee) 14–16, 22, 34–6, 40, 44, 50, 55, 134, (1848 committee) 155–6, 168, (1851 committee) 159–61, 168, 170; penal reform, 57, 92, 95, 114, 126, 138, 142, 158; penal site, search for, 15, 17, 50, 54, 57, 63, 95, 101, 130, 133–5, 141, 149–59 *passim*, 167–9, 175; penitentiaries, 45–6, 54, 58, 61, 67, 87–8, 106, 115, 125–8, 133, 137n, 151, 155, 169, (Auburnists) 137, (Philadelphia system) 138, 167, (solitary confinement) 138–9, 141–2, 152, 156; philanthropes, 42; police, director of, 39–40; political unrest, 130, 155; President, 158; prisoners, 14, 21, 28, 46, 87, 116–17, 129n, 138–9, 152, 158, 161–7 *passim*, 171–2, (political) 19, 56, 129–31, 141, 155, 157, 159, 168, (*réclusionnaires*) 19, 39–40, 57, 151, 156, (women) 175; prisons, 3, 12–14, 19, 24, 42, 46–7, 56, 62, 76, 86, 128–9, 138, 140–1, 147, 156, 166, (overseas) 130, 133, 142, 159, (reform of) 42–7 *passim*, 66, 86, 94, 116,

128, (*travaux forcés*) 17, 162; Republic, Second and Third, 155; Restoration, 12, 14–15, 34, 41n, 56, 131, 134; Revolution of 1848, 138, 142, 155, 157; scientific expeditions, 7, 35, 38; transportation, 1, 3, 8, 12–13, 24, 31, 43, 46, 67, 71, 115, 117, 141–2, 147, 149, 152–75 *passim*; whaling, 149–50; *see also* Australian penal colonies, Botany Bay, New Holland, New South Wales
Franchet d'Esperey, François, 36n
Franklin, Benjamin, 46
French Guiana, 1, 16–18, 28, 38, 130, 134, 160–2, 164–5, 169–74
French Revolution, 2, 8, 12, 41n
Freycinet, Louis de, 11–12, 26, 43, 54, 146–8

Gabert, —, 75
Gaimard, Joseph-Paul, 45
Gaudichaud, Charles, 45
Geneva, 87
Germany, 30, 173
Gibbon, Edward, 89
Ginouvier, J.-F.-T., 28
Gondinet, A., 28n
Great Britain, 9, 16, 64, 76, 87, 100, 104, 107, 146, 174; army, 111; Colonial Office, 48n, 109–10; crime, convicts, 1, 43, 49, 99n, 105n, 107–9, 112n, 125, 134–5, 144, 148; England, the English, 8, 15, 17–19, 22, 26, 32, 36n, 38, 40–1, 43, 48, 52–64 *passim*, 78, 80, 86, 97, 100–2, 105, 119–20, 124, 131–7 *passim*, 144n, 148–52 *passim*, 159–67 *passim*; government, 37, 46, 81, 87, 98, 107, 109, 117, 129, 132, 146, (House of Commons inquiries) 98, 103–4, 121, 124–7, 129n, 139, (Parliament) 163, 173–4, (Parliamentary Papers) 3, 64, 75, 104n, 109n; migration, 143; navy, 41, 102, 149; penal practice, laws, 15, 42, 105n, 106–7, 117, 144n; prisons,

Index

penitentiaries, 85, 105n, 107–8, 112, 133n, 152, 159, 163, (prison hulks) 46, 58, 105n; possessions, 174; society, 117; transportation, 1–4, 8, 12, 15, 19, 22, 24, 29, 33, 37, 40–72 *passim*, 80, 86–117 *passim*, 121, 124–35 *passim*, 139, 144, 159, 162–7 *passim*, 173–4, (cost of) 88, 98, 115, 139; *see also* Australian penal colonies
Greece, 82, 122n
Greenland, 174
Grelier-Dufougeroux, —, 158–9
Guémard, *see* Gaimard
Guiana, *see* French Guiana

Harcourt, B.-J.-M. d', 168
Haussonville, Othénin d', 140
history, historians, 89–91
Hobart, 58, 82, 143–4; *see also* Van Diemen's Land
Holland, Dutch, 16, 131
Horner, Frank, 10n
Hugo, Victor, 157
Hull, James, 110
Hunter, John, 73, 79–80, 98, 121
Hutchinson, Mark, 74n
Hyde de Neuville, Jean-Guillaume, 51n, 53, 55

India, 149, 165
Ireland, 100
Isle de Bourbon, 130

Japan, 9
Journal du Havre, 137, 151

Kelley, Augustus M., 93
King George Sound, 36, 39–40
King, Philip Gidley, 98, 121
King, Phillip Parker, 54

Labrador, 174
Lacoudrais, A., 141n
Lainé, Joseph-Louis-Joachim, 16–17
Laisné de Villevesque, —, 31–2
La Lozère, Pelet de, 134
Lamartine, Alphonse de, 139–40, 157

Lang, John Dunmore, 121–6 *passim*
Lapérouse, Jean-François de Galaup de, 7–8
Laplace, Cyrille Pierre Théodore, 143–5
La Rochefoucauld, Gaëtan de, 59–60
La Rochefoucauld-Liancourt, L.-F.-S. de, 59, 61
Lausanne, 87
Lavaud, Charles François, 151
Leeuwin Land, 36n
Le Havre, 137
Lélut, Louis-François, 164–5
Lémontey, Pierre-Édouard, 9
Lesson, René Primavère 36, 45, 75, 148
Lieber, Francis, 93, 95n
London, 26, 79, 105n, 138n, 148
London and Paris Observer, 75
Louis-Philippe, *see* France, King of
Lucas, Charles, 43–7, 66, 83, 88, 103, 119n, 127–8
Lyon, E. Wilson, 51

Macaulay, Thomas Babington, 73
Macintyre, Stuart, 72–3
Mackintosh, James, 46n, 119
Mâcon Society of Agriculture, Science and Literature, 29
Macquarie, Elizabeth, 147
Macquarie, Lachlan, 78, 80–1, 121–2, 147
Madagascar, 16, 38, 133
Maitland, 110
Malays, 9
Malouines, *see* Falkland Islands
Marchant, Leslie, 35–6
Marquesas Islands, 71, 152, 157
Martin, R. Montgomery, 167
Mauguin, François, 63–4
Mauny, —, Count de, 136
Mediterranean, 41, 156
Mellish, —, 45
Melville Island, 36
Mérilhou, —, 64–5
Mestro, —, 160, 165, 171–2
Michelet, Jules, 89

missions, 149
Moniteur universel, 9, 161
Mont Saint-Michel, 18, 20, 23, 129
Montyon Prize, 46n, 83, 91–2, 95
Mortemart de Boisse, —, Lieutenant, 52–3, 137

Nanto-Bordelaise Company, 150–1; *see also* New Zealand
Napoleon: Napoleon I, 166; Napoleon III, 155, 160–2, 167, 172–3; *see also* Bonaparte
New Caledonia, 1, 159–60, 165–8, 172–4; French occupation and Australian reaction, 168; missions, 167n; penal settlement, 172–5
New Holland, 9, 17–19, 22–6 *passim*, 30–8 *passim*, 44–5, 53–4, 61–2, 122, 131, 134, 145, 157; *see also* Australia, Australian penal colonies, Botany Bay, New South Wales
New South Wales, 8, 21–2, 28, 32–3, 39–40, 50–9 *passim*, 80, 102, 109, 111–12, 124–6, 139, 143–51 *passim*, 158n, 163, 167; conditions in, 21, 124; women, 22; *see also* Australian penal colonies, Botany Bay, New Holland
New Zealand, 36, 38–51 *passim*, 55, 60, 71, 131, 135, 137n, 149–52; France in, 149–52; Great Britain in, 149–51; Maoris, 39n, 150; North Island, 149; South Island, 149–51
Nicholson, —, 37
Niger River, 174
Norfolk Island, 111
North America, 49, 89; *see also* America, United States of America
Nouvelles annales des voyages, 75

Oceania, *see* Pacific Ocean

Pacific Ocean, 7–8, 9, 132, 149–50, 167, 172
Paris, 14, 71, 129, 148; insurrection 1848, 156, 169

Pariset, —, 166–7
Passy, Louis, 75
Patagonia, 61, 135
penal colonies, 3, 12–14, 29–31, 37, 43, 79, 87, 89, 94–105 *passim*, 114, 119, 125, 136; cost of, 97–8, 113; recidivism, 96; sickness in, 39; *see also* Australian penal colonies, France
penitentiaries, 106–7, 119, 125
Pentonville, 163
Péron, François, 9, 11–12, 16, 26, 58, 121–2, 143
Philadelphia, 93; Philadelphia system, 94, 105, 114, 117, 128, 137, 141, 152; Western Penitentiary, 105
Phillip, Arthur, 73, 78–9, 98, 136
Pilorgerie, Jules Luette de la, 4, 71–2, 85, 118–27, 133, 136
Podenas, — de, 61
Pondicherry, 130
Ponérople, 122
Port Famine, 135
Port Jackson, 9–11, 16, 19, 23, 37, 147; *see also* Sydney
Port Lincoln, 124
Portal, Pierre-Barthélemy d'Alberèdes, 16–17, 41n, 166
Portland, 163, 174
Portsmouth, 105n
Portugal, 16
Pougens, Charles, 8
prisons, 29, 114, 116; *see also* France, Great Britain

Quarterly Review, 29, 53n, 75
Quentin, —, Lieutenant-Colonel, 29–31, 55
Quérard, J.-M., 28n

Ranke, Leopold von, 89, 91
Rémusat, — de, 65
Revue britannique, 29, 41n, 45–6, 53–4, 75
Revue coloniale, 173
Revue des deux mondes, 75
Revue encyclopédique, 28n
Richmond, 87

Index

Rigodit, —, Captain, 135–6
Ruse, James, 80
Russia, 148–9

Salut Islands, 171; see also French Guiana
Salverte, —, 66
Schéfer, Charles, 16n
Sellon, Count de, 43n
Senegal, 16, 23, 61, 130
Seven Years War, 7
Shaw, A. G. L., 111n
Siberia, 157
Sidmouth, Lord, 81
Siméon, Joseph-Jérôme, 17
Sinamary, 170; see also French Guiana
slavery, 31, 161n
Société de la morale chrétienne, 42
Société royale pour l'amélioration des prisons, 42, 47, 53, 94; see also France
South Pacific, see Pacific Ocean
Southern, Henry, 84–5, 105n
Spain, 16, 32, 41n
Stockdale, John, 8
Straits of Magellan, 135
Swan River, 35, 41n, 54, 124, 131
Sydney, 10, 16–17, 26–9, 33, 45, 58, 61, 75–82 passim, 120–4 passim, 132–48 passim, 168, 175; see also Australian penal colonies, Port Jackson
Sydney Cove, see Sydney
Sydney Gazette, 147
Sydney Morning Herald, 168

Tahiti, 7, 152, 156
Tench, Watkin, 8, 73
Terre de Witt, 54
Terres australes, see Australia, New Zealand
Thierry, Augustin, 89
Thierry, Charles, 39
Thiers, Adolphe, 155, 158
Tocqueville, Alexis de, 4, 71–2, 76, 83, 87–9, 91–117, 119, 124–38 passim, 141, 156
Toulongeon, Citizen, 9n, 10n
Tracy, — de, 62
transportation, 4, 85–7, 95, 98–9, 104–19 passim, 164–5; see also France, Great Britain
Tremewan, Peter, 150n
Tupinier, Jean-Marguerite, 130–3, 150
Turkish Empire, 16
Turnbull John, 12n

United States of America, 46, 62, 94n, 100, 128, 163; penal systems and practice, 42–3, 46, 53, 83, 93–4, 104–8, 115–16, 118, 126, 128; see also Auburn, Philadelphia

Van Diemen's Land, 49–50, 97, 109, 124–5, 143, 163, 168, 173n; convicts in, 97, 111n; see also Australian penal colonies, Hobart
'V. B.', 137
Villeneuve-Bargemeont, A., 147
Voltaire, 89
Voyage pittoresque autour du monde, 148; see also Dumont d'Urville, J.-S.-C.

Warden, D. B., 84
Waterloo, Battle of, 148–9
Wellington, Duke of, 148
Wentworth, William Charles, 29, 37, 45, 73–5
West, John, 73
whaling, see France
Whately, Richard, 108–9, 112n
White, John, 8, 73
Willaumez, Jean-Baptiste, 16